MASCOT NATION

MASCOT NATION

The Controversy over
Native American
Representations in Sports

**ANDREW C. BILLINGS AND
JASON EDWARD BLACK**

**UNIVERSITY OF
ILLINOIS PRESS**
Urbana, Chicago, and Springfield

Library of Congress Cataloging-in-Publication Data
Names: Billings, Andrew C., author. | Black, Jason Edward,
    author.
Title: Mascot nation : the controversy over Native American
    representations in sports / Andrew C. Billings and Jason
    Edward Black.
Description: Urbana : University of Illinois Press, 2018. | Includes
    bibliographical references and index.
Identifiers: LCCN 2018020260| ISBN 9780252042096 (hardback :
    alk. paper) | ISBN 9780252083785 (paperback : alk. paper)
Subjects: LCSH: Indians as mascots. | Sports team mascots—
    Social aspects—United States. | Sports spectators—United
    States—Attitudes. | Indians in popular culture—United
    States. | BISAC: SOCIAL SCIENCE / Ethnic Studies / Native
    American Studies. | SPORTS & RECREATION / History. |
    SPORTS & RECREATION / Sociology of Sports.
Classification: LCC GV714.5 .B55 2018 | DDC 305.897—dc23
LC record available at https://lccn.loc.gov/2018020260
E-book ISBN 978–0–252–05084–8

CONTENTS

ACKNOWLEDGMENTS

The process of researching, writing, and advancing a book manuscript like this one is a constant evolution. During the multiyear process in which *Mascot Nation* unfolded, we found ourselves regularly readjusting the narratives to accommodate new information, breaking stories, and school-by-school and team-by-team developments in the mascot controversy. The development of the project, at its core, involved being willing and able to adjust to shifting ground and public sentiments, which made the constants in our process all the more meaningful.

Luckily, we both experienced many constant sources of support and encouragement as we endeavored to advance this fairly ambitious project. We wish to thank University of Illinois Press—especially Danny Nasset—for embracing the project from its conception and for aiding us at many turns in the writing and revision process. We thank our anonymous reviewers, of both the proposal and the final product, whose contributions were as constructive as they were informative. We also must thank our two institutions, the University of Alabama and the University of North Carolina at Charlotte, for providing us with the time and financial resources to be able to make this book a reality; we are also thankful that the Alabama Crimson Tide and Charlotte 49er communities embrace mascots with which we did not have to grapple and whose politics we did not have to dispute.

Andrew also wishes to thank the College of Communication and Information Sciences and the Department of Journalism and Creative Media for their steadfast support. Moreover, he extends thanks to the donors who made his Ronald Reagan Chair of Broadcasting a reality, as it provides the flexibility and resources to tackle issues such as this one with minimal compromise. He also had two doctoral students, Lauren Auverset and Fei Qiao, who worked as research assistants on various parts of this project and proved invaluable with their time and efforts. Andrew also extends heartfelt appreciation for the contributions from Jacqueline Pata, executive director of the National Congress on American Indians; her interview was essential, formulating one of the core contributions early in the book formulation. Finally, he thanks his wife, Angela, and sons, Nathan and Noah, for their constant support and interest in the mascot debate that subsumed many a dinner or car conversation.

Jason wishes to thank Danielle Endres, Casey Kelly, and Mary Stuckey, whose work on indigenist-centered contexts has been invaluable both to this project and others and, most vitally, whose friendship over the years is treasured. Two of his graduate students, Jinjie Yang and Elizabeth Ballard, assisted with gathering primary texts; both performed their tasks with precision and innovation. He also thanks C. Richard King for paving the way for indigenist-centered scholars for nearly two decades, and to Laurel Davis-Delano, who leads a weekly conversation among scholars exploring representational issues related to Native American mascots. Jason also thanks the Department of Communication at Wake Forest University, the Department of Communication at the University of Utah, and the Native American House and Department of Communication at the University of Illinois for sponsoring colloquia on his mascot work. To his colleagues and students, past and present, at the University of Alabama and UNC Charlotte, respectively, Jason expresses appreciation for the abundance of mascot conversations they have had for well over a decade. Finally, Jason is grateful to his family—Jennifer, AB, and Amelia—whose love and support make life worth living and remind him that justice is something for which we daily ought to fight.

Overall, we are very pleased to present this book to audiences in a manner that heightened our authorial autonomy, allowing our vision to come into focus. We hope you find this book as meaningful as we found the process of researching and writing it.

MASCOT NATION

INTRODUCTION

For Whom Does the Indian Stand?
For Whom Does the Mascot Stand?

The rituals have a modicum of variance, yet common elements persist within the majority of them. For a school or a team with a Native American mascot, there typically is a drumbeat—not a snare drum but rather something more of the tom-tom, bongo, or bass drum variety. Sometimes there are weapons, ranging from spears to tomahawks; occasionally these weapons are set on fire for added effect. There is almost always a chant or song; it becomes difficult to imagine a Florida State University (FSU) football game, for instance, without humming along with the earworm that is the Seminole War Chant. Proponents of such names, images, and rituals find kinship within these consistent practices, noting that all teams enact them in some form. Opponents of Native American mascots find cause for concern, often contending that they represent issues that are disturbing, insensitive, or outright racist.

Within American sports media, there are certain topics that are assured to kindle debate among the masses. For instance, whenever a sports radio host is struggling with a slow news day, a small swath of topics are ready-made media segment fillers at any time. Some prime examples of these topics range from whether Pete Rose should be eligible for Baseball Hall of Fame induction to disagreements as to whether college athletes in revenue-generating sports should be paid a stipend for their contributions. Listeners queue up to provide their stance on such topics, convinced that their position is undeniably nuanced in comparison to the thousands of others already espoused over the course of many years. This handful of subjects consistently motivates public conversation yet rarely results in any meaningful advancement of dialogue and, certainly, any sense of conclusiveness. Such stagnation is the reason why the topics are tried-and-true controversies: resolutions are seemingly nowhere to be found.

One of these decades-long controversies has surrounded the use of Native American mascots. Sports fans debate the merits of changing the mascots in comparison to the value of maintaining the status quo; ultimately, however, little happens when it comes to making any meaningful changes. With both sides firmly entrenched in their views and with ample evidence to bolster each of their cases, there appears no easy middle ground. Perhaps one aspect that makes the mascot debate somewhat anomalous to others, though, is that both sides of the argument are seemingly undergirded with the same question posed to the other side: *why do you care so much?*

If this book were solely about that debate, it would simply be adding to a cacophony of media bluster, more noise largely signifying empty conclusions. However, at its core this is not what *Mascot Nation* is about. Yes, discussions of the acceptability (or lack thereof) of Native American mascots will permeate virtually every chapter, yet the binaries of should change/should not change and should *have to* change/should not *have to* change are secondary to the broader landscapes of what Native American mascots represent. We aim in this book not to just be descriptive but rather to engage surveyed and public voices, to examine the foundations of the Native American mascot, to critically study the debates, and to assess the possible middle grounds of the controversy.

Core within that discussion involves formative questions ranging from "What meaning is typically ascribed to mascots?" to "Does everyone get equal voice in this debate?" to "Can the acceptability or offensiveness of anything be determined via national poll?" In sum, the goal of this book is to reformulate the terms of the debate, to reframe a discussion in a manner to which different types of arguments can be applied. In doing so, ramifications of the debated acceptability of Native American mascots can be ascertained.

• • •

When we began writing this book, the latest iteration of the debate stemmed from a May 2016 *Washington Post* poll; it was harkened as a closing salvo from the proponents of Native American mascots, who claimed this poll ended the debate once and for all.[1] The results were startling, as 504 self-described Native Americans were queried about the acceptability of the perceived-to-be most egregious of all mascotting cases: the National Football League (NFL) franchise, the Washington R-dskins. The headline read, "9 in 10 Native Americans Aren't Offended" by the name. The sub-narratives were easy to translate: If Native Americans do not care about the issue, why should anyone else? Moreover, if the name "R-dskins"—regarded by many historians and even comedian Chris Rock as the rough equivalent of the N-word—was fine with Native Americans, surely all other cases would yield even more consensus. If "R-dskins" was the lowest-hanging fruit, the finding that nine of ten Native Americans did not find it worth picking was hailed as closure.

Once one examined the survey more closely, however, doubts quickly emerged. For instance, Jacqueline Keeler noted that no safeguards were offered to ensure that the respondents were, in fact, Native American.[2] Other items within the survey seemed to reveal an atypical sample, with 56 percent of respondents unable to name the tribal nation in which they or their ancestors' claimed heritage. Other methodological questions emerged as well: the median age of a Native American is twenty-six, yet only 15 percent of the survey results came from respondents age twenty-nine or younger.

Beyond the manner in which the poll was conducted, even larger questions pertained to how it was constructed and interpreted. The survey incorporated forms of semantic differential items, asking people to rate their feelings between two polar opposite terms. However, the *Washington Post* did not always use direct polar opposites. The key item asked people to choose between "offensive" and "does not bother." One would surely assume that one could be "bothered" by the name without finding it formally "offensive"—or vice versa. Indeed, the same poll asked about whether the name was "respectful"; nearly one-third of the respondents indicated it was not.

Nevertheless, this poll sparked much commentary, with each side clinging to the results or critiques immediately levied about the survey. Washington R-dskins owner Daniel Snyder was quick to claim victory: "The Washington Redskins team, our fans and community have always believed our name represents honor, respect and pride. Today's *Washington Post* polling shows Native Americans agree. We are gratified by this overwhelming support from the Native American community, and the team will proudly carry the Redskins name."[3] Meanwhile, Native American groups worked fervently to negate the findings and the interpretations therein. Brian Pollard, board member of the Native American Journalists Association and former *Cherokee Phoenix* executive editor, was quoted by Keeler, arguing that the poll should be disregarded: "What they've created is a piece of data that drives a narrative they desired. This is pretty much frowned upon in the world of journalism to create a story in this way. It would be different if Stanford did a poll and *The Washington Post* covered it. That to me would be much more ethical from a journalistic standpoint. But this was way beyond that. This was something they manufactured from the beginning."[4] Enough doubt was inserted into the poll that Jay Rosenstein ultimately asserted the growing sentiment that "I have no idea exactly what percentage of Native Americans approve or disapprove of these mascots and nicknames. But I can guarantee something else with even greater certainty: neither does the *Washington Post*."[5]

By the end of our writing, the biggest news regarding Native American mascotting was a related Supreme Court decision that was widely viewed as a harbinger for the future of the Washington franchise's mascot. The decision, rendered in June 2017, found that an Asian American rock group could still name itself "The Slants," regardless of the fact that some were offended by its origins as an anti-Asian taboo phrase (reducing Asian people to the size/width of their eyes). The Supreme Court ruled that to eliminate the name was to also limit First Amendment rights; the presumption was that this decision also widened the possible acceptable trademarks to include the Washington R-dskins.[6] Similarities and differences between the two circumstances are discussed briefly in chapter 4 and in more extended fashion in chapter 8, yet the court's decision helps to place mascotting controversies in an appropriate context for this book. In the back-and-forth game regarding the viability of Native American mascots, pro-mascot advocates were scoring the most points.

Nevertheless, *Mascot Nation* is not singularly focused on whether the NFL team in Washington should change its mascot but rather on the presumptions cultivated within those discussions and those within the hundreds if not thousands of Native American mascotting circumstances embedded within American sports culture. For instance, can the acceptability of a name, image, or ritual be ascertained via public polling? Moreover, are such contentious issues rightly founded upon a "majority rules" mind-set? If nearly a third of Native Americans find such a name disrespectful, a majority is not constituted yet a constituency is. At a wedding, one would not opt to tell a joke during a reception toast if they knew nearly a third of the room would find it disrespectful. Somehow, still, debates about Native American mascots reside in different cultural spaces.

The debate is labeled as one of change versus the status quo, but the real question is one of representation: whom does the mascot represent? In the desire for a streamlined singular answer, slippery-slope fallacies abound. If the mascot is honoring a given group, one would presume that Americans are immense animal enthusiasts, with the five most-implemented mascots for all teams being, hierarchically: Eagles, Tigers, Bulldogs, Panthers, and

Wildcats.[7] The bald eagle's status in U.S. lore, symbolizing the strength and freedom of America, could explain the fascination with the Eagles as a team name, but the list becomes troubling when expanding to the top ten most-implemented mascots, as Warriors (#6) and Indians (#8) join this otherwise animal-driven list.

If the mascot is viewed as diminishing the group, relegating it to stereotype, one would presume that Native American mascots would indeed be problematic, yet so would many others. Such slippery-slope arguments inevitably ensue.[8] Proponents of the Native American mascot argue that Notre Dame should change the name of its sports teams, as people from Ireland should be offended by the "Fighting Irish" moniker. They contend that the University of Miami "Hurricanes" is offensive to storm victims, or that the Duke University "Blue Devils" is either satanic or, at a minimum, an inaccurate color representation of Lucifer. The lunacy of the slope encompasses all seemingly unfathomable, albeit real, nicknames. The mascot of Richland High School (WA) is the Bombers because the location provided plutonium for the detonated bomb over Nagasaki; its logo is a mushroom cloud. Centralia High School (IL) is the Orphans, with girls' athletic teams dubbed the Annies. Laurel Hill High School (FL) is the Hoboes, replete with the backpack on a stick. Proponents of Native American mascots argue that to claim such names are offensive is to say such high schools are, respectively, mocking nuclear war, parentless children, and the poverty-stricken within each of these exemplars.

The slope continues to the absurd: the Minnesota Twins could be mocking progeny of multiple-birth pregnancies; Bakersfield assemblyman Roy Ashburn once noted while debating a California bill seeking to ban Native American mascots that his diminutive height led him to believe they should enact a ban on "Giants" as well.[9] The comment was purportedly facetious, but the bill was nevertheless blocked once deliberations ended.

Debating Political Correctness and Agency

Thus, the Native American debate has evolved from one largely about two entities, sport and indigenous peoples, to one that some perceive to be a struggle over American identity, liberalism versus conservatism, and how agency is determined. Brendan O'Neill fuses such concepts, leading his overview of the debate with this passage: "If you want to know how unhinged and divorced from reality political correctness has become, look no further than the controversy over sports teams with offensive names."[10] When then president Barack Obama opined that if he were the owner of the Washington R-dskins, he would "think about changing" the name, the remark sparked an oppositional side that may not even care about football or the Native American mascot debate at all.[11] Instead, the comment was placed within a much larger culture war, tinged with grander disputes about free speech, political affiliations, safe zones, and trigger warnings. Lynn Bartels ultimately tells stories about the continued use of the Lamar High School (CO) Savages through the lens of the "harsh glare of the culture wars," with decisions on whether the name should remain divided clearly down political party lines: Democrats advocating for a change, Republicans embracing the status quo.[12]

Depending on both time and circumstance, agency is either embraced or voluntarily rescinded, as one seeks agency only when one believes that they possess the power to do what they believe is right, along with a sense that they will be rewarded for asserting said power. John Oliver, host of the comedy/news show *Last Week Tonight with John Oliver*, summarized the problematic issues of agency in asserting that "one person remains unmoved and, unfortunately, he is the only one that matters. . . . The word 'Redskins' isn't potentially disparaging to someone; it is currently disparaging to specific individuals. . . . Intending to honor something is a lot different from actually honoring it."[13]

Names vs. Images vs. Rituals

This book is only partly about the R-dskin controversy; it is even only partly about the names involved. Rather, the names beget other potentially more troubling aspects of Native American mascotting—that is, the images and rituals attached to each moniker. Laurel R. Davis studied the manner in which names produce images, which then result in the creation of indelible logos for fan bases, finding the consequences of mascotting particularly troubling when words become visual representations.[14] Such issues still reverberate a quarter century later; Major League Baseball (MLB) commissioner Rob Manfred responded to concerns about the Cleveland Indians logo when the team was in the 2016 World Series, saying, "Fans get attached to logos. They become part of a team's history. So it's not [as] easy as coming to the conclusion and realizing that the logo is offensive to some segment."[15]

An offshoot of the nexus in which the names and logos intersect can also be found in the third core element within this book: the rituals that unfold within the overarching process of Native American mascotting.[16] While names and logos are largely passive to the overall sports fan experience (embodied largely by apparel or single utterances), rituals become active processes that repeatedly unfold over the course of years, leading to large swaths of non-Native peoples falsely feeling authentic kinship with their Native American–mascotted team. Such actions become serialized as repeated measures that problematically unfold at each and every home game—often multiple times during each contest. The rituals become sanitized versions of unsanitized histories; for instance, "the tomahawk chop, where fans mimic scalping their opponents, relies on cultural memory of the violence of colonization where whites and Natives alike lost their lives."[17]

Historical Principles Informing the Native American Mascot Debate

The most common and inherent historical tie to the Native American mascot debate is to colonialism and then, ultimately, postcolonialism from a communicative perspective.[18] Debates percolate now regarding what mascotting means to an individual in the twenty-first century, yet how such names, images, and ritualistic traditions unfold is central to untangling the core concerns on both sides of the debate.[19] Underscoring this warrant, Jennifer Guiliano writes, "It is vital that we return to the historical roots of mascotry to understand its colonial contexts."[20]

Such specific connections to postcolonial traditions are made in much greater detail in chapter 2, but other historical realities also tinge the silhouettes of mascotry. For instance, scholars such as Ellen J. Staurowsky and Michelle Renee Jacobs chronicle how the Cleveland Indians mascot is based on misrepresented and misremembered histories.[21] Without such cultural literacy, the end result can be the whitewashing of Native American legacies. Steve Wulf uses just one issue—tribal lands—as an exemplar for explaining this larger concept:

> The Washington football team, for example, plays on land taken by sword from the Piscataway tribe. Progressive Field, where the Cleveland major leaguers play home games, sits on territory that belonged to the Algonquins. (Some say it's an actual burial ground.) The past, present and future abodes of the Atlanta baseball team were once on the property of the Creeks—until William McIntosh, the son of a Scottish trader and a Creek Indian woman, sold land he didn't really own to the U.S. government.[22]

Such knowledge is not commonly shared, as is the case for the majority of Native American realities, both past and present. Within such sanitization of the Native legacy, "overtly racist acts generally gave way to color-blind, covert racism in the maintenance of white privilege."[23]

Consequently, R. W. Connell's conceptions of entrenched power within a gendered realm can be coupled with George Gerbner and Lawrence Gross's labeling of "symbolic annihilation" to explain the historical roots of disenfranchised indigenous peoples whose objections were often overruled or stifled because of the power dynamics within the formation of a nation in which all must live and coexist.[24] As Erik Brady offers, "Native Americans did not object as these team names multiplied—partly because they were in no position to object, partly because collective names such as Indians and Braves did not seem to implicate them."[25] The result is a uniquely American construct—certainly Australians, for instance, could claim cultural and historical negotiations of identity with Aborigines; however, such histories involve altered angles, trajectories, and outcomes that make the Native American plight singular in nature. Given such a unique tie to the formation of a nation and sports it holds dear, it is clear to see how one could argue that "it is only in America . . . where the image of the defamed and destroyed original people becomes so central to their popular professional sports teams."[26]

Therein lies the crux of the dilemma, a unique, unparalleled case of debate within a sporting context that is based on fun, leisure, and the pursuit of all things seemingly nonserious and apolitical. Endemic within such discussions is the warranted delineation between what people *intend* as a message and how that message is *received*. Very few doubt that Washington R-dskins owner Dan Snyder honestly believes his team's name honors Native American cultures; however, there is a necessary nuance to such a discussion facilitated by understanding the implied meanings and the evolution of language in what Steven Pinker would characterize as a euphemism treadmill.[27] James McWhorter delves even deeper into such evolutions of meaning to make ties specifically to the debate over the name "R-dskins":

> It isn't illogical to wonder, deep down, whether Native Americans are fashioning a controversy . . . [but] "Oriental" came to be associated with stereotypes of the people in question, such that it was felt that a new term was necessary. Long ago, the same thing happened to "Chinaman." What's wrong with calling a man from China a "Chinaman"? Nothing, in the literal sense—but as always, life is more than the literal. "Chinaman" signifies the subservient, exotified "Ah, sohhh!" figure from Charlie Chan movies; out it went and few miss it. . . . This, then, is why "Redskins" qualifies as slur despite not being a literal insult. Words have not only core meanings, but resonances of the kind that may not make it into the dictionary but are deeply felt by all of us. Sometimes

we need to get back down to cases with a new word. It may not be mean to tell someone their skin happens to be reddish. But it's mean to call someone a Redskin. There's a difference.[28]

As a result of this difference between denotative and connotative definitions, sharp criticisms from comedians such as Chris Rock are sometimes prescient to a portion of the population while failing to resonate with others. When Rock argues, "Redskins? That's not nice. This ain't cool. That's a racial slur. That's like having the 'New York Niggas' or 'Denver Dykes,'" he is largely persuading the people who already concur that R-dskin is the equivalent of the other terms he mentions—terms society now generally agrees to be offensive. People on the other side of the issue dub such arguments as a false equivalency, failing to address the euphemism treadmill that Pinker advances.[29]

Depictions of Native Americans in U.S. Society

One would be tempted to limit problematic renderings of Native Americans to the sporting arena, but it is important to note that there are difficulties throughout American media and society at large when depicting, understanding, or claiming empathy for unique Native American experiences in contemporary America.[30] Part of the difficulties emerge due to a lack of understanding about core issues of Native culture, but part of them arise via characteristics of Native American identity that are co-opted or more overtly stolen by mainstream society when finding an element that seems appealing to non-Native populations (such as an Indian headdress).[31] These elements are then submerged in a cultural performance regarding what it means, or should mean, to be a Native American.[32]

The remedy for many non–Native Americans is to claim color-blindness, arguing that all elements of all cultures are welcome to be subsumed into one collective culture that one dubs the "American experience," a feigned panacea with no memory, history, or timeline to muddy the waters. Such utopian notions are highly problematic, because they assume a level ground for all when hegemonic principles infer that this is far from the case. Inequities in terms of gender, age, ability, and sexual orientation are also ameliorated in such a flawed conception, but race certainly appears to rise to the fore more than any other identity-laden American issue, and rightly so. As Amy Bass asserts, "It can be a problem when our personal and professional lives collide. . . . [Race] magnifies things in your daily routine that many people do not deal with, whether when admitting that 'your' team has a history more racist than most or when watching the African American actor in the 'buddy' role die first and realizing you still like the movie."[33] Thus, generalized notions of race and what it means to be Native American become blanket assessments on everything from political correctness to what it means to feel otherness in the twenty-first century.[34] Mascots appear as the most direct embodiment of this experience, as "each [Indian mascot] weaves and reweaves Indigenous Peoples into already-existing universalist narratives that depict 'Indians' in narrow masculine terms—as intrinsically violent, as endlessly fierce."[35]

Yet it is the notion that Native American mascots are predominantly indicative of racialization that some would argue limits the scope of the overarching debate and narratives that ensue. Given the tendency for contemporary Americans to embrace the present and eliminate elements of an ugly past, history is relegated to a footnote—with a desire to forge ahead in a post-racial world winning the day in some circles. Thus, Native American history is taught less than racism and is learned through reductionist myths such as Thanksgiving and Native vision quests. Put more directly by a spokesperson for indigenous peoples:

> It has been the great failure of the Indian-mascot debate to connect the issue to something other than racism and the self-esteem of individual Indian people. What remains unaddressed is the true history of Indian Country, which is to say the true history of the United States: a story of abrogated treaties, of tribal sovereignty limited by Congressional law and of specious Supreme Court decisions, all of which have either hampered or destroyed the ability of tribal people to govern themselves as political sovereigns on their own land.[36]

The need to fuse history becomes central to the debate. Thus, a warrant for advancing this book follows from David Anthony Clark, who astutely notes, "There is no such thing as an 'Indian' athletic mascot that is a perfectly functional object without supplementary, and thus controversial, meanings."[37]

The Desire for Common Ground

To decipher the general orientation of the voices fighting against the use of Native American mascots, we conducted an interview with Jacqueline Pata, executive director of the National Congress of American Indians (NCAI) on February 8, 2017. We queried her about the general strategy of NCAI, as well as the organization's assessment of the progress it believes it has made toward its ultimate aims regarding Native American mascotting. Pata said that a key tactic in NCAI's long-running and multifaceted anti-mascot initiative involves focusing on the most outrageous and high-profile offenders, with the name of the NFL team in Washington, D.C., at the top of the list. In Pata's view, "The worst offender is the Washington team and its name. We believe that if the name of the worst offender goes away, then the others will follow suit. The domino effect has already started because of the growing national conversation about the Washington team, and it's happening state by state, city by city, and school by school." She also was quick to share that NCAI's approach to the mascot issue—like all of its work—is bipartisan, with no favor shown to either political party:

> We are a bipartisan organization; this helps us get things accomplished with the administration and Congress. When Congress is struggling to agree on various issues, federal Indian policy often is one of the few areas where Democrats and Republicans can come together in bipartisan agreement. We've never been able to get one major piece of legislation passed without bipartisan support. I truly believe that the Independent "I" is for Indian; we don't go down any specific party lines.

Such a belief in apolitical views about the issue seems somewhat at odds with how the public views it; Guiliano writes, "Alternative defenses often chide that the attempt to do away with mascots is about 'political correctness,' often code words for politically liberal."[38] According to Pata, the rise of Native American mascots was emblematic of "the federal policy era known as termination. It was a policy designed to assimilate Native people, erode our cultures and traditions, appropriate tribal lands, and extinguish tribal governments. Native-themed mascots that distort and dehumanize Native people informed that policy. They were never about honoring us." Consequently, Pata noted, NCAI's approach has always been based on making society more aware about the complex histories and challenges, enduring cultural diversity and vibrancy, and contemporary life of tribal nations and peoples. She explains:

> We always felt that our best strategy is to educate America about who we really are. Educating the common fan, educating the schools, educating the cities, and the other people who care about their home teams. A lot of times, these fans haven't yet considered the breadth of the impacts of the team's mascot, especially on the mental health of Native youth. Once they open themselves up to learning about, for example, the origins and history of the term that the Washington team uses as its name—a racial slur that treats Native peoples as less than human—we find them willing to support our cause. They can now make educated decisions about how to treat Native people. It is through education that we truly get our message across to people.

Within this overall schema of public education, Pata stresses that she believes there is common ground to be found within the broader Native American–themed mascot controversy and even the seemingly most egregious of cases regarding the name "R-dskin." It appears respect is also at the core of what NCAI hopes to attain:

> Even with the Washington team, we never wanted it not to be a win-win solution. Perpetuating that name is not a winning solution for Indian Country. At the same time, we don't want to punish fans for supporting their home team; we want to create a conversation about how to respect people. Native people are sports fans too. This issue is not about sports. It's much larger than that. This is about respecting people. A part of healing America involves understanding one another and being respectful of one another. America is an extremely complex country, with complex histories, and finding mutual respect between fans and Native people is part of that healing. I just want the fans to find a name and mascot that we can all rally behind when it's football season.

When asked whether the *Washington Post* poll diminishes any sense of momentum the NCAI may have felt toward the elimination of the Washington NFL team name, she instead urged people to read the comments in the qualitative portion of the survey, indicating that when she did so, the message was devastating. Pata indicates that the poll underscored how "many Native Americans feel totally disenfranchised. When they see a poll like this, they say, 'My voice doesn't matter in this. Nobody's going to care anyway.' It's defeatism. It's that feeling of being conquered, which is a common theme in the history of America. People don't care about who we are as twenty-first-century Americans."

Even beyond the beleaguered sentiments in the survey, Pata challenges the overarching premise of not only the *Washington Post* poll but also all similar mechanisms for measuring public sentiment about the issue. She believes such practices are at best flawed or at worst fundamentally misguided, and asks, "Do we really poll to find out our values? Would we have polled values on segregation? Would we have polled the women's right to vote? You can poll to your heart's content, but if it's not right, it's not right."

In making such a claim, Pata echoes the well-tilled concerns about the accuracy and relevance of not only the *Washington Post* poll but also of other polls taken over the past several decades.[39] Moreover, the concept of polling values is something Pata and many others within the anti-mascotting movement argue cannot be accurately captured by traditional polling practices. James V. Fenelon summarizes such trepidation about substituting public opinion for policy by noting, "Nowhere else in American society do we poll a general population to see what they think about using these racialized words and icons. Imagine asking White southerners whether Jim Crow language and imagery was "racist" or not during the Civil Rights movement."[40]

WHAT DOES A MASCOT (RE)PRESENT?

One aspect of this book will appear to have little to do with sport, as the context and history of Native Americans appears most pertinent to understanding how all other elements of the debate unfold. The mascot issue often becomes virtually synonymous with voicelessness, apathy, and generalized systemic problems facing Native Americans in the twenty-first century. Pata also weighed in on the frequent refrain expressed by some that argues that the mascot issue is of minuscule importance compared to other, larger issues facing Indian Country. On the contrary, explains Pata, the two are inextricably connected and feed off of each other:

> At first, I wanted to prioritize other issues. I felt that there were so many other critical issues that needed to be fixed in Indian Country. Fixing the education gap and addressing the health disparities our people face were some of my initial priorities. But soon I realized that the undercurrent of disrespect fostered by mascots will never enable us to fix anything and make progress as long as we continue to be disrespected and discounted in this way. Mascots feed the antiquated, unenlightened notion that Native people are second-class citizens, skewing how the public views us. Placing human beings on the same playing field as animals creates a public perception that we are not twenty-first century Americans that deserve basic human respect.

Pata recalls the moment she realized how much the debate over the Washington NFL team mascot mattered to her and the people she advocates for:

> We talk about generational trauma and what it does to future generations. Generational trauma is when older generations pass down very complex posttraumatic stress to the next generation. This impacts Native people in very real and destructive ways. One day, when I was working for the Clinton administration, we had a number of military servicemen who were building roads and houses on a reservation for a training mission. Once the project was completed, the local tribe hosted a powwow to thank the servicemen for coming out to help and for their service. During Grand Entry, the beginning of a powwow where the colors are presented, the military servicemen were recognized for their contributions to the community. It was such a powerful feeling. I saw proud Native leaders wearing headdresses, having earned every

eagle feather in that headdress, acknowledging and honoring the service that the servicemen had done for our country. That is what respect looks like. When I came back to Washington, D.C., from that experience, I attended a Fourth of July parade featuring the Washington team. They were marching down the street in their fake headdresses and singing their banner song. I cried. It was such a stark contrast from the Grand Entry I had just seen. Non-Native people were mocking the very act that had moved me so much. Seeing the fake headdresses was such a contrast to the men I had just seen who were truly dignified. The parade wasn't dignified and it certainly wasn't respectful.

Thus, the seemingly trivial world of sports is viewed by many in Indian Country as mocking Native people, doing so in the name of fun and presumed honor; however, people like Pata believe the issue causes harm that ripples far outside the confines of athletic fields and arenas:

> To sports fans, this is about sports, but in reality this is not about sports. This is about respecting a group of people. Respecting our identity. Respecting America's heritage. Respecting those that were here before—and that still are here. American history is Native history. Many people don't know who Native peoples truly are, don't know that we have persevered. The imagery that the Washington team and other teams [present] perpetuates false, distorted, and destructive images about who we are. It matters in how policy makers, our neighbors, our classmates, and our fellow Americans view and treat us.

Pata believes there is hope for reaching common ground largely because while "there is an older generation that feel pretty tied to the memories of the Washington team, for example, the younger generations are going to be the ones to make the change, and they are already starting to do just that."

In many ways, national polls conflict with Native American needs through what Stuart Hall argues as three "circuits of culture": uncritical acceptance, negotiated acceptance, and resistance.[41] Many fans of the R-dskins (and other Native American mascot names) follow their team without any sense of the names' origin or historical undergirding, most aptly fitting Hall's circuit of uncritical acceptance. For decades many Native American tribes and individuals worked for the abolition of the names, images, and rituals that teams were using, clearly fitting under the rubric of Hall's sense of the resistance-oriented circuit of culture. Such polls seek to end the friction via Hall's purported middle ground within these circuits: negotiated acceptance. However, Native American entities are likely to view this view not as compromise but rather as a capitulation, because such polls infer that Native Americans are the ones who must "get over it" to move the debate to a sought-for resolution.

This book responsibly focuses on many of the seminal cases of contested Native American mascotting, yet the scope of the use of such names should not be understated. For instance, Mike McPhate reports that not less than 140 California schools still support Native names, including the Durfee School Warriors, the Washington Elementary Little Aztecs, the Ripon High Indians, and the Cherrylee School Chiefs.[42] Joely Proudfit, who leads the California Indian Culture and Sovereignty Center at the California State University at San Marcos, argues that even at these smaller high school levels, the consequences are potentially quite large in terms of the marginalization of indigenous peoples. She notes that her "big issue is, if you dehumanize us, then you're never going to make policies for us. You're never going to give us a seat at the table. You're never going to see us as human beings."[43] C. Richard King writes extensively on such ramifications, arguing that one "cannot disregard context" in their attempt to make the use of offensive Native American names acceptable.[44] His formative and seminal work was an edited volume with Charles F. Springwood in which the authors create a strong warrant for "reinterpreting the forgotten histories of many of these 'invented' Indians."[45]

Mascot Nation: An Overview

This book is coauthored with good reason, as neither of us could conceive the same project without the other. *Mascot Nation* represents a fusion of ideas stemming from two parts of the academic world: empirically driven social scientific data and a humanistic approach undergirded by both rhetorical and cultural criticism. Such a pairing may initially seem odd but ultimately provides a multitude of vantage points, ranging from macro-level surveys to deeper, closer examinations of the struggles that are endemic within each particular Native American mascotting debate.[46] Because of this merged sense of epistemology, multiple theories (self-categorization and postcolonialism) are utilized, as are a large variety of methods (ranging from surveys, to textual analyses, to case studies, to interviews). The reason for such epistemological fusion will, hopefully, become evident as the survey becomes a baseline for understanding (yet somewhat reductionist for most numerical measures) while the case studies provide nuance for the survey results, offering a sense of how each Native American mascotting issue unfolds within its own context and unique time frame.

Our goal is for *Mascot Nation* to bring together conversations from multiple fields and forms of investigation. We are not naïve and myopic enough to believe we can endeavor to offer consensus-driven answers, but we are optimistic enough to believe that this book can at least help people identify the common terms of the debate—the key questions and concerns that must be allayed for any sort of path forward to emerge. In doing so, we seek to honor both sides of the issue by navigating contested terrain; for instance, we will refer to the "Redskins" when the text specifically pertains to surveys about the name or is in quoted text from people who used the word, yet we will otherwise refer to the name as "R-dskin" when not in those delineated circumstances in order to honor the wishes of many indigenous people who consider the fully spelled word a substantial slur.

In the following eight chapters, we explore the tenets of debate and argumentation concerning the Native American mascotting controversy. We do so within a wide array of contexts and through multiple cases, fusing these two epistemologies that rarely are combined within the academic sphere: empirical and humanistic approaches. Regarding the former, the core methodology involves a survey of 1,073 individuals regarding their attitudes about Native American mascotting and also includes qualitative surveys of attitudes within specific sports fan bases. Regarding the latter, rhetorical and critical cultural strategies punctuate the case studies and critical analyses within specific elements of the controversy.

The opening two chapters provide theoretical applications of core understandings regarding mascotting. In chapter 1 the mascot is framed within the lens of self-categorization theory, a mechanism for comprehending in-group preferences and out-group derogation.[47] Controversies about sports team naming are explored, with three case studies then unfolding to illustrate how in-group and out-group statuses have been used to leave the Native American mascot discussion in a stage of intransigency. Specific cases of the University of North Dakota Fighting Sioux, the Pekin High School (IL) Chinks, and the Florida State University Seminoles explain how the typically desired in-group status that is purported to exist in other spheres was not a major factor when determining the accessibility of the mascot, with out-group status often used to abdicate responsibility. In doing so, the chapter provides an understanding of how sport fandom is formed with in-groups and out-groups (causing favoritism and derogation, respectively), juxtaposed with the racial frameworks in which Americans often inherently define themselves. Such divisions within and among groups are used to potentially explain how groups find little room for consensus when arguments are merged within the confluence of identity issues. The chapter and its macro-framework serve as the silhouette of the book's more audience effects–based contribution to the mascotting controversy.

The latter of the pair of theoretical chapters, chapter 2, then contextualizes both Native American cultures and, most vitally, Native American mascots in Western public imaginaries. Particular attention is paid to the history of the Native American mascot and how it frequently complements a largely American narrative of survival and victimhood. Introduced here is the macro-framework of postcolonialism. The concept is then underscored by case studies of Native American mascotting emanating from FSU and the University of Illinois. Ultimately, chapter 2 serves as the theoretical bedrock of the book's more critical-analytical contributions to an exploration of the mascotting controversy.

Chapter 3 then attempts to set the terms of the mascotting debate, using an analysis of comments on user-generated media (YouTube) to explore the common themes the general public rendered in response to two point/counterpoint media messages: an anti-mascotting ad titled "Proud to Be" and a pro-mascotting ad titled "Redskin Is a Powerful Name." The focus of the chapter is less on the construction of each message and more about identifying the common themes each side offered as primary arguments within the comments sections of each YouTube page. Those themes are then applied throughout the remainder of the book as they shed light on the common fault lines that continually occur in the discussion of the Native American mascot.

The next three chapters delve into the core particulars of the mascotting issue, dividing the discussion into the names ascribed, images attached, and rituals embedded within Native American mascotting structures. The first of these chapters, chapter 4, pertains to names and textual fields. The chapter attends to the ways that Native American mascot names and the texts surrounding them create meaning within the public sphere. The chapter unfolds in three stages, with the first being results from a national survey of 1,073 respondents used to shape responses to the current names employed as Native American mascots, determining where public sentiment stands regarding acceptability and potential offensiveness but also what such names mean to them as well as their specific stances regarding blanket bans on names and specific cases such as the NFL team in Washington. Their comments are then reported as categories of meaning, with specific cases of contested Native American names as examples, and then with an extended case study (an in-depth exploration of the name "R-dskin") analyzed through a postcolonial framework.

Chapter 5 focuses on the second of the three-pronged structure for deconstructing the mascot, concentrating on the visual symbols encompassing a Native American mascot and how such symbols create meaning and are assessed by the public. Similar to chapter 3, the chapter unfolds in three stages, with the first being results from the same national survey of 1,073 respondents used to shape responses to the current visual symbols used by teams—specifically, the logo. Historically discontinued logos are assessed to determine longitudinal trends; multiple logos for a given team are studied to show differences between some primary and secondary logos. A hierarchy is ultimately created to be able to predict overall acceptability and offensiveness based on the presence (or lack thereof) of Native American faces, bodies, objects, and actions. Those results are then reported as categories of meaning, with specific cases of contested Native American symbols as examples. Finally, the chapter concludes with an extended, in-depth exploration of the caricatured Cleveland Indians logo. Again, this case study is analyzed through a postcolonial framework.

The final of the analytical chapters, chapter 6, attends to the ways that the rituals and performances that append to and generate from Native American mascots generate public meaning and are subsequently assessed. Again, following the three-stage structure, the chapter features results from the same national survey of 1,073 respondents who were shown video clips (ranging from fifteen to thirty-five seconds) of various rituals performed at games and contests featuring Native American–mascotted teams. In doing so, the chapter determines where public sentiment stands regarding not only the acceptability but also the offensiveness of such acts. The final two parts of the chapter include specific cases of contested Native American rituals as examples and an extended case study involving a postcolonial assessment of Native American mascotting rituals performed at and by FSU.

Chapter 7 moves into the qualitative survey realm to aid in determining the presumed stakes involved in the (dis)continuation of a Native American mascot. Two fan bases received a predominantly qualitative survey (albeit with several quantitative items): 92 respondents who were self-identified fans of Illinois and 147 respondents who were self-identified fans of FSU. The former was selected because of the decision over a decade ago to discontinue the use of Chief Illiniwek, retiring him as a mascot yet retaining him as a "symbol." The latter was selected because of the still-in-use Chief Osceola mascot, despite many calls for his elimination. Collectively, the surveys provide a sense of answering the question of "What is lost?" or "What is *potentially* lost?" within the overarching scope of the Native American mascot debate.

The closing piece, chapter 8, attends to conceptions of the Native American mascot in the future, presenting larger findings related to the book's driving questions—namely, *what* does the Native American mascot actually mean to U.S. public culture? *Why* does the mascot inscribe meaning in the way that it does? And *how* does the public interpret the names, images, and rituals surrounding Native American mascots? Based on a summary of the findings in the preceding chapters, the conclusion outlines implications of and for the Native American mascot controversy, moving into the future by positing pertinent questions Americans should seek to answer and by providing inroads for change to consider with regard to Native American mascots.

Mascot Nation: The Stakes

Overall, the aim of *Mascot Nation* is threefold. We seek to (1) advance a theoretically driven dialogue as to why contestations of Native American mascots not only persist but seemingly rise in presumed stakes and with fervor; (2) delineate survey-based understandings of presumed fault lines, semantic shifts, and notions of presumed power that are subsumed within the controversy; and (3) interrogate case studies in which the Native American mascot deliberations took different turns depending on the time, place, and actors involved. As previously asserted, this volume offers no definitive answers; however, we do believe that it crystallizes notions of why various camps and positions have been formed, what is at stake when we debate the Native American mascot, and whether common ground can be found when one uncouples names from images and rituals when determining what is acceptable and feasible within sports culture. What follows is a sincere attempt at moving toward resolution—even when that common ground is not clear or immediate.

1

Framing the Mascot through Self-Categorization

Lawrence Baca writes of the racially charged environments created by Native American mascot debates within American schools and in the public sphere, yet the continual friction found within the dialogues about mascots cannot be condensed to the "other side" simply not "getting it."[1] Admittedly, historical and traditional notions of hegemony play integral roles in the lack of consensus on using indigenous names, images, and symbols; however, each debate offers nuance and variation on themes involved within seemingly contradictory discourses.[2] Jackson Miller notes a "performative struggle" for control and ownership of Native American history, and both concepts are explored in the subsequent pages.[3] While the introduction provided some context regarding the history of Native American marginalization, minimization, and fragmentation of Native Americans through the mediated lens of sport, chapter 1 is designed to explore how modern hostilities are cultivated with underpinnings not only in communication but also in sociology and psychology research streams. More specifically, this chapter employs the theoretical underpinning of self-categorization to explain the many layers of binary opposition that ultimately form in-groups and out-groups within the modern debate surrounding Native American mascots.

In essence, this chapter attempts to explain theoretical issues of sociological and psychological commonality. An argument can be postulated that while each Native American name, visual representation, or ritual retains unique dynamics, modern arguments begin with the simple opposition of "us vs. them" and then (d)evolve into more complicated notions of who and/or what constitutes "us" or "them."[4] According to Stephanie A. Fryberg, Hazel Rose Markus, Daphna Oyserman, and Joseph M. Stone, each core argument is frequently offered in the binary.[5] As Scott Freng and Cynthia Willis-Esqueda note, "The stereotype of American Indians historically falls under two broad categories: one with a positive evaluative component, that of the noble savage (brave, religious, silent, and nature loving) and the other with a negative connotation (lazy, lecherous, superstitious, untrustworthy, thieving, drunken Indian)."[6]

In such depictions, even seeming positivity is tinged with negative notions of otherness. For instance, in the positive evaluative "component," indigenous communities are pivoted between violent prowess or demure stoicism, punctuating the ways that Native Americans are further marginalized as antithetical to "civilization" in Western public imaginaries. Thus, the debates become intricately layered and essentialized into pure latitudes of the acceptance or rejection of key arguments depending on one's membership (or lack thereof) in a core in-group or out-group.[7] The chapter begins with core explanations of self-categorization theory before moving those debates into the sports domain and then into the more specific realm of the use of Native American mascots until finally offering emblematic case studies of these embodied theoretical ties. Within this final section, core examples such as the use of the University of North Dakota (UND) Fighting Sioux, the Pekin High School (IL) Chinks, and the Florida State University (FSU) Seminoles are used to illustrate how binary tensions unfold in a much more complex mixture of "us vs. them" dichotomies—well beyond the dichotomy of Native Americans vs. non–Native Americans. Ultimately, discussions of who exerts voice in the debate as well as the volume at which that voice is heard are used to undergird this first of two theoretical chapters.

Self-Categorization Theories

Over the course of many decades, a program of communication theories has been developed that collectively attempts to explain how humans seemingly and innately divide one another into various groups. Leon Festinger developed social comparison theory with these types of segmentations in mind, as the theoretical underpinnings emphasize how one defines oneself either by presumed similarities or differences within the world in which they interact.[8] Central to Festinger's theory is the notion that cognitive dissonance is reduced by discovering similarities within a preferred group or by finding dissimilarities with an undesired group.[9] Shelli E. Taylor and Marci Lobel found that both forms of self-evaluation function simultaneously; humans create numerous upward contacts (creating satisfaction through positive association) along with downward comparisons (creating satisfaction through disassociation with groups perceived to be undesirable).[10]

Henri Tajfel and John C. Turner utilize the psychology embedded in social comparison theory to offer social identity theory, which introduces the concepts of in-groups and out-groups more directly.[11] The theory is a notable advancement in the predictive aspect of its conception, positing that people's actions are often attributable to the group with which they identify, making cognitions and behaviors more foreseeable.[12] A year later self-categorization theory was formally introduced in a manner that made in-group and out-group characterizations more general (as the associations are often loosely defined and inherently malleable) yet also more accessible (as different types of groups, ranging from demographic, to educational, to social, to familial, and well beyond can be more easily delineated).[13] Self-categorization was dubbed a form of social identity of the group in that it specifies that one's personal associations are inextricably linked with one's group associations, showing how one cognitively defines oneself within not only the group in which they identify (in-group) but also by the one in which they do not consider themselves to be similar (out-group).[14]

At the core of this program of theories is the view that there are two ways to cognitively define oneself: by who one *is* and by who one *is not*. Arguably, there is no place more directly submerged in "us vs. them" dichotomies than the sporting arena. Rachel A. Smith and Norbert Schwartz do an excellent job of highlighting how collegiate allegiances are built around not just constructed similarities with one's own institution but also, quite crucially, in the amplification of differences with a rival institution.[15] These scholars found linguistic distinctions in how one describes their "own" team/school yet also found differences in behaviors, finding, for instance, that a win would result in more people within the in-group wearing university-oriented clothing. Such results mirrored the three football studies conducted earlier by Robert B. Cialdini, Richard J. Borden, Avril Thorne, Marcus Randall Walker, Stephen Freeman, and Lloyd Reynolds Sloan, in which they found associative pronoun use increasing as the result of a win and decreasing when a team failed (e.g., "we won" vs. "they lost").[16] They dubbed the concept BIRGing, or Basking in Reflected Glory, to explain such attachments—which certainly exist in sport but also permeate virtually all other aspects of modern society, particularly in the contexts of political partisanship and nationalism.

Self-Categorization Applications to Sport

Schisms formed under the lens of self-categorization are sharpened in the sporting arena, a realm in which "us vs. them" dichotomies are perhaps most formalized, along with American political distinctions of Democrats and

Republicans, which coalesce around "red team" and "blue team" connotations.[17] Alberto Voci studied the phenomenon within a soccer team, focusing on fans as well as team employees.[18] The study illustrates a seemingly two-pronged conception of self-categorization where similarity with the in-group (the soccer team) resulted in depersonalization—molding those within the amalgamated group into a homogenous, single unit with bolstered similarities while simultaneously strengthening perceived differences with the other team. As Voci notes, "The more the in-group was perceived as homogeneous and, at the same time, distinct from the out-group, the more the self was depersonalized. . . . The more the self was depersonalized—that is, the more the self was perceived as different from the out-group and similar to other in-group members—the stronger were group phenomena."[19] In sum, the study highlights how group membership can form a sense of black and white with little gray distinctions in between.

Other studies have shown how sport hardens divisions while escalating emotions. Within college football, Shaughan Keaton and Christopher Gearhart found anger linked to self-categorization tendencies, a connection not found with more moderate emotions such as happiness or sadness.[20] These strong emotions are amplified when the stakes of a sporting contest are higher; for instance, highly identified fans were more likely to lose control of their behavior particularly in playoff or other high-stakes sports scenarios.[21] The result is that fans often experience a game entirely differently depending on which team they root for and specifically relating to the degree through which team identification unfolds in self-categorization. More specifically, "Due to shared group membership (and the positivity extoled toward those categories with which an individual possesses membership), fans of a team will be more likely to interpret the behaviors of that team favorably relative to fans of an opposing team."[22] Thus, a clear binary appears inherent in any discussion of sporting loyalties.

Michael A. Hogg and Barbara A. Mullin find that accessibility, both chronic and situational, shape identity salience.[23] The inherent temporality of sports fandom—the embodiment of the temporary loss of the here and now—can be used to explain not only the division between the in- and out-group but also the embodied rift between one's "normal" self and the person they can become when heavily invested in sports fanship.[24] Clifford Stott, Paul Hutchison, and John Drury explore soccer hooliganism, finding that while self-categorization distinctions are fluid for sports fans, dependent on both time and circumstance, World Cup soccer fans often become caught in a maelstrom of nationalism and sports fandom, activating those in-group affiliations above most other potential perceived kinships.[25] The scholars found that overt hostility toward out-groups was cultivated while those who defended any in-group players or beliefs were regarded as heroes. In attempting to psychologically decipher what occurs in these scenarios, the authors claimed that "the nature of the social relations in the intergroup context for both groups was such that it functioned, in part at least, to shape the normative dimensions of the social category driving collective action."[26] As such, one's loyalties are not only fostered by the in-group but also performed to external constituencies that threaten in-group cohesion.

The notion that self-categorization is in some sense "activated" is essentially an acknowledgment that the number of groups with which one identifies is so immense that one cannot navigate modern society with each element of group membership (or lack thereof) central in one's mind. Thus, the ability for sport to seemingly trump all other aspects when game day commences underscores the power of affiliation.[27] In such scenarios, cognitive and affective dimensions are generally inseparable—a metacontrast dimension formed as a predictor of intergroup bias.[28] When sporting allegiances cause other ties to be less relevant (albeit temporarily), sports fans become less sensitive to other in-groups with which they identify, "blasting friends and family who are supporters of rival universities (i.e., not strangers); although they share group identities with these individuals (e.g., same hometown, gender, social class), these commonalities are pushed aside when engaging in blasting behaviours."[29] In sum, the greater the athletic stakes, the more aggression is manifest within games.[30]

Thus, it is crucial to discern instances when schisms between groups are more likely to become salient. For instance, John C. Turner found that competition was unlikely to naturally occur when in-group and out-group perspectives were considered to be within some range of each other in terms of perceived quality.[31] However, this is in direct contrast to most sports conceptions, where rivalry games create magnified allegiances at least in part because the two teams wish to occupy the same lofty terrain/ranking/playoff position.[32] Indeed, Turner noted the possible paradox in sports, arguing that "an 'easy' victory in sport is often valued less than a victory in a close, hard-fought contest—presumably because under certain conditions positively valued distinctiveness requires that the out-group not be depreciated."[33] The tension created through a game that is considerably in doubt bolsters these positive feelings, allowing rivalries and other primary contests to kindle greater "us vs. them" distinctions.

Studies have also shown how self-categorization is stronger (at least in the United States) for university affiliations than for city or state affiliations, as well as how the threat of a home loss increases in-group favoritism.[34] Scholars have found that being cut from playing on a sports team resulted in an immediate drop of in-group allegiance because "self-protection processes may be related to short-term changes in domain-specific self-concept measures such as athletic identity."[35] Such an eclectic group of variables illustrates how circumstances can shift overall in-group perceptions in sport, as well as perceived out-group derogation behaviors and cognitions.

Many of the distinctions summarized in this section relating to sport and self-categorization could be classified as negative traits, because they often create kinships with those in which one may have little in common while also creating enemies with fairly little justification.[36] However, potential unintended positive consequences are also possible; E. Nicole Melton and George B. Cunningham found that identification with sport could help to counteract negative feelings about stigmatized demographic groups, such as people within the LGBTQ community.[37] For instance, fans of the University of Missouri football team could have more positive feelings about the inclusion of gay athletes after one of their own, Michael Sam, publicly came out as a gay athlete. Thus, it appears that such team connections could blunt other levels of friction within groups, including those divides by issues of gender, race, heritage, and culture.

Self-Categorization and the Native American Mascot Debate

The possibility of using sport for social change provides a seamless transition to understanding the theoretical underpinnings of self-categorization as it specifically relates to the use of Native American mascot names, images, and rituals. John S. W. Spinda found that self-categorization theory can be used to predict stances and biases, which is certainly the case with the aforementioned mascots, as those on the "inside" of such fan bases may feel threats that others may not.[38]

Identity is often, in some sense, performed; a young boy experiencing physical pain might adopt masking techniques to perform a sense of hypermasculine power, thwarting the conveyance of the emotions he feels. Just as one performs one's identities within other realms of society, so, too, is mascotting a performative act. As such, "performances of sport mascots borrow from history, but they also create new versions of history which are paradoxical and the selected/new histories are forwarded as authentic."[39] The problems become engrained within the mascotting struggle at that point, fostering friction between old and new histories.

Table 1.1: Dichotomies at Play in Native American Mascot Debates

Native American	vs.	Non-Native American
Racial Minority	vs.	Racial Majority
Non-Sports Fan	vs.	Sports Fan
University Alumnus	vs.	Non-University Alumnus
Corporate Interest	vs.	Societal Interest
Historian	vs.	Contemporarian
Politically Correct Advocacy	vs.	Politically Incorrect Resistance
Liberal	vs.	Conservative
Change Embracement	vs.	Status Quo Embracement

History mixes with issues such as contemporary fan identity and team identification to create a unique blend of self-categorization regarding who "owns" the mascot and, thus, who becomes the temporal and possessive arbiter of whether a mascot should continue to be used.[40] For instance, one clear dichotomy of self-categorization pertains to whether one is Native American or not. Even ardent supporters of the use of Native American mascots seemingly cede the highest terrain to local and national Native American tribes and associations. However, other types of dichotomies play at least some sort of secondary role in the negotiation of the offensiveness or acceptability (or lack thereof) of Native American mascots. Table 1.1 illustrates a mere sampling of the potential binaries that make arguments that arise during the debate both byzantine and potentially convoluted.

As one can see from table 1.1, many issues are activated depending on time, history, and circumstance. Seemingly, one element of the debate pertains to whether one's being of Native American descent should be a primary form of self-categorization or whether it should be the only form of self-categorization—making all other dichotomies not only secondary but irrelevant. Such distinctions unfold in a manner that clearly establishes that even if one believes only Native Americans should be able to voice their opinion on various indigenous mascots, that stance is more optimal than realistic. Study after study shows that different groups feel as if some level of ownership can be claimed in a debate beyond the central notion of Native American vs. non–Native American stances.[41] Three short case studies illustrate the various binaries that are often activated when disputes occur over whether a Native American mascot should be retained. The first involves the now defunct UND Fighting Sioux (abolished in 2012), the second renders the ethnic parallels within the debate over the Pekin Fighting Chinks, and the final case incorporates the still widely used mascot for FSU: the Seminoles and the use of Chief Osceola in image and ritual performances.

Case #1: The Intransigent Donor and the University of North Dakota Fighting Sioux

First, much insight can be taken from the evolution of the debate surrounding the UND Fighting Sioux.[42] Before 1930 the university officially claimed the nickname "Flickertails," a type of squirrel found in that region of the country. That changed to "Sioux" in 1930, and then "Fighting Sioux" in 1999. Since then, the name has been retired and reinstated at least three times, with most of the debates surrounding the argument of who constitutes an in-group for having the power to decide the fate of the mascot.[43] At various points it appeared that local Native American tribes could effectively protest the name, arguing for its elimination for not honoring their heritage, yet other forms of interests often trumped the feelings of the indigenous local tribes.[44]

David Wahlberg chronicles one of those deviations, specifically the case of UND alumnus and former college athlete Ralph Engelstad, who made a $100 million donation in 2000 for the construction of a new arena, at the time one of the largest donations ever given to a public school and certainly one of the very few for a school not occupying the highest divisions of collegiate sports competition.[45] Engelstad had a condition to his gift, though: the name "Fighting Sioux" must be retained in perpetuity. Using Steven Fink's book illustrating stages of crisis management, Wahlberg chronicles the negotiations that followed, attempting to navigate different stakeholder interests while keeping the arena construction progressing.[46] The facility ultimately opened in 2011 but not without many constituencies noting that corporate interests seemed to speak more loudly than all others within the debate. As one newspaper report summarized, "If [UND is] going to sell its soul, $100 million is a good price to fetch."[47]

Various types of in-groups were activated in the coming years as statewide ballot initiatives, state senate votes, university Board of Higher Education decisions, and attempts to lobby local indigenous groups resulted in the status of the mascot changing nearly once a year. Finally, in 2012 the "Fighting Sioux" was retired and five new names ("Fighting Hawks," "Nodaks," "North Stars," "Roughriders," and "Sundogs") were deliberated upon for years after that (seemingly final) decision.[48] In late 2015 the team and its mascot were renamed the "Fighting Hawks."[49]

From a communicative point of view, the intermittent salience of a variety of in-group constituencies within the debate unfolded under a guise of myth and heritage.[50] The meaning and sense of history surrounding that perceived meaning shifted based on one's standpoint and overall levels of cultural sensitivity.[51] Raul Tovares identifies the context of this negotiated terrain, arguing that "the Fighting Sioux logo is a cultural artifact created over time within a social context. . . . Like all artifacts, the origins and development of the Fighting Sioux logo are rooted in a dynamic interaction of cultural, political, and economic conditions."[52] Those conditions are both temporally and contextually sensitive and determinant.

Case #2: All Politics (and Mascots) Are Local within the Case of the Pekin Chinks

Another instructive case that can be used to exemplify issues of agency and ownership within conceptions of in-groups and out-groups arises from the complex—and yet now largely decided—case of the Pekin mascot that until the 1980s was dubbed the "Chinks." While not Native American specifically, the controversy proves useful in identifying paths to remove names, mascots, and rituals considered to be offensive by an ethnicity. James Loewen believes the case is highly illustrative of race-based mascotting controversies, functioning as "an in-your-face example of White privilege."[53]

Richard B. Stolley chronicles the various origins and arguments surrounding the rise and eventual fall of the word and mascot over the course of time.[54] The town of Pekin, Illinois, itself was perceived by its founders to have connections to China; in the 1820s founders named the town "Pekin" because they believed it was geographically on the other side of the Earth from Peking, China. That was later proven not to be the case; the opposite side was the Indian Ocean, yet early settlers embraced the name to the point that when a high school was established in the 1930s, the nickname "Chinks" was seemingly viewed as honoring the now century-long history of the city in which people resided. For many decades, little documentation of any controversy can be found, likely because very few (if any) Asian Americans had made Pekin their home. From a theoretical perspective, the name seemingly stood (despite growing national sentiment that "Chinks" was indeed an ethnic slur for people of Chinese descent) predominantly because there was no perceived out-group instigating dissent or feeling direct effects of the nickname and the selected mascots, Chink and Chinklette, who banged a gong whenever something positive happened for a Pekin High School sports team.

As again summarized by Stolley, dissonance began more formally in 1974, when representatives from the Organization of Chinese Americans (OCA) visited with Pekin officials about the mascot. The officials from Pekin reportedly were stunned to hear the mascot was offensive to the OCA representatives but took no direct action to change it. The city mayor and boards were made aware of the issue yet claimed they lacked agency, contending that they did not have the power to make the school change its nickname. Again, self-categorization theory comes to the fore as different officials did not feel as if they were part of an in-group that could directly change the culture (and, in this case, mascot) of the people within the smaller subsection that would be most directly affected by any change.

Shortly after the visit with the OCA, Chinese Americans met with the Pekin High School Student Council, arguing that students held the power to change the name. A decision to vote on the name change occurred, with the school newspaper advocating for the end of the use of the name and mascot. However, the results indicated a strong preference for keeping "Chinks," with 85 percent of juniors and seniors voting in favor of the status quo.[55]

By 1975 the *Journal-Star* (Peoria, IL) indicated they would no longer print the mascot name; the Illinois Commission on Human Relations threatened a lawsuit if the name remained. The name had become a national story and larger governmental investigation. However, the Illinois Department of Health, Department of Education, and Department of Welfare's Office for Civil Rights concluded that the name was not discriminatory against Asian American students, because there were no Asian Americans at the school. Again, the lack of a direct, local perceived out-group appeared to be a crucial lacking component to enacting change.

Finally, in 1980 James Elliott was hired as superintendent and immediately changed the name to the "Dragons."[56] After years of controversy, debate over who was part of the in-group as well as whether there was a constituted out-group, and national attention, Pekin High School swiftly and immediately changed. Teachers largely accepted or tacitly endorsed the decision, yet the community struggled with a perceived loss of identity, with parents vowing to fight to protect their children's rights to be "Chinks." Several hundred student protesters represented the group who felt they had moved from in-group to out-group status through a perceived loss of agency. Students picketed with signs that said things like "Old Chinks never die, they just drag-on."[57]

However, elements of the name still live, particularly from graduates of the high school who feel part of their identity is tied to the distinctively monikered mascot. In the 1990s, Pat Hagen, a Pekin graduate, referenced one of the most famous Pekin graduates, former senate minority leader Everett McKinley Dirksen, as a core in-group member shaped by his connection to the mascot: "He was born a Chink; he died a Chink; he's known around the world as a Chink."[58] Some residents of Pekin still harbor resentment of the decision, yet the controversy has largely subsided.

Similar debates and trajectories between the Pekin High School case and current debates about Native American mascots offer parallels between malleable notions of in-group and out-group statuses and whether Native American mascots should be eliminated. In endeavoring to crystallize the parallels between the cases, Jonathan Zimmerman asks, "How is the Chink any worse than the Redskin, the feather-clad mascot of Washington's pro football franchise? It isn't. The only difference is that the Redskin purports to be American Indian, not Chinese. And unlike any other ethnic group, Native Americans remain fair game for bigotry on game day."[59] Thus, there is a perceived uniqueness of the Native American mascot that ostensibly makes the parameters of the cases different from the Chink or other mascotting labels based in ethnicity.

Case #3: Lack of Tribal Agreement within Debates about the Florida State Seminoles

These same cultural, political, and economic conditions develop within a similar, yet distinctly different, example in our final illustrative case of self-categorization theory in action within the debate: the ongoing clash between different stakeholders regarding the Seminole mascot at FSU. Within this long-standing dispute, FSU claims to have in-group Native American support through partnership with the Seminole Tribe of Florida (STF) while still attempting to squelch contention surrounding the name (and the images and rituals surrounding it) by other non-regional Seminole groups, most specifically the larger, Oklahoma-based Seminole Nation.

Here, the region of the country in which one resides becomes central to a sense of who deserves and has earned a voice in the debate. Michelle R. Jacobs found that indigenous populations residing exclusively within urban settings were less likely to resist romantic portrayals of Indianness of the Cleveland Indians mascot than were Native Americans who lived on or near a reservation before moving to Northeast Ohio. It seems that one's locality shades judgments.[60] Thus, regionality and proximity become key functions within the FSU case study. Most FSU fans believe the name, the embodied mascot (Chief Osceola), and the rituals and chants that accompany the moniker are socially acceptable through an agreement with the STF, which established a partnership with the school. (See chapter 6 for an extended discussion of the agreement.) David Zirin, however, disagrees with the notion of what he terms a "racism amnesty card," noting that the agreement is with the STF and not with the much larger group known as the Seminole Nation of Oklahoma.[61] The Seminole Nation of Oklahoma has offered a consistent stance against the use of the Seminoles mascot (and the pomp and circumstance surrounding it), yet a 2005 ruling from the National Collegiate Athletic Association (NCAA) argued for a unique relationship between FSU and the STF's tribal council, determining that the university could maintain all aspects of the status quo.[62] In contrast to virtually every other Native American mascot controversy, FSU offers a unique claim of in-group endorsement, which could help "explain why, if Native American mascots keep ebbing in the United States through the 21st century, 'Florida State Seminoles' could be the last one standing in the 22nd."[63]

Thus, the FSU case becomes one of whether in-group status should best be determined by groups that are the most local (STF) or groups with the largest constituency (Seminole Nation). The majority of Seminole Indians reside in Oklahoma yet are argued to be not as geographically central to the Florida-based group, prompting a larger question of whether FSU is a regional brand or a national one. Moreover, economic advantage is also part of equations such as how the local tribe benefits from the partnership, but the Seminole Nation of Oklahoma does not.

Debates also persist as to whether FSU is educating locals on Seminole histories or, instead, is building unfounded myths regarding Seminole culture.[64] For instance, Chief Osceola plants a spear into the football field while riding an Appaloosa horse, even though Seminoles in that area of the country rarely rode horses because of the swampy terrain. He carries a spear and inspires a "tomahawk chop," even though Chief Osceola was a crack shot with a rifle. Visually, the Seminole logo mirrors a Plains Indian caricature by way of a head feather, hooked nose, and agape mouth (not to mention the updated 2015 version that sports what appears to be a Mohican coiffure). Such inconsistencies are regarded as more than reinterpreting history but rather a reimagining of Seminoles that thwarts attempts to teach their history. As Zirin concludes, "No one is getting educated about Osceola or the Seminole Wars. Instead their heroic resistance has been translated for football purposes to being 'tough.' This 'respect' for their toughness not only reduces a rich and varied Seminole culture to a savage culture of war, it is also an unspoken way to praise out won ability to engineer their conquest."[65] In the embodiment of this quotation, Zirin establishes one of the core issues facing those favoring Native American mascot elimination: even the positive attributes problematically connect with conceptions of bellicosity and savagery.

Implications of Self-Categorization Theory

This chapter illustrates the various binaries present within in-group and out-group status and distinctions within the debate. Beyond issues of demographics ranging from race, to cultural history, to region of country, the groups seemingly diverge on several interrelated central notions: Who has the right to speak? Who has the power to enact change or preserve the status quo? Who "owns" the legacy of the Native American mascot? Even if and when such multifaceted issues are somewhat successfully negotiated, society tends not to wholeheartedly validate such decisions for many years. For instance, Jessica M. Toglia and Othello Harris performed qualitative interviews after the name of the team mascot for Miami University of Ohio was changed from the "R-dskins" to the "RedHawks."[66] Groups were divided into three different constituencies based on when a person had graduated, finding varied yet continual resistance to the change at all levels. They note that "even though the athletic team nickname changed, views did not necessarily change accordingly. . . . Simply changing an athletic team nickname does not necessarily coincide with a change in practices if structural changes are not made in addition to the name change."[67]

There is no definitive position as to why such resistance remains entrenched. Certainly some scholars have claimed that the core of such issues is based on a tangled legacy of myth and misunderstanding, articulating that "vicious resistance to this challenge occurs because the myth is central to the shaping of American and hegemonic masculine identity."[68] Such core conceptions of American identity are difficult to alter in any demonstrable manner.[69]

Thus, self-categorization (embedded in broader notions of social identity theory) is crucial for understanding debates within and among disagreeing groups; one's standpoint is frequently employed as a trump card, arguing that when two or more groups seem hopelessly at odds, the faction with in-group status should inherently win the debate. Sometimes these in-groups are not built on demographics but as elements of the status quo contrasted against a change-oriented position. Such stances are predicated on histories (if it has been used for X years and the Earth kept spinning, that is an argument for maintenance of current policies); other times they are founded on cultural myths (if people believe something to be true/authentic, then it seemingly "becomes" acceptable as entrenched over time). As a result, different groups enjoy varying levels of status based on their ability (or lack thereof) to garner in-group status within society.

The three specific case studies in this chapter illuminate how such groups unfold. With the first, UND, a donor's stance on the issue was used to thwart indigenous populations who felt otherwise. With the second, status quo was embraced for the Chinks' mascot name by various populations arguing that they were not in-groups and therefore could not work to enact change. In the final case, society seemed to acknowledge the STF's in-group status but then disagreed on which tribe of Seminole (local vs. national) enjoyed that status more imminently. All cases underscore the power embedded within the theory, illustrating how Native American mascot debates are often decided not by who shouts the loudest but by whose voice should be "rightly" elevated within the cacophony based on a determination of privilege that some tacitly have and others explicitly seek.

2

The Native American Mascot in the Western Gaze

Reading the Mascot through a Postcolonial Lens

Chapter 1 framed the mascot through sociological and psychological research streams dedicated to a study of self-categorization. Self-categorization helps us to discover how and why people define themselves within an in-group, especially as opposed to another group imagined as an enemy or at least an antagonist—a perceived "threat" to the supremacy or cohesion of the in-group. As was explained, self-categorization seamlessly connects to sports and sport culture when fans of one particular in-group are inoculated into a positionality, or team "camp," in relation to other out-groups who do not share the same relationship to a team identity as well as its traditions, history, and instantiations of its fans' culture. The implications of this theoretical link to fandom hold productive potential for better exploring Native American mascots—that is, self-categorization provides the contours of the debate over the propriety and efficacy of the Native American mascot. When one asks why fans activate their opinions on Native American mascots' textuality, visuality, and ritual in the ways they do, perhaps it is an in-group/out-group dynamic that catalyzes their entrenched positions. Western dichotomies of "right and wrong," "winning and losing," "ethics and immorality," "respect and impertinence," and "heritage and hate" become polar ends of a rope that opponents pull on in a cultural tug-of-war, an apt metaphor because both its tenor of sport and vehicle of "camps" involve in-groups and out-groups.

The present chapter engages not *why* people self-categorize during the mascot debate but rather *how* the Native American mascot controversy is contextualized within an ideology of colonization that sets cultural parameters for those in-groups and out-groups. As a sample of deeper critical analyses to come later in the book, this chapter delves into the rhetoric of pro-mascotters as an in-group, including how pro-mascotters constitute their own identities and roles in the mascot milieu and how they configure the out-group of anti-mascot agents. To accomplish this aim, the section proceeds by (1) discussing postcolonialism as both a historical apparatus unto itself and as a particular critical theory, (2) tracing a few nineteenth-century colonizing ideologies that inform the contemporary Native mascot debate as a colonial space, (3) offering an example of two case studies—the social-scapes at Florida State University and the University of Illinois—as examples of how the Native American mascot debate can be seen as neo-colonizing through the *hows* of pro-mascotter rhetoric, and (4) presenting some implications for postcolonialism as a critical lens.

Postcolonialism as a Critical Framework

The critical and theoretical perspective of postcolonialism derives from the work of scholars such as Gayatri Spivak and Edward Said, who, in the late twentieth century, examined the Western world's intervention into non-Western or "oriental" cultures in both historical and contemporary eras. Their topical interest mostly involved the British Empire and its colonial ties to nations in Africa and Asia, especially India. Said was most fascinated by what he deemed "Orientalism"—the representation of people in the "non-Occidental" world by Westerners for the purposes of controlling the imagery and, thus, the material bedrocks of colonized cultures. The logic of Orientalism proceeded by homogenizing and scripting the "other" as generic in order to construct them as "inherently vulnerable to scrutiny," thus making them available as an objectified resource of exploitation by dominant publics.[1] In many ways, such theoretical means of understanding colonial power through representation translates to Native-U.S. affairs, both historically and contemporarily.

Backing up a step, though, Orientalism is rooted in traditional colonialism, or the bonds of land, labor, and bodily use/abuse between dominant publics (empires) and subaltern groups (typically, colonies). A foundational way to explain this mechanism for control comes from Derek Buescher and Kent Ono, who write, "Colonizers appropriate land, conquer indigenous people, and found colonialist governments to oversee the efficient operation of property and labor."[2] In other words, colonization proceeds through the physical and visceral, a realm that equates to the raison d'être of a colonial relationship in the first place: to bring economic resources back to the *metropol*, or center of the empire.

Typically there comes a point in imperial history where a conspicuous and discernible control of material resources on the part of the colonizers comes to an end, or at least ceases to be as stark. Perhaps resources become depleted or colonials are killed off or are merged with another colony; perhaps an empire is defeated by another, more powerful empire. Alternatively, it is possible that resistance efforts help end the material consequences of colonization through a process called *decolonization*, or when "a presentation of resistance can unmask governmental cycles of abuse concerning indigenous cultures and can challenge the ways that this relationship has functioned over time."[3] However, even when material ties cease to endure, an empire generally replaces the tangible and identifiable acquisitiveness of colonization with more cultural forms of imperialism. In a U.S.-based context, one example is the movement from slavery to post-Reconstruction Jim Crow laws and black codes in order to extend physical slavery into the practices of social segregation; another perhaps more direct example, given the subject of this book, involves efforts from Indian removal and land allotment policies to the instigation of assimilation programs to control Native customs when all Natives were corralled into concentrated spaces once and for all.[4]

Susan Silbey reminds us that "control of land or political organization . . . is less important than power over consciousness and consumption."[5] This process is called *neocolonization*—when "rationalizations of colonialism involve the symbolic, as both a precursor to and extension of the material realm," and when these symbolic structures come to function as ideological mechanisms of control.[6] The complication presented by neocolonization for colonized cultures is that their representations and narratives, their historical characteristics and contemporary lifeways, their ethos and morality, their appearance and intelligence, and their usefulness or uselessness (to a dominant public) are all managed by forces operating outside of that culture. It is not as if such coordination is for nothing; the management of subaltern symbols is meant to maintain hierarchies of supremacy.

Postcolonialists study both colonization and neocolonization, as well as decolonizing efforts to dismantle the logics of imperial oppression. Any postcolonial lens examining contemporary milieu, therefore, is fixed on situating texts in a larger colonial landscape in order to demystify the neocolonial "moves" made by the colonizing power.

In Native American contexts, postcolonialists such as Glen Sean Couthard, Emma LaRocque, Duane Champagne, Linda Tuhiwai Smith, and others are concerned with Native agency and how colonization strips indigenous people of their voices and stymies their abilities to frame their own pasts, presents, and futures.[7] They do so by studying the language of the Native-colonial relationship, and these relationships clearly have consequences. Couthard explains the relationship as one ultimately locating Native self-determination at the center of confrontation: "A settler-colonial relationship is one characterized by a particular form of domination; that is, it is a relationship where power—in this case, interrelated discursive and non-discursive facets of economic, gendered, racial, and state power—has been structured into a relatively secure or sedimented set of hierarchical social relations that continue to facilitate the dispossession of indigenous peoples of their lands and self-determining authority."[8] Notice how power here is both generated and sustained by discourse. In many ways, write Mary E. Stuckey and John M. Murphy, neocolonizing discourse *represents the power* in and of itself. That power—as a hegemonic contrivance—is typically invisible, especially because, unlike the materialism of early colonization, neocolonization is assumptive and imperceptible. Of this idea, Stuckey and Murphy argue that such entitlement "remains largely hidden; not so much concealed as buried within a taken-for-granted culture that views any oppressive or potentially oppressive practices as either the exception . . . or as the province of other people, in other places."[9] Therefore, postcolonial criticism, especially in Native-U.S. contexts, unveils neocolonization and, in so doing, calls it into presence and interrogates its significances for Native American cultural lifeways.

As noted earlier, part of postcolonialism also "reads" Native American voices as resistive or decolonial in a neocolonial landscape. And following Jason Edward Black's suggestion that we must "reveal the presence and agency of Native discourses," deeper analysis in later chapters engages anti-mascot rhetoric as decolonial.[10] As a start to examples of postcolonialism as a critical lens, though, the following case studies attend to pro-mascot rhetoric and how it replicates neocolonialism as an ideological formation. The cases proceed with a brief illustration of some early and foundational colonial entailments and then with a textual analysis of pro-mascot voices at FSU and Illinois.

Foundational Colonial Ideologies in the United States

Expansion, territoriality, paternalism, and benevolence combined to define, in part, some of the colonizing ideologies of the United States in the nineteenth century. These ideologies scaffolded the government's colonial lording over the North American continent.[11] The brief discussion that follows spotlights the relationship between Native Americans and the U.S. government that was constituted through these ideologies, because it is important in comprehending the way the Native American mascot controversy can be situated in a context of neocolonization.

EXPANSION AND TERRITORIALITY

Expansion can be traced to the government's self-professed mission into new lands and the civilizing of so-called savages in the "wilderness" with the aid and support of divine providence. This mission was used to justify how the United States "conquered" others and "establish[ed] and perpetuate[ed] histories" naturalizing a hierarchy where the federal government possessed considerably "greater [cultural] importance" than Native Americans.[12] The mission of progress as a nationalistic concept has been deemed "manifest destiny" and involved the notion that the United States could control an open "frontier" along with cultures upon whom to inscribe American principles.[13]

Expansion led to a connection between territory and "othering" in the same way Said theorized the concept—that is, as American settlers occupied these new spaces, Anglo property holding became a vital component for the nation.[14] This move toward a *"white* republic" was defended "in terms of racial superiority" that placed whites on a higher cultural plane.[15] For Natives, then, their occupancy with regard to land meant little in terms of territoriality to the U.S. government. The government used ethnic categories to *otherize* Natives based on territory; as Andrew Jackson noted in 1829: "Indians . . . lacked the honest industry" of white citizens, and therefore "the children of the forest cannot hold territorial power because they had seen land from a mountain or passed it in the chase." Whites, he wrote, were the "true" Americans; Natives had only "artificial distinctions" as weaker subordinates.[16]

PATERNALISM AND BENEVOLENCE

As ideologies, paternalism and benevolence also guided U.S.-Native relations. According to Francis Paul Prucha, paternalism involved a rhetoric infused with "policies and practices of treating or governing people by providing for their needs without giving them responsibility."[17] Such paternalism functioned by naturalizing familial imagery within political contexts and likening "what is done by colonial powers to what goes on in the family, giving it a moral justification that it otherwise would have lacked."[18] The U.S. government mimicked the family relationship to control its "minor" Native "children."[19] The paternal persona of the U.S. nation during the nineteenth century complicated identities, signaling a hierarchy. From one perspective, the U.S. government asserted an aberrant control over Native communities using the sardonic relationship of a father to his child.[20] In this vein, Natives were constructed as veritable wards who "as children were ignorant; they could be deceived or treated in a way that served the interests of the adults"—what Mary Jackman calls "a kind of exploitative paternalism."[21] As the United States managed its own paternal relationship with the continent's numerous Native nations, it additionally constituted these nations as inferior and uncivilized, controllable and animalistic.

At a cultural level, the denigration of Natives allowed the United States to exert its territorial influence. Benevolence could justify this—that is, acting on the behalf of Native Americans, protecting them, civilizing them, saving them, honoring them, and speaking for them. These actions would make might "right." As Prucha argues, the government thought that so-called "children were defenseless . . . required support, and since they were not fully responsible . . . required guidance."[22] We can see this in the 1880s, when the U.S. government sought to uplift and rescue Natives (in a veiled way) to secure more land for settlers. During this time, for instance, Senator Thomas Skinner argued that "the Indian must either perish or depend on the Government for support, abandon his thriftless habits . . . and finally rise to the level of civilization that surrounds him. . . . We as guardians must choose for him."[23] Similarly, Senator Joseph Dolph contended that "[Indians] are wards. . . . We control their persons, and their property."[24] The idea of a nation as a "family" justified U.S. governmental power.[25] Needless to say, protecting Native nations in the nineteenth century conferred supremacy on the dominant public.

Neocolonialism in Pro-Mascot Rhetoric: A Sample from FSU and Illinois

Chapter 6 closely interrogates the unique mascotting performances at FSU (whose Chief Osceola remains, along with the "Seminole" nickname). For this chapter, we attend to how pro-mascot rhetoric at FSU and Illinois manifest homologically with nineteenth-century ideologies to exhibit a neocolonialism, a discursive imperialism that privileges "U.S. public space" over Native American symbols and cultures.[26] This neocolonialism moves through discourses of possession and appropriation as well as paternal benevolence.

POSSESSION AND APPROPRIATION

Neocolonialism in the mascot issue is fomented by the possession and appropriation of Native representations. These devices had been foundational to the territorial and expansive ideologies of the nineteenth century. John

Forsyth, Georgia senator and co-sponsor of the Indian Removal Act of 1830 (that forced eastern Native nations onto trans-Mississippi reservations) exemplified these ideologies. In 1830 Forsyth said, "The European doctrine of the right conferred by the discovery of new countries, inhabited by barbarous tribes is a reason to take land. The lands, the streams, the woods, the minerals, all living things, including the human inhabitants" are all the "property of, or subject to, the government of the fortunate navigator."[27] Ostensibly, this Jacksonian argument was posited as "possess it and use it for U.S. national ends."[28] Of course, this was a different age, and a different issue was at question in this argument—the colonization of land—but the taking and use of something "Native," such as imagery and names, resonates in the current mascot debate as colonial.

THE COMMODIFICATION DEVICE   The process of mascotting possesses Native signifiers as "commodification tools"—ciphers advancing a contemporary manifest destiny by co-opting Native cultures as American identity.[29] To this point, Ono and Buescher argue that "Euro-American culture has consistently appropriated and redefined what is 'distinctive' and constitutive of Native Americans. This strategy of appropriation relies on culturally specific views of ownership and property."[30] In this observation "mascot-users" might be said to reconfigure Native nations, a practice institutionally supported by the long history of prejudices against Native peoples, a practice that finds a home in U.S. territoriality.

Typically, universities argue that Native mascots stand as synecdoches of respect, stoicism, and honor that represent those qualities for which a university strives. Mascot supporter and former FSU Booster Club columnist Charles Barnes demonstrates this view, writing, "No athletic team chooses a name or mascot in order to bring contempt or disrepute on itself. . . . They depict Indians and by extension themselves as noble, courageous, and fierce."[31] Illinois's Honor the Chief Society made a similar argument in its FAQs following Illiniwek's 2007 removal, claiming, "Chief Illiniwek embodies the attributes valued by alumni, students, and friends of the University of Illinois. The tradition of the Chief is a link to our great past, a tangible symbol of an intangible spirit, filled with qualities to which a person of any background can aspire: goodness, strength, bravery, truthfulness, courage, and dignity." In these two instances the universities claim an authentic link in justifying the appropriation of Native cultures as truly admirable symbols for what remains "good" in society and on the playing field: strength, ferocity, nobility, and courage.[32]

Thus, the question becomes, Are Native Americans being honored, or are they being appropriated as "discursive territory" for universities to use in order to couch their identities in some imagined mythos of the past? If Natives are being honored, is it principled to do so through a reliance on the classic double-hydra myths of the "noble savage" or "bloodthirsty savage"? In either case, one needs only to look to the rhetoric employed to defend the Seminole and Illini monikers. These discourses frame the mascots at FSU and Illinois in what Laurel R. Davis calls "a form of American identity that is linked to narratives about the Western United States."[33]

On the one hand is the "noble savage" myth that constitutes Natives as silent and stoic, tepid and innocent, accepting and accommodationist.[34] "Hinton," a poster on the Inside Higher Ed blog, contends that Illiniwek "stands as a tribute to the American Indian in his finest tradition. . . . The Chief states silently, but eloquently, that although we may be defeated, we will not be vanquished."[35] Here the "Indian's finest tradition" is "defeat," which seems inconsistent with the practices of honoring and lauding Illiniwek as, what poster "Brinkmann" calls "someone being *all about* the good of the University."[36] Similarly, FSU's Alumni Group contends on its website that "the Seminole people have suffered many hardships and injustices, but they have remained dignified and proud."[37] In these quotations, injustices have occurred, but stoicism—essentially a euphemism for inaction—was the result. Ultimately, this myth grounds the mascot in a gloss of despondency. In a way, then, mascots become reminders of the U.S. government's colonialism of, and conquest over, Native Americans as well as the reduction of Natives to flora and fauna. The "noble savage" is a telling myth to connect with Native mascots, because "Indian names" in collegiate sport culture occurred on the heels of what Ellen Staurowsky deems "the last of the Native American nations being conquered or subdued."[38] Therein lies a colonial-to-neocolonial connection.

On the other hand, pro-mascot discourses often rely on "savage" characteristics attributed to Native Americans.[39] In this mythos, past Native nations are recognized for their acumen in battle—for how they demonstrated aggression, violence, and bravery in times of war. This "dark and dangerous [Native] antithesis," argues Brenda Farnell, has been "pregnant with fascination" in the Western eye, especially when it is safe to approach and is, therefore, controllable.[40] For pro-mascotters at FSU, the story line of the Seminole Nation's "refusal to relent" to the U.S. military in the 1830s and 1840s is what makes it, along with Osceola, a prototypical mascot. Barnes remarks, "When we speak of Osceola . . . we speak of that unconquered spirit . . . symbolizing the brave Florida Seminoles, the only unconquered Indian people." Barnes limits those "positive qualities to which we aspire" to the bodily realm.[41] Osceola is remembered for his efforts in war, in fighting back the tide of U.S. military forces during conflicts such as the First and Second Seminole Wars. In a way, then, the Chief becomes defined with the aid of his interactions with colonial figures. Similarly, a poster on a Chief Osceola Facebook page argues, "As the Seminoles painted themselves, were great warriors and . . . used tomahawks . . . and sharpened spears . . . and performed the scalp dance," so, too, do we "honor" that "spirit in our war chant" whose "long version title is rightly called 'Massacre.'"[42] In this instance, there is no mistaking the way that Seminole culture is constituted and steeped in bellicosity, especially as words like "warriors," "tomahawks," "spears," "scalp," "war," and "massacre" establish a link between Natives and violence. Of this warrior persona, "GreenStreet" argues on an ESPN Illiniwek Conversation site that "what protestors call violent antics, I call the great remaining preservation of a Native American culture."[43] In this quotation, hostility inheres in what is to be remembered and honored—not only that, but it is also the "great remaining" vestige of Native histories.

The myth of the warrior/savage could be seen to obscure traces of white violence committed against Native Americans.[44] The violence is actually invisible; what we get is a "culturally comfortable and comforting myth of the American Indian warrior"—something to praise rather than remember as a target of U.S. colonization.[45]

CO-OPTATION THROUGH OVERLAP   Simultaneously, the neocolonization of Native cultures through possession of the mascot involves the overlap of Native and university communities—that is, universities appropriate their mascots as extensions of their collegiate constituencies. Upon entering FSU or Illinois, a person *becomes* a Seminole or Illini. This identity entrenches the university community and plays out not only in the classroom, student union, or university sporting event but also well beyond the physical boundaries of the university itself.[46] An Illinois alumnus posting on the Save the Chief Facebook page once wrote, "I will always be an Illini. . . . I am proud to be an Illini!"[47] Or as one FSU graduate living in Chapel Hill, North Carolina, mentioned, "I defend our Seminole symbol. . . . Although everyone here lives for [the UNC Tar Heels], it's fun being the lone Seminole."[48] The identity of "Indian" becomes intrinsically tied to university publics; a University of Utah graduate is forever a "Ute," whether reminded by oneself or by another, such as the alumni newsletter or the coworker who comments, "Hey, I graduated from Utah, too. Looks like there are two Utes here."

The neocolonial move in these instances is that universities pack their mascots full of the traits they see as being shared by both the Native icons and the university. The mascot embodies traits that manifest as a part of the hard sell, which alludes to tinges of commodification. Consider Barnes's comments about the tie between the Seminoles and the FSU Seminoles: "We routinely honor the Seminole Tribe of Florida in public by raising them as the one tribe, among all the indigenous peoples, which was never conquered. The Seminoles never surrendered, we say. They never gave up. The public, main-stream America, sees this as a great tribute to them. . . . Refusing to surrender is admirable. To never give in is a virtue that we admire, that we exult."[49] A syllogism exists here: Seminoles are admirable. We are Seminoles. Hence, we are admirable. However, the syllogism functions through neocolonialism. FSU Seminoles are not *Seminole* until the Native can come to represent them; the university perpetuates this bridge by weaving the "Seminole" into FSU culture—FSU "raise[s] them as the one tribe." The university creates the FSU Seminole and traditions like the tomahawk chop to provide its constituents with some semblance of its authenticity. Soon, constituents—as well as the public that views the mascot fanfare—cannot think of the Seminole Nation without bringing to mind the grandiose pre- and mid-game pageantry of the FSU Seminoles. The university and mascots become eternally joined, but the university possesses this Native currency on its own terms.[50]

Universities claim that the appropriation of Native cultures honors tribal customs by uniting the past with the present. In a temporal sense, univer-sities—at least those, like FSU and Illinois, employing the synecdoche of a specific nation—argue for an intrinsic and natural extension of the Native as a "symbol" of the university. The Honor the Chief Society posits a temporal and spatial bond between the Illini and the Illinois Illini: "As a reminder of our only common geographical ancestor, Chief Illiniwek reminds us of the high ideals of the First Nation people who made up the Illini confederation of tribes for which the state of Illinois is named. The Illini tribes took their sustenance from the same land we share today. Although the original Illini disappeared from the region long ago, they are remembered through the Chief Illiniwek tradition."[51] Illinois seems to say that the Illini "called to it" to appropriate the image, "thus taking the onus for choosing the Native off of the university and placing it on Native peoples themselves."[52] Randall Lake, in examining Native mythos, writes that the Native narrative "grounded in time's cycle, seeks to renew the ties between past and present to enact a future."[53] Indeed, universities have appropriated this myth by allowing the mascot to come to represent all that the university wishes to embody. In fact, though, "rather than dealing with the painful reality" of these myths, universities have done nothing more than cling to "sentimentalized stereotypes and caricatures" of their own making.[54] Native cultures have been made into a vessel for the possessor: they have become appropriated to satisfy the "possessive," "consumptive," and "hegemonic" desires of the neocolonizer.[55]

Once this occurs, Seminoles and Illini "become both Indian and white. . . . Everything in their world is now in conflict."[56] In the confusion of blended identities, do universities—emboldened by U.S. neocolonialism—get to control Indianness on their own terms?[57] This query might be answered if one thinks about the possibility that universities co-opt Native identities.

PATERNAL BENEVOLENCE

Pro-mascot discourse also moves the paternal benevolence of the nineteenth century—regarding land and assimilation—into the mascot milieu. In the 1880s, during the allotment era, Interior Secretary Carl Schurz claimed that, left unprotected from "bad and destructive whites," Natives would be "dwarfed and shriveled" in the face of the "glare of civilization above and beyond his comprehension." He said that benevolence was needed because "the knowledge possessed by the white man is necessary for self-preservation. . . . The Indian needs it to save him."[58] As a paternal force, the government was willing to step up and "appreciate as it never has before our duty and responsibility in this respect."[59] This ideological structure carries through to the present mascot debate; Farnell calls it "the positive moral high ground . . . predicated on a constructed narrative of the past, typical of settler colonialism, which supports a strong emotional desire on the part of Whites to feel legitimate" in a landscape.[60]

SAVING THE "INDIAN" One of the ways that pro-mascot discourse reflects this benevolent neocolonialism is through the assertion that the mascot saves/preserves the Native and the surrounding narratives. This move, of course, echoes ideological justifications of expansion and control—from Western European "discoveries," missionary work, and U.S. interventionism in Cuba and the Philippines through "Small Wars," "conflicts" in Southeast Asia, and "missions" in Iraq and Afghanistan.[61] In terms of nineteenth-century governmental discourse, such pro-mascot discourse exudes from Senator Wilson Lumpkin's position in support of the Indian Removal Act in 1830: "To those Indians whose good we seek, the subject before you is of vital importance. It is a measure of life and death. Pass the bill on your table and you save them. Reject it and you leave them to perish. Reject this bill, and you thereby encourage delusory hopes and evil consequences. . . . Delay is pregnant with danger to the Indians; what you do, do quickly, before the evil day approaches."[62] This rationalization demonstrates Susan Ryan's contention that "asserting what will contribute to the well-being of another . . . is best understood as an exercise of power in itself."[63]

In the mascot milieu, numerous chat board posts replicate this benevolent rhetoric. For instance, "Lanier125" notes on a National Coalition on Racism in Sports and Media site, "The white race has eliminated the Seminole in the past, and we will watch as it happens again."[64] Similarly, "GDang" sarcastically says of Chief Illiniwek's retirement, "It's nice to see the U.S. continue their long-standing tradition of forcing out the American Indian."[65] And on the same chat board, "The Tanker" argues that "by getting rid of those school names or teams, in 10 years time, people will forget about the American Indian. . . . [The mascot would have kept] people connected to the heritage."[66] In these cases, anti-mascotters are maligned as the oppressors, as the catalysts for eradicating Native cultures.

In this move, pro-mascotters concomitantly free themselves of colonial ties and suggestions that keeping the mascot in place yields deleterious effects. Poster Chris Smith even unites Native oppressions with subjugation on a larger scale: "I think it is a good honor that any institution recognizes Native American cultures and uses a sports name as a reference to a difficult and hard traveled road. This meaning is a reminder of the tragic history that all of our people have suffered."[67] Supporters of this idea claim to occupy a different discursive field from either vulgar racist discourse or racializing processes, accomplishing this through "the rhetoric of honoring," the use of which enables supporters to claim a moral high ground to effectively mask the underlying racializing discourse.[68]

To remedy what poster "Gann" calls this "gross injustice," pro-Native-mascotters attempt to represent the mascot and speak for Native cultures.[69] Such "standing in" positions pro-Native-mascotters as dominant agents of neocolonialism. Alumnus John Brinkman wrote on a "Save the Chief" website that he "hoped to keep the Tribe's rich cultural history alive for all to learn from."[70] The problem here is that a seemingly non-Native would retain the privilege of saving the Illini. And, of course, the conception of just what constitutes the Native is predicated on university (and university constituents') constructions, so the benevolence is spurious in that it actually saves the *university's* "Indian." Former FSU president Sandy D'Alemberte even went so far as to articulate an economic benefit of saving the Seminole Nation, writing in 1998, "Mascotting promotes the tribe and gets it more recognized by our

Seminole name."[71] A 2005 editorial in *FSU Notes* claimed that "the identity of FSU helps with recognition and tourism for the tribe in Florida."[72] Within such a postulation, there is a hierarchy inscribed that constitutes universities as benefactors, which, in the paternal ideology, subordinates the group that is seemingly the beneficiary.

Likewise, "RW," posting on the "Save the Chief" Facebook page, connected the saving of Illini cultures with the saving of all members of the university community. The poster wrote, "If Illiniwek does not keep alive the very thought in people's minds of the Illini, then it will die. . . . We must step into the breech and promote the memory of the Illini. I, for one, will not let the memory of the Illini people die. That memory is our heritage too and that is something no one should be permitted to take from us."[73] Notice how both the agent performing the "saving" and the victim here is "us"—the university community. In this instance, there is a sense that "whites own the imagery; . . . the white majority has inherited the right to appropriate and control Native American imagery."[74] Keeping the mascot "alive" becomes a way to sustain university identities through a possession of the mascot. The mingling of a neocolonial figure with historically oppressed and inaccurately constructed Native cultures reveals for whom this benevolence functions.

FOMENTING ANALOGOUS CONDITIONS   Pro-mascot responses also tend to make smooth the racialist practice of mascotting by couching representations of the mascot in what can be dubbed analogous conditions.[75] These conditions involve non-Natives demonstrating how the appropriation of their identities is not deemed offensive. Such an argument deflects colonial legacies by aligning Native mascots with Anglo mascots. This strategy is reminiscent of Andrew Jackson's colonial and benevolent justification for removal in his Second Annual Message to Congress, in 1830:

> Doubtless it will be painful to leave the graves of their fathers; but what do they more than our ancestors did or our children are now doing? To better their condition in an unknown land our forefathers left all that was dear in earthly objects. Our children by thousands yearly leave the land of their birth to seek new homes in distant regions. Does Humanity weep at these painful separations? . . . Far from it. It is rather a source of joy that our country affords scope where our young population may range unconstrained. . . . These remove hundreds and almost thousands of miles at their own expense, purchase the lands they occupy, and support themselves at their new homes. . . . Can it be cruel when the Indian is given new territory . . . and their expenses are paid? How many thousands of our own people would gladly embrace the opportunity of

removing to the West on such conditions! If the offers made to the Indians were extended to them, they would be hailed with gratitude and joy.[76]

Of course, the irony is that European and American settlers *chose* to relocate in the West. Their "removal" was not forced under colonial conditions.

In the same way, pro-mascotters replicate this coded ideology in their neocolonial justifications. A common incidence of this goes something like "as a Norwegian-American, I am not offended by the Vikings. Please lighten up, go after real and true racism."[77] Here, poster "Tronson" elides the notion that mascotting in itself is racialized. Or as "rcw3006" exhorts, "Why do you never hear of other ethnic groups complaining? The Vikings' Scandinavian heritage or the running rebels of UNLV's southern heritage, or the Fighting Irish using a drunk fighting leprechaun probably the most insulting? Do you hear any of these people complain? NO! They are proud of their heritage and teams. What are you, not proud of your heritage?"[78] And further still, a post on the "Save the Chief" Facebook page argues, "We have those mascots which mock religious groups. While many claimed that Chief Illiniwek was somehow offensive to Native American religious beliefs, no one seems to find the Wake Forest Demon Deacon offensive. Personally, I think describing Baptists as evil and demonic is a pretty clear ringer for offensive. But the NCAA doesn't consider Wake Forest to have a hostile and abusive mascot."[79]

Such comparisons activate what can be characterized as "the Fighting Irish argument."[80] The problem is an issue of agency—of deciding for oneself whether a mascot should stand as a representation of one's culture. Irish Catholics founded Notre Dame and decided on their own mascot. The North Carolina Baptist Convention founded Wake Forest and named themselves "Deacons" to reflect its culture. The university added "Demon" when the Methodist college a short journey down Tobacco Road, Duke University (formerly Trinity College), called themselves the "Blue Devils."[81] Ole Miss was founded in 1844 and its team named "The Rebels" in 1877, reflecting a sense of the college's own Southern heritage in the face of Reconstruction.[82] There remains a qualitative difference in terms of ownership and the right to name when it comes to Western or Anglo-based mascots.

Implications of Postcolonial Criticism

To summarize these brief FSU and Illinois case studies, pro-mascot rhetoric can be seen as predicated on property and ownership. Postcolonial analysis indicates that the U.S. government colonized Native nations during the nineteenth century and that the larger U.S. public culture presently extends this imperialism into neocolonial practices or representations.[83] Similar to U.S. governmental discourse in the nineteenth century, such possession and appropriation is justified in a benevolent gloss of "savior-ship" and unification. In this view, colonization emerges again in the mascot milieu as a neocolonial possession of Native cultures through the "discursive." Of this idea, Laura Whitt argues that "those who appropriate (and do so in a benevolent justification) use what they have stolen, feel good about the act of stealing, legitimize and maintain colonial privilege, and then divert attention away from the consequences of such behavior." The net result is that benevolent means "enable the dominant culture to mask the fundamental oppressive nature of its treatment of subordinated cultures."[84] C. Richard King and his colleagues summarize well this effect of the collegiate mascot: "they fit within a broader context of control and consent in which the dominant (a) silences the histories of indigenous peoples, (b) appropriates their cultures, (c) teaches White supremacy, and (d) prevents Americans from understanding the legacies and significance of Natives."[85]

We began chapter 2 with a discussion of what postcolonialism, neocolonialism, and decolonization mean for a study of Native American mascots. To wit, postcolonialism as a critical apparatus provides us with one of several lenses through which to view the *how* of the mascot controversy—how the mascot controversy comes to us as public consumers, but also how the public itself expresses its polyvocal views on the controversy. This symbiosis of invention and consumption comprises a circuit of cultural meaning regarding the Native American mascot. Whereas chapter 1 outlined the importance of self-categorization for *why* in-groups and out-groups form their identities and attendant opinions based on those identities in a contested, spatial mélange, this chapter took up aims to contextualize the rhetorical moves that are made in groups' self-categorization, at least from a pro-mascot perspective.

From here, the book discovers in-group and out-group voices of pro-mascotters and anti-mascotters—through surveys and public textual examples—to improve our grasp of how Native American mascot names, visuals, and rituals come to have meaning through self-categorization. The postcolonial lens that this chapter has adopted, complete with its focus on neocolonization and decolonization, is drawn upon to read the variety of data we gather in our case studies, which range from professional sports to collegiate sports, from baseball to football, from generic mascot names to tribal-specific names.

3

Online Debate on the Acceptability
of the Washington NFL Mascot

It is the hottest of hot buttons when it comes to the Native American mascot controversy. Even if people believe "Warriors" is not necessarily a Native American name or conceive "Brave" as something that is an adjective more than it is a noun, one struggles to encapsulate the vitriol that surrounds the debate over the National Football League's Washington team: the R-dskins. Many individual high schools have moved to change mascots away from the name; the entire state of California complied via a 2015 bill banning it.[1] At a meeting where the decision was made to eliminate the mascot from Goshen High School (IN), Native American Rochelle Hershberger summarized the resistance: "Please don't tell us how to feel or argue we are being too sensitive. Don't use the R-word to my face. I am not your mascot, my family is not your mascot, and my children are not your mascot."[2]

The debate raged for decades, yet the crescendo began in 2013. In that year, *Sports Illustrated*'s Peter King joined a chorus of journalists announcing they would no longer use the Washington franchise's nickname. One year later, NFL broadcasters, including Hall of Fame quarterback Phil Simms and Super Bowl–winning head coach Tony Dungy, announced they were considering the same. Revelations were also disclosed; highly regarded referee Mike Carey asked not to work any Washington games for the final eight years of his career because of his stance on the controversy. And August 2014 found the team's own local newspaper, the *Washington Post*, barring the use of the mascot's name in its editorial pages, though not its sports page.

Whether one refers to Washington's NFL team as the "Redskins," the "R-dskins," or simply "Washington" with no nickname attached, the decision about whether to highlight the mascot—and questions about how to do so or not—underscores the height of the percolating debate over Native American history and culture and the labels attached to modern renderings and memories about indigenous communities in the United States. Thus, this chapter explores the specific case of Washington as an example of the types of arguments that encompass Native American mascotting as a whole. Positioned after one has received theoretical grounding via self-categorization (chapter 1) and postcolonialism (chapter 2), yet before exploring the results of a national survey (in chapters 4–6), this chapter is much less concerned with reaching consensus regarding the name than it is with illuminating the venues in which such debates now take place and, specifically, the arguments that encapsulate both camps within the controversy.

Positioning the "R-dskin" as Central for Debate

As Jason Edward Black notes, in 1968 the National Congress of American Indians began a campaign to address troubling depictions of Native Americans in sport.[3] Nearly a half century later, some changes in collegiate mascotting practices have occurred, ranging from the elimination of names such as the St. John's "Redmen" (changed to the "Red Storm" in 1994) to the retirement of the University of Illinois's Chief Illiniwek in 2007. Yet, primary debates remained, particularly related to what was perceived by many in favor of the elimination of Native American mascots as being the lowest-hanging fruit given its historical racialism and metonymically reductive tenor: the Washington R-dskins. Such an argument is intriguing in terms of understanding movements for change or stagnation. For instance, one could argue that R-dskins represents the most grievous of claims, representing a point on which all could agree even if failing to reach consensus on names such as "Braves" and "Indians." However, one could also view the moniker as one to cause an avalanche of change, because one could potentially view it as repugnant while still being sanguine about other names less likely to be construed as slurs. Eliminating one of the "higher-hanging fruits," such as "Braves," could be seen as more likely to result in all mascotting practices being altered. That is, if one could claim that "Braves" is problematic, then surely one could not justify retaining "R-dskins" within that same syllogism.

A confluence of pro and con arguments have been marshaled regarding the placement of "R-dskins" within the broader Native American mascot controversy, including the voice of Ellen Staurowsky, who contends there is an element of white privilege and power punctuating the discussion of whose votes or voices should be counted within debates about potentially offensive mascots.[4] In the 1990s that debate moved online, where oft-anonymous voices sometimes adopted stances about the mascot that were even more vehement and polarized.

However, in January 2014 a commercial spot, "Proud to Be" made a two-minute case for eliminating the Washington nickname. The commercial, funded and produced by a group called Change the Mascot in conjunction with the National Congress of American Indians, aired during the online broadcast of the Super Bowl but received even more attention when shown during ESPN's coverage of the NBA Finals.[5] The ad listed names attached to Native Americans, each with powerful complementary images; words ranged from tribes (e.g., "Navajo," "Sioux"), to adjectives (e.g., "survivalist," "patriot"), to names of Native American legends (e.g., "Sitting Bull," "Hiawatha"). The final line of the spot says, "Native Americans call themselves many things. The one thing they don't?" The spot then concludes with a shot of the Washington Redskins helmet, revealing the answer to the previous question.[6] As of this writing, the spot had received roughly five million views on YouTube, with "likes" outnumbering "dislikes" by a 13:1 ratio.

In August 2014 Washington's NFL franchise responded with its own two-minute commercial, "Redskins Is a Powerful Name," claiming that many Native Americans not only were unaffected by the nickname but also garnered empowerment from the depiction.[7] This spot focused more on first-person testimony, with a Native American claiming, "It's never been an issue for anyone in my family," and a fan who was also from the Blackfoot Nation arguing that "the intent has never been to degrade people."[8] As of this writing, the spot had received 1.1 million views on YouTube, with "likes" outnumbering "dislikes" by a 3:1 ratio.

Both commercials received attention in mainstream and online press, jointly receiving millions of views—and thousands of comments via their primary location on YouTube. Moreover, the majority of the people watching each spot found the arguments and delivery of the message compelling, at least enough to warrant more "likes" than "dislikes." This chapter explores the themes embedded within the comments from both sides of the mascot issue. A clearer sense of where the debate currently resides can be ascertained by analyzing the primary arguments espoused by both sides.

Arguments for Change

Arguments against the "Indian" mascot—whether articulated by Native-identified folks themselves or members of the larger U.S. public—have remained fairly consistent throughout the nearly four decades since the NCAI began its inquiry into the harmful entailments of the mascot. The overarching claim has always been that the mascot relies on centuries-old stereotypes of Native people as savage yet conquered, bellicose yet silent, to questionably honor indigenous cultures. Anti-mascot activists contend that filtering these historical stereotypes through more contemporary professional and collegiate sports images, names, visages, symbols, and slogans only serves to retrench the ways that the U.S. government and public have treated, and therefore continue to consider, Native people.

The R-dskins mascot is a special case for anti-mascot activists. Black argues that while Native-identified protesters such as Charlene Teters and Suzan Shown Harjo have explained how mascot names like "braves," "Indians," "warriors," "chiefs," and "redmen" "harmed Native communities and recirculated their identities in disreputable, materially harmful ways, one mascot name has ascended above the rest: *r-dskins*."[9] This particular mascot name activates stereotypes based on a term that *Merriam-Webster* notes is a "very offensive" metonym that "should be avoided." Plainly put, most literary, colloquial, historical, political, and cultural sources point to "R-dskins" as the ultimate racial slur concerning Native communities. One may now add to that a government source, as the U.S. Patent and Trademark Office canceled six of the Washington team's trademarks in June 2014 based on its mascot, which the office labeled "disparaging . . . to a substantial composite of Native Americans."

At this point in the "Indian" mascot debate—and certainly within the context of the Washington R-dskin issue—the primary *what* of the anti-mascot position is clear. Nevertheless, questions remain, and the resurgent controversy surrounding the Washington team's defensiveness has been reignited since 2013: *How* does the anti-mascot position unfold? In other words, how do the categorical claims of these activists and of a doubtful public function to serve the anti-mascot position? Do certain critical structures help us to make sense of the *how* question? Of the latter query, we argue that the renascent anti-mascot position advances through what we call a decolonial framework. This framework then helps us discern four main categories of mascot critique: humanization, homology to other cultural groups, ironic sentiments, and alternate naming.

As discussed in chapter 2, decolonization as a framework results from a cultural environment in which colonization has been historically present and continues to maneuver as a major undercurrent. Colonization in a U.S.-based context has previously involved the control of Native communities through mechanisms such as the Indian Removal Act, reservationism, unfair treaties, assimilationism, and the allotting of indigenous land. Ostensibly, colonization in this Native-U.S. past demonstrates how the dominant powers associated with the U.S. government and U.S. public have served to regulate the land, labor, and bodies of Native people. Over time, this past environment has motivated powerful groups' contemporary symbolic control over Native communities, a process called neocolonization. Raka Shome contends that "whereas in the past imperialism was about controlling the native by colonizing territorially, now [it is] more about subjugating the native by colonizing discursively."[10] The "Indian" mascot fits squarely within this logic of control. The Washington R-dskins controversy, for instance, reminds us that the symbolic use of Native names and images in sport can reflect our colonial pasts.

Anti-mascot activists resist this control through decolonization, or "the process by which those who are colonized or oppose colonialism attempt to demystify master narratives."[11] One of the ways that decolonization can function is, of course, discursively: arguing back with rhetoric. In the mascot milieu, anti-mascot individuals have generally placed their critiques in the framework of decolonization, seeking to question and offer solutions concerning the "Indian" mascot. Those who responded to the "Proud to Be" and "Redskins Is a Powerful Name" commercials are no exception. Their decolonizing comments can be organized into four main categories.

ARGUMENT #1: HUMANIZATION

The most prominent anti-mascot theme in decolonizing arguments attends to the ways that the "Indian" mascot can come to dehumanize Native communities through stereotypes and caricatures. Therefore, anti-mascot commenters attempt to work through humanization to reveal the problems of the R-dskins mascot. For instance, one individual noted, "We Indigenous Peoples are human beings. Calling a team the Redskins is just as bad as calling another the Slaves." Another poster wrote, "We are a race that has culture, language, heritage, and beliefs. I am not your mascot." Yet another took the critique a step further by specifying just what that "people" might look like: "There are 558 different tribes in North America, 52 million descendants from the original Indigenous People in the Americas, so the term redskin is offensive just because it ignores the many cultures and traditions of the natives." In all three of these iterations, the posters center their criticism on the assumption that the mascot makes flat, static, and reductive Native peoples. Notice how the first commenter capitalized the identifier "Indigenous Peoples" (perhaps to remedy this) and how the second closed their remark with "I am not your mascot," a sentiment that seemingly echoes beyond Washington, as this chapter opened with the same statement regarding a high school with the same R-dskin moniker. The third worked to dismantle the prevailing ways in which "Indian" mascots come to essentialize all Native people into a compact package—how mascotters can cipher and commodify Native cultures.

In these three brief narratives we get a sense that anti-mascot activist rhetoric attempts to resituate Native communities as people. The assumption, therefore, is that in the face of the Washington R-dskins' red-hued, hook-nosed, and sallow-cheeked logo there exists an almost racist relic of the past. As one poster quipped, "Anyone who supports the name is ignorant and racist." The dehumanizing position here gets linked to racism. The corrective, it seems, is to consider how, in the words of one poster, "R-dskin is a racial slur that is being taken lightly because of the open use of it." The "open use" mentioned is a use in which the colonizing context of Native-U.S. relations is ignored or forgotten. Black has called this open use "discursive territory." He argues that a team such as the Washington R-dskins can "mark generic Native identities. . . . This pretty much captures our public's ocular frame of Native people."[12] In sum, the humanization theme speaks to anti-mascotters' efforts to fight against the reduction of Native communities to things—to mere symbols ripped from their context and removed from culture beyond stereotypes of savagery and the bestial realm.

ARGUMENT #2: HOMOLOGY TO OTHER CULTURAL GROUPS

A common argumentative practice in the Western world is that of the analogy, or the comparison of two or more people, places, things, or ideas in like, kind, content, substance, structure, and style.[13] Indeed, anti-mascotters maneuver through this line of argument in their remarks about the R-dskins moniker and symbolism. In fact, they do more than analogize Native communities to other groups of color; rather, they equate them through contexts of colonization. A comparison that adds the important tint of context is called a *homology*.[14] African Americans and Asian Americans, like Native peoples, have been susceptible to U.S.-inspired colonization for centuries. Whether through contrivances such as slavery, forced internment and exclusion, or removal (respectively), these groups in particular have been caught in a fabric of control stitched with the needle of colonization. Thus, the homology between Native peoples and other potentially racist mascots makes argumentative sense.

We see these homological sentiments in the anti-mascot rhetoric appended to the "Redskins Is a Powerful Name" video comments. The typical comments perceptible are comically or glibly written ones, such as "The 'black skins,' the 'white skins,' the 'brown skins.' See . . . doesn't sound nice, huh?" or "If you don't think [that removing the mascot name is important] then why don't we start naming teams cr-ckers, k-kes, w-tbacks, and n-ggers?" Another individual wrote, "Calling a football team the 'Blackskins' and using Buckwheat as a caricature wouldn't stand even if they changed the mascot to a more dignified caricature of Morgan Freeman." Ostensibly, these anti-mascot posters decolonize by turning the tables on those who are vehement about or are complicit in the naming of Native peoples as team mascots. Comparing the contexts of other racial, ethnic, or disenfranchised groups, the anti-mascot activists demonstrate that turnaround is fair play. Of course, in their lampooned examples, the insinuation is that a larger U.S. public (and certainly the U.S. government and, while we are at it, the NFL) would not stand for such a mascotting practice.

All of this led one poster to punctuate well what we perceive to be the spirit behind the homological argument. That person stated simply, "Do not treat us like we are inferior to any other race of human beings on this." The deductive riff here is that Native peoples are oppressed by the mascot but are doubly so by the assurance that other marginalized groups would be protected if their cultural symbols, lifeways, and names were being mascotted.

ARGUMENT #3: IRONIC SENTIMENTS

When faced with the task of arguing against slavery (on Independence Day, no less) after a twenty-plus-year career of making that same exact argument, abolitionist Frederick Douglass once famously said, "What we need now is not reasoned argument, but scorching irony."[15] The use of irony, or the comparison of things to demonstrate hypocrisy or an opposite or differing meaning, can be simple yet telling. Irony can certainly reveal the problems of a particular practice. This argumentation device was useful in the early Native-U.S. relationship when Native leaders spoke against colonization by reminding U.S. officials of treaty promises that were later broken in the midst of practices such as removal and allotment. Neocolonially, because the mascot has been shown to function in controlling ways, anti-mascot activists have also engaged in irony as a decolonizing tactic.

In the video comments, we witness this most clearly in a post that speaks to how Native people helped early American colonists and later the U.S. government and U.S. public. The post claims, "[Native people] helped us, taught us, and fought for us. And we won't change the mascot of a sport team." This passage communicates the irony in the Native-U.S. context. That is, after everything indigenous communities have done for the larger nation—actively done and interminably suffered—our public cannot get a sports team to change its mascot. It seems simple, insinuates the poster: centuries of pain and suffering in exchange for a modest mascot name change. This ironic rhetoric reaches into comedy in another posters' narrative. In this one, the individual argues, "Michael Jackson got in trouble for saying k-ke. Paula Deen lost her empire over the N word. And people are offended about the use of the word Gay," but our public lets the "R-dskin" name off the hook. This comment connects with the homology category discussed above, but it also underscores the importance of making an ironic point. If veritable celebrity castles have fallen into the sea over racial slurs, how can the Washington R-dskins organization and its owner, Dan Snyder, get away with continuing the mascot's use?

One of the starkest ironic points made in the comments is also one of the most succinct and yet powerful in its brevity. The comment reads, "Native Americans were nearly eradicated from this world. How much more should we suffer?" The irony in this instance is that despite how our public memories sympathize with the plight of Native nations and peoples, they are often still ignored. This sentiment is corroborated by yet another poster who wrote, "[Native people] have been asking to have this name removed now since 1968 and what does it tell you that only now in 2014 [their voices are] starting to be heard?"

ARGUMENT #4: ALTERNATE NAMING

The above three themes ultimately lead to the bottom line of the anti-mascot position: changing the "R-dskin" moniker along with its logo and rituals. This argument is a *what*, but exploring the *how* of this theme reveals a decolonial tactic of great poignancy. Essentially the anti-mascot comments attached to the "Proud to Be" and "Redskins Is a Powerful Name" videos call on the Washington team to be honest. As we discuss later, one of the pro-mascot positions is that by mascotting Native communities, a team honors, respects, and "saves up" said Native communities. Some mascot scholars have questioned this practice.[16] If, for instance, the U.S. government justified going to war with Native nations because of their bellicosity, then why do teams now honor a Native nation for its might in war and for its savage resiliency in battle? This pairing does not make sense and, in fact, might smack of hypocrisy. Scholars are one group of agents in the mascot controversy, but most vital to consider are those agents who have the most stake in the debate: Native people and their allies. These people, too, notice the inconsistency and, thus, weave this observation into their insistence that an alternate name be considered for the Washington football team.

In the video entries, posters ask, "How about the Washington Warpath?" or "How about the Washington Bravehearts" or "If Redskins is such a proud 'Warrior' name (as was stated in your video) then change the name to the Washington Warriors." These mascot critics are arguing for a change of Native imagery; they are motivating the team owners to consider being honest. If the mascotters are going to honor the stereotypes of Native savagery, imply the anti-mascot activists, at least make the name more generic and less incendiary. Other anti-mascotters suggest less-intrusive names ("Perhaps they should call them the Washington Reds"), while others link the possible name change to the region ("Washingtonians! An excellent name for a football [team] in D.C."). Still another poster suggests, "If you want to honor [Native communities] change it to an indigenous tribe name and be respectful of its portrayal." Regardless of the politics associated with these alternate suggestions, the one common denominator is the desire to keep the team honest about whom it purports to honor. One seemingly exasperated poster closed by suggested the name should be "just anything not racist."

In the end, the four themes articulated in the anti-mascot narratives emblemize a decolonizing argumentative frame whereby the R-dskin moniker is challenged and called into question. At the same time, the remarks remind us that neocolonization is still alive.

Status Quo Arguments

Despite the aforementioned arguments for changing the mascot name, public sentiment at the time of this writing still favored maintaining the name "R-dskins."

Majorities of NFL players (58 percent) and the general American public (71 percent) indicated they did not believe Washington should change its name.[17] Both polls asked whether Washington "should" change its nickname, which could yield more nuanced responses than if asked other types of questions, such as whether they would *like* to see the nickname changed even if they do not feel Washington should *have* to do so.

Nevertheless, the majority of Americans seemingly fall on the side of some form of maintaining the status quo. Comments within the YouTube sections for the two advertisements were compiled into a taxonomy of four key themes of the resistance to any proposed change.

ARGUMENT #1: INOCULATION

A primary strategy employed by those favoring the maintaining of the name emerged around the concept of inoculation, using Native Americans as surrogates for making their arguments. Such a strategy was also heavily used within the "Redskins Is a Powerful Name" advertisement. For instance, one person simply posted, "I'm proud Ojibwa and yes, we have no problem with calling ourselves Redskins." Some comments consulted polls (such as those articulated in the previous paragraph), arguing that if Native Americans had no problem with it and if public sentiment was on the side of maintaining the name, then the issue should be considered resolved, with the status quo emerging as the victor.

Interestingly, it appeared that these arguments seemed to view "don't care" and "in favor" of keeping the name as being one and the same, essentially arguing that any presumed tie vote should defer to the maintenance of the status quo. One argument exemplifying this conflation of terms was this: "The funny part is that all the white people and media think its racist, but the actual Native Americans really don't care. There are literally Native American high schools on reservations with Redskins as there [*sic*] mascot."

Another strategy used in this inoculation involved arguing that the name "R-dskins" was not ignorant but the advertisement for "Proud to Be" was not wholly accurate or respectful. As one commenter noted, "No, [Redskins] is not a direct insult to anybody. A direct insult is calling Jim Thorpe, Crazy Horse, Tecumseh, and Geronimo a Redskin." Thus, in making these types of arguments, proponents of maintaining the name are not only arguing that being in favor of the name "R-dskin" is consistent with Native American stances, but that the position on the other side is ahistorical or at least not entirely accurate.

ARGUMENT #2: INCONSEQUENTIALITY

Another trope arising from the YouTube comments involved the notion of inconsequentiality, asserting that there are much larger issues for Americans to be concerned with than the name of a football team's mascot. Some of the comments pertained to other concerns specifically for Native Americans (e.g., "Why don't you worry about education, poverty, health care, and crime on reservations and leave the Redskins mascot alone?"), while others vaguely referenced generalized issues in which they believed all Americans should be concerned (e.g., "Just stop, seriously stop. The world has a lot more to worry about than the name of a football team").

Interestingly, some comments pertained specifically to a federal government role in pushing this agenda, even though there had not been a formal role at that time (as of 2013). Comments in this vein seemed to express the view that the government was specifically making this an issue, noting, "It's too bad our government spends more time forcing sports teams to change their names than it does actually trying to help indigenous races." Other comments pointed to a governmental role but with the comparative other issues that they believed should receive a greater bulk of attention, particularly emphasizing the Democratic executive branch of the government (at the time) more than the Republican-controlled House of Representatives: "They should just stop and [focus] on what is important like permanently ending Obamacare [and] solve the Benghazi attack." In sum, major economic, social, and foreign affairs issues were frequently juxtaposed with the mascot debate in an attempt to diminish any attempts to enact change.

ARGUMENT #3: CELEBRATIONS

Another popular claim of people believing the mascot should not be changed involved arguing that the name "R-dskin" is not a slight against Native Americans but rather a compliment. Some cited the chant used frequently at games, noting, "The Redskins say 'Hail to the Redskins.' They are honoring them! The name Redskins is powerful and it is an honor to all natives! HTTR!"

Others invoked historical origins of the name to denote that it was always meant to be a commendation (e.g., "If people did there [sic] research in the early 30's, the name was giving to Boston (the Redskins first home) to honor the Indians that lived there"). This historical assertion was then used to emphasize entrenched precedent, believing that "it's been along so long. Why change it now?" Others believed the logo used for the R-dskins provided further evidence of the compliments that were intended by the establishment of the name, with one commenter believing "there is nothing offensive about the nickname of the 'Redskins' especially in the connotation of the logo how the Redskin is strong, determined, powerful, and brave." Debates have persisted for years about the denotative definition of the word "R-dskins," yet comments like these attempt to shift the conversation to the connotative definitions, which are not as easily ascertained, because they are inherently more personal in nature.

ARGUMENT #4: THE STIFLING OF FREE SPEECH

A final theme emerging from the pro–status quo comments involved the claim that the movement to change the name was representative of political correctness gone wild. Many of these comments argued that this was a liberal versus conservative issue, with liberal politicians assumed to have ulterior motives (e.g., "They want the Native Americans' support in politics") and that liberals were pushing an agenda of promotion of ethnic minorities (e.g., "Hey Americans. How about we elect a Native American president[?] It's absurd that there hasn't been a Native American president yet [at] all. This ad represents is [sic] liberals wanting more attention."

The notion of the "Proud to Be" ad being a direct affront to free speech was mentioned by several commenters, with one saying, "That ad is meant to touch at the hearts of the uninformed. This is a manufactured controversy because they want to control speech." Other beliefs were more opaque; for instance, one person commented, "People, don't let yourselves be fooled by this new wave of political correctness. The people promoting this nonsense have a hidden agenda. Be careful!" Overall, this theme was almost universally painted as a liberal agenda for change, with the aims of this presumed agenda ranging from garnering votes to vague notions of agendas beyond winning elections.

Conclusion

As schools continue to remove Native American nicknames, particularly those with any reference to R-dskins, the debate over the name "R-dskins" continues on the grandest of all American stages: the NFL.[18] This chapter has offered two contradictory sets of emerging themes (for or against changing the mascot), yet it is clear that far more deviations from these two stances exist, just as there are more than only dual histories at play. Interestingly, Michael A. Robidoux calls for saturation of these types of images in both sport and fashion, not because they are empowering or trivial, but because "it is only then that their signifying potential of a reality that never was can be erased, giving way to new systems of meanings."[19]

Perhaps this is the most significant lesson that can be derived from the analysis of comments arising from the advertisements for and against a Washington mascot change: that there is far more being contested than merely a nickname, logo, or ritual. The next three chapters springboard into how each of those three elements (names, images, and rituals) play out in different manners, with problematic receptions unfolding in nuanced ways for each of these core areas of the mascotting controversy.

Deconstructing the Mascot, Part 1

Names and Textual Fields

From a reductionist perspective, debates regarding Native American mascots all start with the name. Florida State University claiming the "Seminole" moniker begets the visuals of Chief Osceola and other forms of Native American imagery, which then begets the rituals within, which finally begets the entrenchment of fan sentiments as inseparable from the performance of one's identity with a school or team. The name "R-dskins" begets the imagery that begets the endorsement of the National Football League (NFL), which begets the mainstreaming of the NFL team in Washington as inherently acceptable. All mascot debates seemingly start with a name: a Native American name with a wide range of intent from honorific to dubious and virtually all elements between.

The purpose of this chapter, though, is less to enter the robust debates regarding whether names represent "heritage or hatred" and more about deconstructing the mascot through a systematic process, starting with the empirical (to gain a broader perspective on public sentiment) before moving to the humanistic (via case studies to explore the messages endemic to mascotting processes).[1] This chapter focuses on persuasive messages embedded within specific mascot names assigned to schools and teams and is followed by chapters focusing on visual imagery/logos (chapter 5) and rituals (chapter 6). After all, much has been made about action steps for eliminating Native American mascots in team culture, informing the subsequent media that cover them.[2] However, examining the influence of Native American mascots relates to overall conceptions of the culture as a whole, meaning it is the perception of names, visual imagery, and rituals that seeps into any constructive mechanisms for change.[3]

As such, each of the "deconstruction" chapters offered in this book begins with the results of a national survey pertaining to public perceptions of the Native American mascotting debate. A total of 1,076 respondents from a national sample (attained via the Amazon Mechanical Turk website) completed a comprehensive survey regarding attitudes about Native American mascots—and also some oft-mentioned mascots as potentially troubling outside of Native American terrain (e.g., the Notre Dame "Fighting Irish"). The survey featured a near-equivalent gender split (544 women, 532 men), with racial demographics very close to census data for the U.S. population (e.g., 69 percent white). All measures had reliable alpha coefficients (exceeding .8). Part of the design of the survey was to blunt any notions of belonging to a given portion of the debate, meaning that Native American voices were neither sought out nor eliminated. The design was intended to provide the best snapshot of American sentiment without privileging any group over another, whether that involved indigenous persons (or not) or sports fans (or not).

General sentiments on Native American mascots were substantially divided. For instance, when asked on an eleven-point scale (with 10 indicating strong agreement) as to whether they agreed that "no team should have a Native American mascot," the mean was 4.08, somewhat in the middle, but leaning against complete bans of all Native American mascots. However, when asked for responses on whether a "new team should not consider a Native American mascot," scores rose significantly, with a mean of 6.09, favoring a ban of any future use of Native American mascots. Thus, it appears there is a sense of being "grandfathered in" to a cadre of teams with Native American mascots, echoing sentiments uncovered in chapter 2. Perhaps a good summary of the bifurcation found was that when presented with the item "calls for removal of Native American mascots are examples of how society has now become too politically correct," the mean score was 5.01, placing it almost perfectly in the center of the scale from 0 to 10. Standard deviation was high (3.89) on this item, meaning that roughly one-third of respondents offered one of two of the poles of this item.

Respondents were then asked to rate both the acceptability and inoffensiveness of such mascots on an eleven-point scale (0–10). More specifically, they completed such items relating to three forms of the mascot debate: names, images (unpacked as logos), and rituals (unpacked as 15- to 25-second video clips of Native American mascotting chants, dances, etc.). The results of these three forms of debate are rendered in this chapter as well as in the subsequent chapters 5 (images) and 6 (rituals), respectively.

First, table 4.1 reports mean scores on fourteen different Native American mascot–oriented names, offering scores on both acceptability and inoffensiveness scales. Higher scores indicate public support for the name in each regard; lower scores indicate the public is much less sanguine about the use of the specific Native American sports mascot name.

Regarding the least acceptable names, the five scoring lowest were "Savages" (M = 4.36), "Redskins" (M = 4.69), "Indians" (M = 5.80), "Fighting Sioux" (M = 5.94), and "Savage Storm" (M = 6.24). In contrast, the Native American name dubbed most acceptable was "Braves" (M = 7.12). In terms of the inoffensiveness of names, the same five ranked lowest, albeit with different means, "Savages" (M = 4.40), "Redskins" (M = 4.47), "Indians" (M = 5.54), "Fighting Sioux" (M = 5.71), and "Savage Storm" (M = 6.21). Again, "Braves" was considered the least offensive Native American name (M = 6.71).

The semantic difference between a name being "acceptable" and being "offensive" was offered as a way to mitigate some of the ways the mascotting debate has unfolded, asking both types of questions and rendering them in synonymous ways even when they could have meaning extracted quite differently. For instance, one could deem a team name to be offensive but still dub it generally "acceptable" under the belief that there are other names even more unacceptable than the one in question, creating an equation in which

Table 4.1: Mean (M) Scores for Native American Mascot Names

| Name | Acceptability (0–10) | | Inoffensiveness (0–10) | | |
	M	Rank	M	Rank	+/−
Braves	7.12	1	6.71	1	.41
Chiefs	6.92	2	6.56	5	.36
Aztecs	6.77	3	6.57	4	.20
Seminoles	6.73	4	6.43	6	.30
Illini	6.68	5	6.74	2	−.06
Utes	6.61	6	6.63	3	−.02
Sioux	6.44	7	6.34	8	.10
Chippewa	6.38	8	6.35	7	.03
Choctaws	6.24	T-9	6.31	9	−.07
Savage Storm	6.24	T-9	6.21	10	.03
Fighting Sioux	5.94	11	5.71	11	.23
Indians	5.80	12	5.54	12	.26
Redskins	4.69	13	4.47	13	.22
Savages	4.36	14	4.40	14	−.04

the "low-hanging fruit" is where change should most likely next occur. Most names rendered similar scores on the two types of measures, yet there were some notable differences. For instance, "Chiefs" was considered more *acceptable* than "Aztecs," "Seminoles," and "Illini" and yet was simultaneously rendered to be more *offensive* than "Aztecs" and "Illini"; in a similar vein, "Illini" was considered less offensive than acceptable, scoring a higher rating on its inoffensiveness than its acceptability, a relatively rare finding (as only "Utes," "Choctaws," and "Savages" yielded higher scores on the second measure than the first).

The survey also featured some pairs of similar names to determine whether the addition or subtraction of a modifier helped or hurt the cause. More specifically, dropping the word "Fighting" in front of the word "Sioux" helped make the moniker a half point more acceptable and had an even greater positive effect on its perceived offensiveness. In an even more deviating example, "Savages" was collectively found to be the most offensive and least acceptable of all tested names, yet when "Savage" was used as an adjective modifying the word "Storm," respondents were far more accepting of the name, indicating scores nearly two full points higher regarding both acceptability and inoffensiveness. Thus, it appears the problem many people have with such a name is not the word "Savage" but rather the word being used as a noun as opposed to a modifier of another non–Native American noun.

Other comparisons can be drawn from measuring respondent scores on oft-incorporated names used to offer potential "slippery slope" arguments infused to hinder the changing of Native American mascot names. Six of these cases were measured and are offered in table 4.2, providing a sense of comparison to determine whether Native American names occupy a unique space among debates over mascot naming acceptability.

As table 4.2 illuminates, virtually all of the tested potential equivalent mascot names resulted in higher acceptability and inoffensiveness scores than the

Table 4.2: Mean (*M*) Scores for Non/Questionably Native American Mascot Names

Name	Acceptability (0–10)		Inoffensiveness (0–10)		
	M	Rank	*M*	Rank	+/–
Mustangs	8.37	1	8.52	1	−.15
Vikings	8.34	2	8.05	2	.29
Warriors	8.29	3	7.72	4	.57
Celtics	8.07	4	7.84	3	.23
Fighting Irish	7.32	5	7.06	5	.26
Quakers	7.00	6	7.03	6	−.03

fourteen Native American mascot names. Indeed, the lowest score offered in table 4.2 pertains to the use of the religiously based word "Quakers," which scored lower (yet not statistically significantly so) than the ratings for the highest-scoring Native American mascot name: "Braves." Other names were statistically more likely to be embraced. For instance, the moniker "Warriors" was tested in this table rather than table 4.1, but some would argue it best fits with the other Native American mascots, because it sometimes is unpacked with indigenous cultural practices and images. However, it appears most respondents did not place the name in the Native American universe given its scores registering above 8 on the eleven-point scale. Perhaps the prevalence of the National Basketball Association's (NBA's) Golden State Warriors (who won the NBA title in 2015 and 2017 and lost in the NBA Finals in 2016) made people less likely to extract Native American connotations from it, as Golden State has resisted any marketing that makes the Warriors in any way related to the Native American mascot debate. Other names of groups of people relating to heritage, such as "Celtics" or "Vikings," were significantly less problematic for people than any of the fourteen Native American names, seemingly a product of defunct cultures more than issues with heritage. Reasons for this could be offered at many levels, but it is likely that the lack of many formal ties to people with those cultural backgrounds created indifference for some to sensitivity issues; the out-groups for "Celtics" and "Vikings" were not readily in most people's minds in same manner as one would picture Native American populations in the United States.

When the NCAA offered a list of eighteen schools deemed not in compliance with the stance against Native American mascots, indicating they would be banned for postseason play if a mascot was not changed by February 1, 2006, the result was that many schools sought new monikers to replace the previous Native American mascots.[4] Several of those cases involved the same label: "Indians." Thus, three replacement names were tested to determine the degree of improvement a replacement name provided in comparison to the previous "Indian" label. Table 4.3 ultimately provides insight as to whether the new names bolstered the acceptability of the selected mascot for a given school and, if so, to what degree.

As one can see in table 4.3, each of the three schools replacing the name "Indians" was successful in bolstering perceptions of both acceptability and inoffensiveness, in varying respects. To reiterate, the name "Indians" was given a composite score of 5.80 on acceptability and 5.54 on inoffensiveness. In contrast, two of the three schools tested yielded nearly identical improvements in both scores.

Table 4.3: Mean (*M*) Scores for Names Replacing Native American Mascots

Name	Acceptability (0–10)		Inoffensiveness (0–10)		+/−
	M	Rank	*M*	Rank	
Crimson Hawks	7.69	T-1	8.05	1	−.36
Red Wolves	7.69	T-1	8.03	2	−.34
Warhawks	6.97	3	7.27	3	−.30

First, Indiana University of Pennsylvania adopted the name "Crimson Hawks," which improved acceptability by 1.89—to a total mean of 7.69—and bolstered inoffensiveness even more so, increasing a total of 2.51 to an overall mean of 8.05. An interesting side note to this selection of "Crimson Hawks" was that the school seemingly did not fully vet the name, later finding that crimsonhawk.com was connected to a pornographic cartoon character and presented a potential new set of problems for the university. Such problems were momentary, as the owner of crimsonhawk.com was willing to change the website domain name without formal legal action or debate from the university, yet they underscore the lack of focus most people place on the origins of a mascot name.

The other case, yielding nearly identical results to that of Indiana University of Pennsylvania, was Arkansas State, who altered their "Indians" label to "Red Wolves" in 2008. The change bolstered acceptability by 1.89 and inoffensiveness by 2.49.

A somewhat less successful rebranding happened in 2006 for University of Louisiana–Monroe, who shifted their "Indians" moniker to "Warhawks." The shift was still successful—elevating acceptability by 1.17 and inoffensiveness by 1.73—both of which are statistically significant improvements but nevertheless markedly lower scores than the other two replacement names. Part of the potential lessened impact of the name change could be lack of knowledge of the out-group. The in-group (in this case, people with ties to the University of Louisiana–Monroe) would be more likely to connect the "Warhawks" label to the person it is intended to honor: Clare Lee Chennault, who used the Curtis P-40 Warhawk in battle during World War II. Conversely, the out-group may be more apt to consider a Warhawk to be honoring conservative principles, as modern politics often labels politicians with pro-war sentiments to be dubbed "warhawks."

Perhaps one of the largest measures of the Native American mascot debate involves the level of disagreement among a population. In other words, it is useful to determine which Native American mascot name is the most polarizing for the overall American population. In the case of this survey, standard deviations were used as a surrogate for such bifurcation, with higher standard deviations representing greater diversity (and, hence, disagreement) among respondents. Table 4.4 offers the standard deviations for both acceptability and inoffensiveness for each of the fourteen selected mascot names.

As table 4.4 shows, the most hotly debated name in any list of potentially offensive Native American mascots rises to the fore: "Redskins." Indeed, the two names deemed most offensive in table 4.1 ("Redskins" and "Savages") yielded the highest levels of disagreement here. Interestingly, the names most apt to yield more consensus within the respondent population were "Utes" and "Illini," both collegiate mascots argued to be problematic less for their name than for the embodiment of the mascot in the form of personas such as Chief Illiniwek.

Another interesting finding outlined in table 4.4 is that the +/- differential showed that it was somewhat easier to find agreement as to which name is acceptable than it was to do so regarding whether a name was offensive; only "Savage Storm" had more agreement on the offensive/inoffensive continuum than the acceptable/unacceptable binary.

Finally, it is also noteworthy to recognize that the two sets of standard deviation ranks were nearly uniform in their consistency. Standard deviation scores changed from name to name within the fourteen tested Native American mascot monikers, yet ultimately agreement over their acceptability or offensiveness scored almost equivalently to form a nearly perfect rank-order correlation. Comparisons of standard deviations can be found in tables

Table 4.4: Standard Deviations (SD) for Native American Mascot Names

| Name | Acceptability (0–10) | | Inoffensiveness (0–10) | | +/- |
	SD	Rank	SD	Rank	
Redskins	3.97	1	4.03	1	−.06
Savages	3.92	2	3.95	2	−.03
Indians	3.71	3	3.77	3	−.06
Savage Storm	3.68	4	3.65	5	.03
Fighting Sioux	3.66	5	3.70	4	−.04
Sioux	3.51	6	3.64	T-6	−.13
Choctaws	3.50	7	3.64	T-6	−.14
Chippewa	3.47	8	3.61	8	−.14
Seminoles	3.36	T-9	3.59	T-9	−.23
Aztecs	3.36	T-9	3.57	T-11	−.21
Chiefs	3.35	11	3.59	T-9	−.24
Braves	3.27	12	3.57	T-11	−.30
Utes	3.30	13	3.52	13	−.22
Illini	3.28	14	3.44	14	−.16

Table 4.5: Standard Deviations (SD) for Non/Questionably Native American Mascot Names

Name	Acceptability (0–10)		Inoffensiveness (0–10)		
	SD	Rank	SD	Rank	+/–
Quakers	3.21	1	3.26	1	–.03
Fighting Irish	3.06	2	3.18	2	.26
Mustangs	2.48	3	2.48	6	–.15
Celtics	2.48	4	2.87	4	.23
Warriors	2.43	5	3.03	3	.57
Vikings	2.38	6	2.79	5	.29

Table 4.6: Standard Deviations (SD) for Names Replacing Native American Mascots

Name	Acceptability (0–10)		Inoffensiveness (0–10)		
	SD	Rank	SD	Rank	+/–
Warhawks	3.23	1	3.25	1	–.02
Red Wolves	2.94	2	2.81	2	.13
Crimson Hawks	2.88	3	2.76	3	.12

4.5 and 4.6 for other mascots (arguably problematic ones and replacements, respectively). In general, one can witness a key trend in each of these two tables: there is significantly less disagreement on the acceptability of these mascot names than the Native American ones rendered in table 4.4.

Beyond items querying the acceptability (or lack thereof) and overall offensiveness (or lack thereof) of given mascot names, additional items were tested to gauge principle elements of the Native American mascot debate. For instance, figure 4.1 features mean scores from respondents when asked the question of who should possess the power to determine the acceptability of Native American mascots.

As figure 4.1 highlights, among the three constituencies offered (fans, players, and Native American tribes), the one group given the most authority is Native American tribes. As previously established in this book, discerning such interests is inherently difficult, because different tribes have different stances and even different relationships with local universities and teams with Native American names. Although consensus can rarely be attained, the respondents offered fairly strong support for the notion that Native American tribes occupy a unique space of authority, with a mean of 7.08 out of ten, far surpassing that of fans (5.21) and players (4.1). It is perhaps equally noteworthy, though, that fans were given precedence over players in ascertaining acceptability—particularly when considering the players are the ones who

Acceptability of NA Mascots

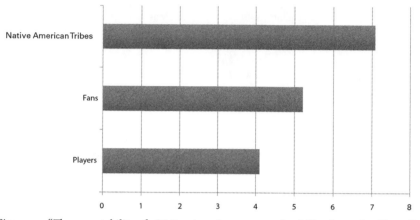

Figure 4.1. "The acceptability of a Native American mascot should be determined by . . ." Key: 0 = strong disagreement; 10 = strong agreement.

must wear the name and logo while being surrounded by the imagery. The players are often the embodiment of a given team, yet respondents felt fans should have more say as to whether a Native American mascot is acceptable, potentially because of presumed greater loyalty to a school or organization.

Delving deeper into the data, questions of local vs. national standing are reflected in figure 4.2, which pertains to a pair of binaries: not only local vs.

Local vs. National Sentiments

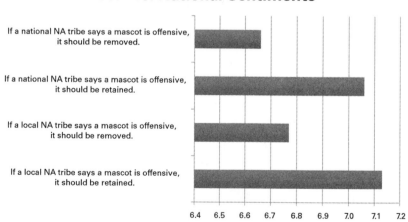

Figure 4.2. Sentiments on removal vs. retainment of Native American (NA) mascots. Key: 0 = strong disagreement; 10 = strong agreement.

national but also removal vs. retention. The semantics appear to shift scores demonstrably within the latter, while the former resulted in a key overarching finding: the more local the concern, the more relevant respondents believed it was to the discussion at hand. Thus, even though an entity such as the FSU Seminoles participate in sporting competitions telecast to the nation at large, precedence is presumably ascribed to the local Seminole Tribe of Florida (which supports the name) over the larger Seminole Nation of Oklahoma (which does not support the name).

Finally, questions were advanced pertaining to the largest naming controversy within the entire debate: the "R-dskins." Some questions dealt with the name without combination with the city of Washington, while others did not. Results of six different measures related to the name "R-dskins" are offered in figure 4.3.

As highlighted within this figure, semantics again played a key role. If asked whether any team should use the name "R-dskins," mean scores were 5.95; if queried about the specific case in the NFL as to whether the Washington R-dskins *should* change their name, the agreement dips to 5.57; if adding two words to the same item "should *have to* change their name," means drop to below the scale median: 4.95. Thus, one could conclude that the majority of people have some level of concern with the R-dskins' name, yet are much less comfortable with the notion of an outside entity forcing a team to change it against its will. Such semantic differences can be noteworthy. For instance, it

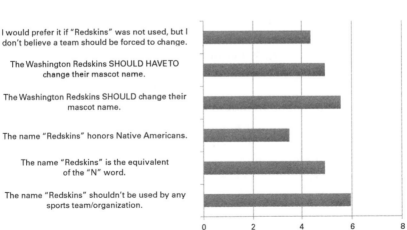

Figure 4.3. Attitudes toward the moniker "Redskins." Key: 0 = strong disagreement; 10 = strong agreement.

is important to note that when a 2016 *Washington Post* poll found that nine of ten Native Americans were "not offended" by the name "R-dskins," the poles of the scale were not direct opposites, with options being "offended" and "not bothered."[5] Thus, it is very likely conceivable that one could be "bothered" or "disapprove" of the name "R-dskins" without being able to argue one is "offended." Thus, results of such polls are less insightful than they could potentially be.

More tellingly within the survey, one could conclude that there is middling support for the notion that the word "R-dskin" was the equivalent of using the N-word ($M = 4.94$). Such confusion with high standard deviation ($SD = 2.40$) seemingly stems from semantic evolution or, as *Washington Post* writer Dan Steinberg puts it, the question of "how did a word that was not offensive for 75 or 80 years suddenly become offensive in 2013?"[6] He goes on to explore the usage of the word, finding that in the early 1970s the debate already raged as to the equivalent of the word "R-dskins," with authors contending if it did not directly constitute the word "n-gger," some other direct correlates could be made with the word "darky," "Dago," or "kike." The result of this study generally concludes that determining whether a member of the lay public would argue "R-dskin" and "n-gger" to be equivalent is roughly a coin-flip proposition.

Nevertheless, it is also fair to conclude that there was a stronger sentiment that the name was the equivalent of the N-word than there was for the notion that the name honored Native Americans through its usage ($M = 3.49$). Perceptions, of course, are different from historical realities, yet calculating such sentiments is useful for gauging the manner in which the public addresses Native American mascot names. Moreover, such survey items underscore how the addition, elimination, or substitution of a single word or phrase can produce significantly different results.

Finally, it is important to note that sports fan identification appears to be a crucial discerning factor in determining relative acceptability and offensiveness of a mascot. On the large majority of the items reported earlier in this chapter, a highly identified sports fan was more likely to consistently, statistically, and significantly judge Native American mascots in a kinder light than would a less-identified sports fan.

As one example of this phenomena, consider the means reported in table 4.7. The table divides respondents into two groups: non–sports fans (less than 7 on an eleven-point scale) and sports fans (7 or greater on an eleven-point scale). This bifurcates the sample almost exactly equally (49.2 percent non–sports fans; 50.8 percent sports fans). Means are then rendered between these two groups as to their perceived acceptability of mascot names.

Table 4.7: Mean (M) Acceptability Scores for Native
American Mascot Names by Sports Fan Identification

Name	Non-Fan M	Fan M	Sig. p
Braves	6.98	7.26	n.s.
Chiefs	6.55	7.29	.002
Aztecs	6.40	7.15	.001
Seminoles	6.25	7.19	.001
Illini	6.30	7.06	.001
Utes	6.00	7.21	.001
Sioux	6.08	6.80	.003
Chippewa	5.99	6.77	.001
Choctaws	5.82	6.67	.001
Savage Storm	6.20	6.28	n.s.
Fighting Sioux	5.58	6.30	.005
Indians	5.37	6.21	.001
Redskins	4.36	5.00	.023
Savages	4.23	4.49	n.s.

Sig. = Significance
p = significance level statistic (chance of error)

Thus, as shown in table 4.7, there is a very clear pattern that emerges, with non–sports fans finding each of the names less acceptable than did self-described sports fans. An analysis of variance (ANOVA) was performed with significance levels determined. In all but three cases the differences between the scores indicated by the two groups was significant. Only the most seemingly benign of all tested Native American names ("Braves") and the two names containing the most detested of all Native American words (as shown in table 4.1—"Savage Storm," "Savages") had non-significant results. For all other cases, if you were a sports fan, you were significantly more likely to find a given Native American name to be acceptable.

An interesting correlate to the results offered in table 4.7 is that the hierarchy of acceptability stays relatively constant. Both groups agree, for instance, that "Braves" is more acceptable than "Seminoles," which is more acceptable than "Choctaws," which is more acceptable than "Redskins." Thus, there is uniformity in the ranking of acceptability but also in the inflation of acceptability that arises through being a sports fan, with the average sports fan rating a name .61 higher than the average non–sports fan.

Such consistent trends occurred for perceived offensiveness as well, yet, interestingly, not with other aspects of names within the survey. No differences between non–sports fans and sports fans were yielded on any names when it came to non–Native American mascot names (e.g., "Celtics," "Irish," etc.), and relatively few of the overarching questions about acceptability of mascots as a whole offered the fan versus non-fan bifurcation. For instance, there was no statistically significant (via ANOVA) difference between fans and non-fans on questions such as whether a new sports team should consider a Native American mascot or even whether teams have a right to choose whatever mascot they wish. One Redskin-oriented question resulted in differences between fans and non-fans, and it related to whether the name "honors Native Americans"; both groups were likely to disagree with this sentiment, but non–sports fans were more vehement in their disagreement ($M = 3.07$) than were sports fans ($M = 3.90$).

The other two items resulting in significant differences depending on fandom related to political correctness. Non–sports fans were less likely than sports fans to connect calls for both Native American mascot and specifically the removal of the "Redskins" name as being equated to a society deemed too focused on political correctness.

Overall, the results from the name-based portion of the empirical survey spotlight the differences between certain types of Native American names. The debate is often constructed as one side against the use of all Native American mascots and the other in favor of the status quo in all circumstances; that simply was not the case in the survey. That is, the gap between the name "Braves" and some of the names scoring the lowest on the scale (e.g., "Redskins" and "Savages") is as wide as the gap between "Braves" and most any other mainstream mascot name. Thus, distinctions between and among Native American mascot names must be made, with some of that nuance offered in the case study portions of this chapter that follow.

Positioning Native American Names in American Culture

Continuing this chapter's theme of focusing on the persuasive elements of mascot *names*, the rhetorical-critical analysis that follows delves discursively into how those opposed to Native American mascots and those in favor of the status quo entrench and then retrench their positions. The analysis is grounded in two frames. First, building from chapter 1, the discourse that will be analyzed assumes that self-categorization as a theory underscores the adamancy, and sometimes vitriol, of "stances and biases" of in-groups in apposition to those perceived to be in an out-group.[7] These stances and biases, of course, are made emblematic in the rhetoric that calls them into public being rather than just being discussed interpersonally among those within the in-group or singularly being gauged by polls, including the infamous May 2016 *Washington Post* iteration.[8] Second, using the theoretical underpinnings organized in chapter 2, the analysis offered here acknowledges that the Native American mascot controversy is firmly ensconced in colonial logics, thus calling to postcolonialism as a critical apparatus to examine the rhetoric on either side of the mascot debate. Danielle Endres reminds us that "analyses of rhetorical colonialism focus on the ways that dominant non-American Indian discourse perpetuates and justifies a racist, hegemonic, and colonial mindset."[9] Glen Sean Couthard agrees that "a settler-colonial relationship is one characterized by a particular form of domination; that is, it is a relationship of power . . . that continue[s] to facilitate the dispossession of Indigenous peoples of their land and self-determining authority."[10] Taking Endres's and Couthard's lead, part of the neocolonial relationship stitched through the Native American mascot controversy thus involves settler-colonial arguments. Moreover, we also witness resistive, decolonial sensibilities within the debate. As Amy Lonetree argues, "Decolonization is about empowerment—a belief that situations can be transformed; . . . it is about transforming negative reactionary energy into the more positive rebuilding energy" to fix deleterious stereotypes and representational practices.[11] This decolonization can be accomplished by Native-identified and non-Native folks alike.

Mascot *names* wield potency and primacy as a first step to publics recognizing and making judgments about Native American mascots. Names generate visual symbols and contemporaneous performances of mascots. The name, thus, is the origin point; there is no documented case of a team beginning with an image or ritual they would like to represent their team and then determining a name that could somehow encapsulate said image or ritual. Therefore, the critical analysis in this book begins with names before proceeding in successive chapters to investigations of the visual images and rituals associated with Native American mascots.

This portion of chapter 4 addresses the Washington R-dskins case from October 2013, when the controversy hit a fever pitch during the Change the Mascot group's increased protest of the Washington team name, to July 2015, when a U.S. federal court denied the Washington team an appeal of the U.S. Patent and Trademark Office's (USPTO's) 2014 ban on the team's trademark rights related to the name "R-dskins." The section unfolds by summarizing a chronology of the R-dskins milieu during this time period before next discussing a methodology of gathering public rhetoric surrounding the Change the Mascot protests through to the Washington team's failure to embrace such appeals. The spotlight of the section, then, is a rhetorical analysis of pro-mascot and anti-mascot discourse, organized thematically. Finally, implications of the R-dskins controversy are contoured.

Case Study: The 2013–2015 Washington R-dskins Context

As we discussed in this book's introduction and in chapter 3, the social topographies and polemics of the Washington R-dskins dispute are not new. In fact, as early as 1933, Washington franchise owner George Preston Marshall was having to answer questions about the R-dskins mascot. At the dawn of the team's existence he said, "So much confusion has been caused by our football team wearing the same name as the Boston National League baseball club [Boston Braves] . . . that a change appeared to be absolutely necessary. The fact that we have in our head coach, Lone Star Dietz, an Indian, together with Indian players has not, as may be suspected, inspired me to select the name Redskins."[12] Marshall's comment appears to strip away the contention that the team was named to honor Native Americans. Rather, the rhetorical choice of the mascot was one of convenience and possibly economics. Either way, discussion of this rhetorical choice was alive and well from the beginning of the Washington franchise. Issues concerning the team name returned to the national radar in 1968 when the National Congress of American Indians (NCAI) and the American Indian Movement engaged in a large-scale campaign to address Native American mascots in sports. The primary agents of their reprobation included the abundant number of universities, schools, and professional teams that marked their identities with indigenous names. There were more campaigns launched throughout the 1980s and 1990s, especially during the R-dskins' successes in 1990, 1991, and 1992 (particularly when and after they won the Super Bowl in 1991).

In the intervening late 1990s and the 2000s, activists such as Suzan Shown Harjo, Charlene Teeters, and the Morningstar Institute continued their efforts to resist the "R-dskins" name in particular, yet there was an incredible resurgence in activist bustle around 2012. It was at this time that 2011 Heisman Trophy winner, Robert Griffin III, was drafted by the Washington team, and, given his and the team's renewed and valiant performance during the 2012 NFL season, it was clear that commentators were focusing more attention on the once-beleaguered team, because it appeared to have a bright future with a compelling young star quarterback. Suddenly the R-dskins team was back in favor, and publics—from fantasy football leagues and jersey collectors to the predictable national sports media and ubiquitous water cooler quarterbacks—were agog about Washington's NFL franchise. In the midst of the fanfare, writes C. Richard King, a watershed moment of scrutiny of the name occurred when sportscaster Bob Costas "offered a sharply worded critique of [the team], describing it as a 'slur' and an 'insult'" during a Sunday Night Football game between the R-dskins and the Dallas Cowboys.[13] Following suit, more and more sports writers and broadcasters began amending the ways they addressed the team in print and on the air, respectively. In fact, the use of the moniker "R-dskins" declined in sports media coverage of the team by some 27 percent as "Washington" became the go-to identifier for the team.[14] Even owners of professional sports teams claiming a Native American mascot chimed in as did Paul Dolan, owner of the Cleveland Indians, who wryly remarked, "If we were the Redskins, the day after I owned the team, the name would have to be changed."[15] For a team that caricatures their "Indians" mascot name with a red-faced, white-toothed, grossly feathered Chief Wahoo (explored in greater detail in chapter 5), such remarks were noteworthy and jarring. In the end, as an increasing number of sports media pundits and stakeholders began discussing the revitalized debate over the "R-dskins" name, a growing anti-mascot fervor took root anew.

The 2013 episode proved a spark of *kairos* for a newly regenerated group called Change the Mascot, a joint campaign of the NCAI and the Oneida Nation. Every social change effort needs a generative moment, a public opening, and a villain, and Change the Mascot found these in the cleavage that Costas had wedged into the controversy, the public outcry it produced, and in Washington team owner Daniel Snyder's acerbic defense of the "R-dskins" name, respectively.[16] The same month as that fateful Sunday Night Football game against the Cowboys in October 2013, when Costas shed even brighter light on the controversy, Snyder wrote a letter to the public, but mostly to Washington fans, guarding the mascot and claiming zealously that he would never change it while he was alive. He said, in part, "Washington Redskins is more than a name we have called our football team for over eight decades. It is a symbol of everything we stand for: strength, courage, pride, and respect—the same values we know guide Native Americans and which are embedded throughout their rich history as the original Americans."[17] This old chestnut, an "honor" argument from as far back as the 1960s, was just the spark that Change the Mascot needed to move ahead with resistive velocity.

A few months later during the same NFL season, in January 2014 Change the Mascot ran an online advertisement during the Super Bowl, and in March the group ran a televised commercial during the NCAA March Madness basketball tournament. This campaign called "Proud to Be" indicated that Native Americans are many things, "but a mascot is not one." The Washington team and Snyder countered with the "Redskins Is a Powerful Name" commercial during the Super Bowl. (The mediated public debate over these competing commercials was described and analyzed in chapter 3.)

The public controversy was now in full-fledged, rancorous debate mode. In May 2014 fifty Democratic and Independent U.S. senators, minus Virginia's two (Mark Warner and Tim Kaine), asked the NFL to consider taking action on the "R-dskins" name. They drew a parallel between the National Basketball Association's no-tolerance policy regarding the racist comments made by Los Angeles Clippers owner Donald Sterling and Dan Snyder's defense of the "R-dskins" name. The group of senators wrote:

> Today, we urge you and the National Football League to send the same clear message as the NBA did: that racism and bigotry have no place in professional sports. It's time for the NFL to endorse a name change for the Washington, D.C. football team. The despicable comments made by Mr. Sterling have opened up a national conversation about race relations. We believe this conversation is an opportunity for the NFL to take action to remove the racial slur from the name of one of its marquee franchises.[18]

The NFL, loyal in spirit if not also in commercial bond with its franchises, responded with the following: "The NFL has long demonstrated a commitment to progressive leadership on issues of diversity and inclusion, both on and off the field. The intent of the team's name has always been to present a strong, positive and respectful image. The team name is not used by the team or the NFL in any other context, though we respect those that view it differently."[19] The public debate had turned political, and it was about to turn legal as well.

Motivated by Change the Mascot and the group of senators, the U.S Patent and Trademark Office (USPTO)—through its Trademark Trial and Appeal Board (TTAB)—decided to cancel six team trademarks deemed "disparaging . . . to a substantial composite of Native Americans" in late spring of 2014.[20] In August 2014 the Washington R-dskins franchise filed an appeal claiming that their First Amendment rights were violated by the TTAB's cancellations. They argued that the company could be an individual and, as such, the individual has freedom of expression. The appeal to the U.S. District Court in Alexandria, Virginia, was put off until March 2015.

In the meantime, the American Civil Liberties Union filed an amicus brief for the R-dskins in March 2015, saying although there is "little doubt that many Native Americans view the word as at least problematic, if not outright racist, the question of whether certain speech is distasteful is entirely distinct from the question of whether the government can constitutionally disadvantage a trademark registration for that reason. Under the First Amendment, viewpoint-based regulation of private speech is never acceptable, regardless of the controversy of the viewpoint."[21] Countering this, more than twenty American Indian and social justice organizations filed a joint amici curiae in support of Amanda Blackhorse and a group of anti-mascot defendants who had worked with the USPTO to file the trademark suit against the Washington team.[22]

The U.S. Department of Justice (DOJ) said that the TTAB did not violate the Washington R-dskins' right to free speech when it cancelled the six trademarks. Ostensibly, the attorney general's office filed a brief addressing the constitutional issues, stating that as commercial speech, the team name (and logo) is not protected by the First Amendment and that a large number of cases support the cancellation of the trademarks. The brief also stated that the court should reject the claim that the cancellation of trademarks constituted an illegal impingement of valuable property, which is barred by the Fifth Amendment. Even aside from the constitutional issues and, instead, leaning more toward cultural dimensions, the DOJ quoted the USPTO, writing, "The term can still be disparaging even if the team says it is intended to show honor and respect."[23] By forging an inquiry into constitutional issues regarding limits on disparaging speech in order to protect the cultural heritage of American Indian populations, the case was poised to make gains for anti-mascot proponents. And, indeed, July 2015 found the district court denying Snyder's and the Washington R-dskins' appeal, therein upholding the cancellation of trademarks. The court agreed with not only the DOJ's constitutional claims but also its indigenist-centered argument that unique Native cultural heritages "ought not be identified by the basest of prejudicial labels."[24]

Snyder and his franchise almost immediately brought a writ of certiorari before the U.S. Supreme Court, and the case was to be heard during the 2016–2017 session. The high court never adjudicated the case, instead choosing to hear *Mata v. Tam*, a similar case that featured a debate about whether an Asian American rock band could use the racially charged and potentially pejorative name "The Slants." Earlier, the USPTO had rejected the Slants' request for a trademark based on the term itself, a stereotypical slur for Asians and Asian Americans. The Supreme Court reported on June

19, 2017, that the USPTO's rejection of the Slants' trademark request was a First Amendment violation. Justice Samuel Alito, writing for the court majority, overturned the trademark cancellation. This ruling and its potential consequences for the Washington R-dskins are addressed more extensively in chapter 8. For now, however, an analysis of public discourse surrounding the 2013–2015 episode of the controversy will be examined.

Tracking the Discourse Surrounding the R-dskins Name

For this portion's rhetorical-critical analysis, we retrieved discourse from public Facebook comments appended to articles between October 2013 and July 2015. While chapter 3's analysis of public commentary dwelled specifically in the realm of two competing commercials, the discussion explored below is geared more toward the overall R-dskins trademark issue. Some of the themes we discuss replicate those found in chapter 3's analysis of YouTube comments affixed to the "Proud to Be" and "Redskins Is a Powerful Name" commercials. More themes, however, were found in the heat of controversy that succeeded the YouTube commercials in spring of 2014 and following the USPTO's cancellation of Washington's and Snyder's trademarks and the slew of resultant legal cases.

Facebook is not only an individual publishing platform but also an arena for public discussion and debate. And, of course, many news agencies have opened public accounts on Facebook and post near-hourly and synchronously with their other online news portals and print formats. Moreover, the comment boards appended to Facebook stories provide an accessible vehicle for users to express their ideas freely and publicly. We accessed the search engine embedded in Facebook with certain keywords—"Native American mascot," "Indian mascot," and "Redskins"—to retrieve related news posts during this time period. We included only news resources from large news agencies, counting NBC, Fox, the *Wall Street Journal*, and the *Washington Post* (which doubled as a local outlet regarding the R-dskins debate) among our sources, and retrieved a total of nineteen core articles. We browsed all of the public comments in the selected posts. Some news articles contained more than two thousand comments, with most reflecting strong attitudes on both sides of the debate. We selected a proportion of discourse that comprised rich messages; saturation typically occurred within the first one hundred comments on any of the given nineteen news stories. Selected comments met the following strict criteria: stating a clear claim and providing some modicum of evidence and reasoning for the claim. Simple and scant comments such as "No! No name change!" or "R-dskins is racist!" were excluded from the final analysis.

In all, we retrieved 228 pro-mascot and 120 anti-mascot comments. On the comment boards, the number of pro-mascot comments overwhelmed the anti-mascot ones. This can be explained most likely by what one finding of our survey indicated: even those who find the "R-dskins" name less offensive and less acceptable thought that no outside entity should *force* change ($M = 4.95$).

However, because we did not conduct a quantitative study in this portion of the chapter, the goal of sampling was neither to obtain a large sample nor to secure representativeness. Rather, we aimed to exhaust all meaningful claims. Our final discursive pool, having exhausted all major themes, helped formulate a comprehensive picture of how people interpreted the debate about the R-dskins mascot. Four researchers read all discourses independently and formed their initial categories of themes. After an in-depth discussion, we reached agreement on seven pro-mascot themes and seven anti-mascot themes.

Analysis of the "R-dskins" Name

As the first section of this chapter indicated, a survey of 1,076 respondents demonstrated that "Redskin" is one of the most contested of names in the Native American mascot controversy. Only the name "Savage" ranked above "Redskin" in terms of least acceptability ($M = 4.26$ vs. $M = 4.69$) and least inoffensiveness ($M = 4.40$ vs. $M = 4.47$). Regarding an explanation for "Savage," it is worth noting that this term is also a modifier that exists outside of settler-colonial logics and contexts. "Savage," in contemporary parlance, is an adjective describing an agent's intentionally hateful, mean, insulting, and incendiary reprobation or humiliation of another agent. The term is popular in online comment sections related to news stories, social media posts, and the like. When a commenter gets "one up" on another commenter by calling out or into question their appearance, character, intelligence, or capabilities (versus the other's rational argument), others might respond with "Dude, that was *savage*." We offer this aside as a possible, though not deterministic, factor to explain why respondents may have seen "Savage" as a bit worse in valence than "R-dskins" during a 2016-era survey.

One thing is certain: the name "R-dskins" has a sordid past and a deep colonial history. As King argues, one cannot separate context from contemporary use of the word itself: "Whatever the word's precise origin is, countless American Indians have suffered the indignity and intimidation of being called a r*dskin by a stranger, classmate, peer, coworker, boss, police officer, or commanding officer. Often said out of anger, meant to target, and designed to hurt, the symbolic violence of the word multiplies when coupled with adjectives like *dirty, lazy, stinking*, and *fucking*. It is very much a living slur. Today, r*dskin is widely regarded as an epithet."[25] Perhaps for this reason, among others, anti-mascot activists—both Native-identified and non-Native—have returned time and again to Washington's mascot as a case study of the toxic representations of indigeneity and the debilitating effects of the R-dskin name. During our interview with Jacqueline Pata, executive director of the NCAI, she explained why her organization and other resistive groups continue protesting Washington's team name. She contended that Washington's nickname constituted "the worst of the worst" and was therefore their "leading claim." The name "R-dskin" is no tepid or neutral term, to say the least.

Still, respondents to our survey seemed uncomfortable (M = 4.95) with a name change being forced by public organizations (i.e., anti-mascot organizations), private parties (i.e., the NCAA), corporations (i.e., the NFL), educational systems (i.e., school boards), or state and federal governmental entities (i.e., the USPTO, state legislatures, and federal courts). At the same time, as reported earlier in this chapter, these respondents were concerned with the "R-dskin" name. For instance, there was roughly the same middling finding that equated the name "R-dskin" with the N-word (M = 4.94) while substantially fewer thought the name "R-dskin" "honored" Native Americans (M = 3.49).

In the end, there are mixed opinions about the R-dskins mascot. This perhaps explains why we found so much public, discursive disagreement in comments appended to news stories about the Washington R-dskins context from 2013 to 2015. Of course, such in-group and out-group dynamics lend credence to self-categorization theory, especially its sine qua non proposition that "sides" constitute identities along lines of debate.[26] We now turn to themes that emerged in pro-mascot and anti-mascot rhetoric.

PRO-MASCOT COMMENTS ABOUT THE "R-DSKINS" NAME

OWNERSHIP The first rhetorical theme employed by those supporting the "R-dskins" name, and thus in favor of maintaining the status quo, involves claiming Native American identity as their own to bolster one's ethos in the controversy. There is no discernible way to verify one's cultural heritage or ethnic identity in such posts. Nonetheless, the theme of ownership stands out as a node of authority in arguments supporting the "R-dskins" name. Indeed, comments adopting such a rhetorical strategy received many "likes" on comment boards, and thus it is one of the most prominent themes among all pro-mascot discourses. For example, one comment offered a straightforward counterargument to oppose the idea of "R-dskins" being a racist slur to Native Americans: "I am part Native American and I would be offended if they CHANGED the name!" Besides those in favor of the name, some commenters refused to see any offensive elements in the word "R-dskins" at all: "I fail to see why this is offensive? It is a known fact that different races are known by the different shades of their skin . . . Asian-yellow, Negro-black, Latin-brown, Indian-red . . . Please, I am of the Cherokee blood line. . . . Why is this offensive, someone please explain this to me . . . ?" Along these lines, other commenters stated, "My grandfather's side of the family were full blood Cherokee" and "As a 1/8 Seminole, I didn't see any problem with the name." This comment connects to the *Washington Post* study that purported to poll only Native Americans, a high percentage of whom could not name their tribal affiliations. The difficulty of self-professed Native Americans unable to name their affiliations borders on the "My Grandmother Was a Cherokee Princess" mythos that some Native American skeptics have often pointed to as potentially white-identified people "playing Indian" to authenticate their rugged and frontier "Americanness."[27]

This theme occupied a prominent place among all pro-mascot discourses, because it countered the core basis of the anti-mascot campaign: If Native Americans are not offended by the name at all, why would other people be bothered by it? If removing the name offended Native Americans, would one still insist on changing the name? These questions were also associated publicly with responses to the *Washington Post* poll from May 2016 wherein nine of ten Native Americans were said to be agreeable or unaffected by the R-dskins mascot. In this instance, claims to Native American heritage shielded the pro-mascot standpoint from question and fortified the "R-dskins" name in a rheto-biographical bedrock of ethos.

As illustrated in chapter 3, such claims of ownership border on larger U.S. colonial ideologies regarding possession and territory of Native American lifeways, places, spaces, resources, and symbols. Even when speaking about Native-identified people being agreeable to a term like "R-dskins," settler-colonial logics still abound. As Endres explains it, "American Indian permission can unintentionally perpetuate colonialism, which American Indian opponents of permitted mascots point out in their arguments."[28] This unfolds, especially when activating a postcolonial lens, because assimilation and accommodation are often necessary—though not always sufficient—for Native Americans to survive in a nation whose relationship with indigenous communities is undeniably colonial in historical memory and contemporary lived experience. Sometimes this type of internal colonization has been so complete that Bryan McKinley Jones Brayboy writes, "Even many American Indians fail to recognize that we are talking up colonialist ideas when we fail to express ourselves in ways that may challenge dominant society's ideas about who and what we are supposed to be."[29] Ultimately, claiming Native heritage speaks to the power and ubiquity of ownership as a pro-mascot logic.

INOCULATION   The second rhetorical strategy used to defend the "R-dskins" name is inoculation, where commenters use Native Americans as ciphers for making their argument. A cipher, according to Kent Ono and Derek T. Buescher, is "a figure through which various commodities with multiple exchange values are marketed, and it is a social concept that circulates like a commodity. . . . It is a metonym."[30] For example, people from other ethnic groups exerted their voices to express what they believed Native Americans thought about the issue. One non-Native-identified person wrote that "99.9% of native [*sic*] Americans have no problem with the Redskin name." Similar to the first strategy, inoculation included under this theme involves people arguing that if Native Americans feel comfortable with the name, there is no real issue to be resolved; thus, maintaining the status quo is a reasonable reaction. Calling for the name change was another "damn media driven problem," some argued, where the media painted themselves as the friends of justice and disrupted the harmony among all racial groups. As one commenter queried, "Please tell me who is offended? I have some Native American friends and they have no problem with the name." These comments reflected how the majority group perceived the R-dskins mascot problem (or supposedly lack thereof), perhaps, from their own life experiences but concomitantly channeled the claim through Native surrogates.

In addition to the argument of Native Americans not being offended by the name, several commenters indicated that instead of being offended, Native Americans should instead be thankful to be called "R-dskins": "Native Americans should be proud that their heritage is being honored by so many teams wanting to be associated with their ferocity and strength!" In other words, according to such commenters, the name "R-dskins" is not only harmless but may also garner benefits for the social status of Native Americans. In the end, inoculation boils down to speaking *for* Native Americans, a colonial maneuver that has persisted throughout the Native-U.S. relationship and arises here as a neocolonial residue of the past.

INCONSEQUENTIALITY The third theme arising from the Facebook posts encompasses commentators' claims that issues exist that are vastly more important for Native Americans and the nation as a whole than the R-dskins controversy. These remarks revolve around the argument that the name of a football team's mascot does not deserve such publicly invested attention. One person wrote, "No! No name change. Somewhere along the line you just have to draw the line. Leave football alone. Mr. President we have bigger, more real problems to deal with than a name change." The commentary suggested that the war on terror and economic crises ought to be approached as political problems instead, and that those politicians and lawmakers who focused attention on the R-dskins were doing so simply because they were not capable of addressing those real problems. Thus, anti-mascot politicians were criticized for shifting the public's attention to trivial topics: "The gov. cannot take care of our major issues therefore it focus [*sic*] on these ridiculous ones!" This theme avoided the debate of whether the name "R-dskins" was offensive or not and concluded that the priority of this issue (of maintaining or changing the mascot) was not comparable to other social, diplomatic, and political problems. Simultaneously, the comment assumes a zero-sum-game argument that politicians can address only one issue at a time rather than tackling a docket of political, social, and economic policies.

This theme seemingly carries with it two implicit messages. First, it represents the haughtiness of the majority (or dominant) group, which was unaffected by the dehumanizing "R-dskins" name. Those commenters perceived the problem as limited to a small percentage of Native Americans who were easily offended; therefore, it was not worth the time and effort to cater to such few people: "There are much bigger problems in this world than a stupid team name. If you don't like it, don't watch it." Second, this theme highlights complaints about contemporary government's incapability of meeting commenters' demands. In other words, those commenters used this debate as a channel to vent their dissatisfaction with the political system. As with inoculation, the rhetorical strategy of inconsequentiality ciphered the R-dskins mascot controversy for something beyond the controversy itself.

CELEBRATION Another popular pro-mascot theme emphasized that using the name "R-dskins" had no single link to discrimination against Native Americans; instead, commenters viewed it as a respectful compliment. For instance, in the following post, a person argued that keeping the name is the best way to honor Native Americans: "Ridiculous . . . the [R-dskins] respect native [sic] Americans in every way. . . . Leave the team alone and let them continue in their traditions and honor the team name as they have always done." This theme located the R-dskins mascot as a symbol of Native American spirit: strong, brave, powerful, and determined. Unlike the sense of indifference expressed in the inconsequentiality theme, the rhetorical move of celebration seems to engage emotions and valence regarding Native American people and cultures as those to be heralded and even emulated. As another commenter argued, "The [R-dskin] is the symbol of all the aspirations of the American people: wisdom, integrity, confidence, presence, belief in ourselves, and American exceptionalism. To cave in to some vocal minority who don't comprehend values would be a travesty." This theme generated numerous productive sentiments by removing the original connotation of "R-dskins" while changing the denotation of the name to something more positive. In a way, though, the settler-colonial ideology of "saving up the Indian" wends its way into this theme as teams like the Washington R-dskins are argued to save Native culture, imbuing the mascot full of positive qualities. Granted, the qualities are those that a seemingly non-Native entity would be privileged enough to mark for itself in spite of the lived experiences—and often discriminatory treatment—of Native peoples. In this case, a team such as the NFL's Washington franchise "has inherited the right to appropriate and control Native American imagery."[31]

POLITICALLY ORIENTED THEMES Politics punctuated a great deal of pro-mascot commentary. We found three subthemes under this category, and each represents an independent but closely related rhetorical strategy.

The first subtheme under this category contains complaints that political correctness had run amok: "No!! Tired of the minority of people getting catered to. That's why this country is on [sic] the shape it is today." Our analysis of YouTube comments in chapter 3 indicates a similar finding that anti-mascotters had "gone too far" with promoting the well-being of Native Americans. In comments of this type, people complained that American society had lost its principium value of e pluribus unum by catering to every demand, reasonable or not, from minority groups. These posters worried that once Native Americans, in particular, felt offended, mainstream society would have to compromise at any cost or they would commit the trespass of being politically incorrect; comments such as "The USA has been taken over by crybabies!" explicitly express such impertinence. Sentiments included in this subtheme further indicate that Americans should learn how to "get over the political correctness" issue and not be so thin-skinned.

The second political subtheme includes comments invoking the value of free expression to defend the team name. In comments under this category, people frequently adopted two strategies to enhance their persuasive power: referring to the Constitution (especially the First Amendment) and using analogies. For instance, the following commenter adopted both strategies: "Canceling the trademark without due process is unconstitutional. . . . This administration [has] gone mad . . . Gestapo style!!!" Some comments illustrate disagreement with the government's public power to affect a name change: "No. People could make a case that any team's name is offensive. It's a privately-owned team, so the owner can have the name be whatever he wants it to be." Washington's football team was seen as a privately owned organization; thus, Dan Snyder had the right to treat his private property as he wished, keeping sacrosanct the name "R-dskins" within that framework. It was believed that the name change under governmental enforcement was a dangerous signal of a totalitarian society. The analogy of the U.S. government to the Nazi-era Gestapo expresses quite clearly the pro-mascotting position's fear of losing freedom of speech. And the politically infamous "C-word" was also invoked along these lines: "Communism! . . . This is not a free country. People need to wake up this is so wrong!"

Third, the larger pro-mascot political theme includes people's complaints about the government and President Barack Obama (whose executive branch had worked to curb and squash the R-dskins' and Snyder's trademarks). This subtheme involves some commenters directly targeting liberals and an essentialized, phantom radical agenda. Such remarks were often posted on traditionally conservative-oriented news sites such as Fox News, including these: "Anyone who supports a name change is an idiot"; "Keep the name 'REDSKINS' and change Obama"; and "Hell No another media driven problem!" This reveals that the debate regarding the R-dskins mascot had perhaps started to move beyond its original cultural landscape and toward a complete topography of ideological warfare between 2013 and 2015.

HISTORY AND TRADITION   Affirmative R-dskins rhetoric also dwelled in the area of history and tradition, as might be expected given that the Washington football team has claimed its mascot name for over eighty years.[32] This category includes two subthemes. The first involves attempts to use historical facts to justify the team name: "No, it's a football heritage. It may not be a PC name now but the US Govt needs a history lesson," and "Research[,] people!! That trademark was designed by a group of Native Americans!! The only discrimination going on here is discrimination against the team and its fans!!!" According to this argument, the team was named based on the choices of Native Americans—they participated in the naming process, and their decisions largely determined the team name, so write the posters. Thus, it would be nonsense to oppose the name, because Native communities had already sanctioned it. Indeed, the Washington team has claimed that Natives helped create some of the pomp and circumstance surrounding the team name. An early example is the insistence of the team's original owner, George Preston Marshall, that when he chose the name, he had Native support. Or former franchise president Bruce Allen, who firmly maintained, "The term redskin originated as a Native American expression of solidarity."[33]

Nevertheless, many people have questioned the authentic links to the franchise's "Native past" of folks like Princess Pale Moon and others who are said to have generated Native input on the mascot and to have eternally promoted the R-dskins name. King calls the logic of this pro-mascotting argument and the claims of Snyder and the team "the invented Indian." Such manipulation of history is said to "reflect and reinforce the fundamental features of racial and gendered privilege in a settler society, particularly a sense of entitlement to take and remake without consent and to do so without the burden of history."[34] Colonial rhetoric of ownership and appropriation clearly move to the foreground in these regards.

The second subtheme includes arguments that changing the status quo would betray the past and poison the sanctity of historical fact, thus leading to an abandonment of glorious tradition. Of this point, one commenter argued, "How very sad and pitiful! 81 years and now some people have an issue! Really! Leave them alone! No harm has been done. I am not a fan of the team but this is just plain crazy!" Commenters supporting this argument insisted that people should respect the team name as a non-denigrating historical compliment. Therefore, the correct attitude toward the team name (as a so-called historical *fact*), insinuates that the pro-mascot position is to preserve the name or add new connotations to it to replace its racist elements. Some commenters argued that those "who appealed for the name change were selfishly depriving football fans of their glories and identities." They could not understand why people suddenly had become so thin-skinned when the term "R-dskins," as used by the Washington franchise, had been uncontested for so many decades. Clearly, these pro-mascotters were not aware of the 1960s-generated campaigns to protest the Washington R-dskins. Their employment of team memory harkens to what mascot scholars call "selective history."[35]

COMPARISON WITH OTHER MASCOT NAMES   In the last pro-mascot theme, people compared the name "R-dskins" with other mascot names. Some commenters used ironic statements to demonstrate how ridiculous it would be if people removed the name "R-dskins" simply because a few people felt offended. "I am upset about the NY Giants, because that offends short people. What about the Carolina Panthers? That conjures up the Black Panthers of the 1960's. What about the New Orleans Saints? That should offend the atheists. When will it end?" Ironic statements such as these could be a useful discursive tool, because they confuse the original issue, making it less dubious by introducing new concepts (a type of rhetorical cookery). The example above introduces three unrelated, non-Native mascot names, specifically "Giants," "Panthers," and "Saints," to argue that every name has the potential to offend someone and that it would be an endless cycle if the public made compromises whenever someone was dissatisfied. Some people argued that there would be a chain reaction if the R-dskins were renamed: "Changing the name is wrong. . . . Changing the name will cause more controversy and will be a chain reaction for other teams." Another commenter used the expression "flood gate" to depict the possible aftermath regarding other terms related to Native Americans: "No way[,] not just because of the team's history but it will open the flood gates. Indians, Blackhawks, Braves, Chiefs, etc." Such an argument borders closely on a slippery slope, as even the least acceptable and most offensive non-Native mascot name ("Quakers") still tested better than the most acceptable and least offensive Native American mascot name ("Braves"). Finally, commenters actuating this theme sometimes did not quite understand the point of the debate. One commenter said, "What I don't understand is the focus on just the Redskins. Why aren't the Braves, Indians, Blackhawks, etc. included?"

The pro-mascotters here fail to engage the racialist complications tied to the name "R-dskins" by presenting a red herring via analogous conditions—rhetorical smoke screens—described in chapter 2 as the practice of deflecting colonial tendencies and legacies away from a direct confrontation of the underpinning denigration that a term like "R-dskin" brings to bear.

ANTI-MASCOT COMMENTS ABOUT THE "R-DSKINS" NAME

HUMANIZATION   Moving to a rhetorical-critical exploration of anti-mascot discourse, one of the most conspicuous themes attends to how the R-dskin mascot can come to dehumanize Native communities as metonymically reduced objects upon whom mascotting practices act. Therefore, anti-mascot commenters attempt to work through humanization to reveal the problems of the R-dskins mascot. Humanization is one of several decolonizing discursive tactics taken up by those who oppose the R-dskins mascot in our sample. As a reminder, decolonization, according to Casey Kelly, is "both a critical methodology for reading texts in the context of colonialism and a strategic rhetoric adopted by subaltern resistance."[36] Decolonial rhetorical tactics expose the architecture of colonial logics, harming indigenous communities in the process.

In that vein, calling out the dehumanizing treatment of Native Americans became a key tactic of anti-mascot commenters. Some mentioned sentiments such as "We've treated native [*sic*] Americans horribly since our initial invasions" and "For all the unlawful things that have happened to native [*sic*] Americans it's the least we can do [changing the R-dskins mascot]." In these instantiations, the veritable landscape of colonization sets the tone for the contemporary ways that the R-dskin mascot animates the same type of treatment. Rooted in the nadirs of the past, the practice of mascotting is set alongside "invasion" (land) and "unlawful things" (removal of Native bodies from ancestral homelands) to constitute the next iteration of what has "happened" to Native Americans.

Dehumanization also involves the metonymic reduction—a diminution of name and form—of Native Americans by way of the R-dskins mascot. One poster wrote, "We are not mascots. We are not animals," thereby underscoring the importance of Native people *not* being objectified shoulder-to-shoulder with costumed characters of mostly dogs, cats, and birds. Moreover, anti-mascot rhetoric demonstrated how mascotting exposes Native Americans to degradation by way of the "R-dskins" slur. One mentioned that "Redskins is the equivalent of the 'N' word and that is no way of honoring a proud group of people." Another similarly wrote, "Do you not understand that this is offensive to all Native Americans? How about you all Google the term Redskins. It's like saying the N word to an African American or any other racial slur." Perhaps the ultimate "devil term" in American history, the N-word as a tie-in to hatred of and bigotry toward Native Americans functions in such comments as a means to express just how dastardly the anti-mascot position perceives the R-dskin mascot to be.

The humanization of Native Americans by anti-mascot voices was also made by critiquing the "celebration" trope of pro-mascotters. The rights of Native Americans to retain and enact agency in the mascot controversy take a centered place in the debate, as does the question of whether a mascot like R-dskins truly honors Native communities. One commenter pointed out the inequity of protecting everyone else's sensibilities while Native Americans are silenced. The poster wrote, "Why is it even a question about that name? If it's offensive to the Native Americans, get rid of it like they're trying to get rid of everything else that offends people. Do Native Americans not have the right to be offended, too? Sounds like discrimination that we can defend one group but not the other." Another poster added the notion of veneration to the dehumanization critique, noting, "If the team really respected native Americans, how about the idea that Native Americans can pick a name that they think is appropriate that will honor their race and culture? Just throwing that out there." In both of these instances, mascotting as a tradition is subjected to critique and adjustment. In the end, these remarks focus on Native Americans as *peopled* subjects rather than *controlled* objects.

HOMOLOGY   As we noted in chapter 3, anti-mascotters operate in part through analogies in their resistive comments about the "R-dskins" name. Not only do they create a link between Native Americans and other people of color in terms of form and style, but they also equate the groups through colonial milieu. Such an analogy that contours a relationship among subjects within a related context is called a *homology*.[37]

The homology of Native Americans and African Americans becomes both stark and clear in analyzing anti-mascot rhetoric. We theorize that commenters spent an inordinate amount of time focusing on the connection between the N-word and "R-dskin" due to the context of both groups' bodies, lands, and labor being colonized by Europeans and European Americans historically. Furthermore, as our survey data indicated, a fair number of respondents saw "R-dskin" as a racial slur parallel to the N-word. The union of these names was not lost on the Facebook posters.

One commented, "This is just my opinion. It's kinda like having an NFL team named the N**ers and having a picture of Buckwheat from the Lil Rascals as the logo. Yeah, that's pretty racist. Same goes for the Native American and the 'RedSkins.'" In a related entry, another person wrote, "We can't call African Americans the 'N' word which is a derivative of skin color! So why OH why, would we dare refer to Native Americans as REDSKINS?????? They are the TRUE AMERICANS!!!!!" And yet another exhorted, "Red skins? . . . How about The D.C. jiggaboos? Or the D.C. Darkies? Of course they should change it—something like 20 years ago." In these instances, we see what Waziyatawin Angela Wilson and Michael Yellow Bird refer to when they argue that decolonization is "the intelligent, calculated, and active resistance to forces of colonialism that perpetuates" subjugation.[38] That is, the posters tactically weave joint oppression through the narratives of both African Americans and Native Americans to emblemize the extent of the R-dskin mascot's inappropriateness. Words such as the N-word, "jiggaboo," and "darkie" are known despicable racial epithets. Perhaps the larger public is not aware, the posters insinuate, that "R-dskin" connotes similar dastardliness in terms of the harsh symbolic treatment and often deplorable material conditions of Native Americans.

In breaking with the homology between Native folks and African Americans, in particular, one poster lobbed a fascinating cultural salvo. This poster wrote, "Redskins is equivalent to us natives [sic] calling Caucasians crackers." If a non-Native member of the dominant public hailed by and from Anglo heritage did not understand the devil terms "R-dskins" and the N-word residing alongside each other—mired in oppression—then perhaps the mirror being turned brought the homology to light a bit livelier. This is not to suggest that all pro-mascot commenters are white-identified or that they all do not see the connection between the N-word and "R-dskin." But in the case that supporters of the Washington team's mascot were unable at first to see the overlap, it might be so that viewing a racial slur related to the dominant public struck a chord.

IRONIC SENTIMENTS   Irony, or the comparison of typically unlikely things to demonstrate duplicity and pretense or a contradictory or different meaning, was long a decolonizing rhetorical tactic of Native Americans throughout the eighteenth, nineteenth, and twentieth centuries.[39] We found in the anti-mascotting Facebook comments that posters also engaged in irony to jostle and question the R-dskins mascot. Though often presented as lighthearted, parodic, or sarcastic, irony communicates a powerful critique; it is an inventional resource speaking to the absurdity of something like the use of "R-dskins" to represent hundreds of Native nations as flat and stereotypical.

To illustrate the lived experience of what "R-dskins" might mean, one commenter posed an experiment to their audience: "Okay people a test. Go find a full-blooded Native American . . . any tribe. Someone who appears to look like a Native American, not a white-skinned person who claims to be ¹/₈ something. Someone who is a stranger to you. Walk up to them and call them a Redskin. Let me know how that works out for you." The ironic point here is that pro-mascotters may hide behind a name (and visual symbol and attendant rituals) that they see as honoring Native Americans. But what if these same folks were asked to utter the name to a Native-identified person directly, having to peer into one's eyes while doing so? This poster argues that any rational human being would not dare utter the word in front of a Native American and that this alone should refute any notion of honor or acceptability of uttering it in a broader sporting context.

Speaking of sport contexts, another commenter used irony to challenge whether pro-mascot proponents actually cared about the embodied people for whom a team is named. Calling into account the ethos of those in agreement with the Washington R-dskins mascot, the poster said, "Been reading the comments and surprise! Everyone who seems to disagree isn't even Native American. So basically, you are more upset over a football team potentially losing their name than you are of a whole Native group feeling insulted over the past couple decades. Oh, ok got it." The lack of diffidence in this remark functionally diminishes the veracity of pro-mascotters' claims to honor and cherish Native Americans by remaining loyal to the "R-dskins" name. Again, challenging their credibility as non–Native Americans, the poster seems to confront and defy the "R-dskins" defenders' genuine sense of concern for Native Americans. In the same vein, another commenter made a blunt, unadorned point about non-Natives' lack of agency in the matter: "And I am SURE [a pro-mascot poster] speaks for ALL NATIVES . . . because they are ALL the same . . . right? Uber sarcasm."

Allied with the "cracker" comment above, we found that anti-mascot comments similarly circulated around turning a mirror on white Americans in various forms and fashions. One person quipped, "I think they should rename the team: Washington Paleskins. The Native Americans used to call the white people that. Time for the white people to take one for the team." Another chided, "Change the names. It offends people. It's a racist ass name. I bet if they had a symbol of the confederate flag being burned, you would be offended. As matter of fact, Burn baby burn!!!" Admittedly, it is unfair to homogenize all white people and to suggest that they all support the Confederate flag, yet the irony here is fascinating, because these posters are navigating the rhetorical tactic of *detournement*, what Kelly defines as "a deliberate slippage of a familiar and revered artifact . . . in which aspects of the original are committed to oppositional or self-defeating uses."[40] The "original" artifact here would be white people—expressly that they are rarely mascotted in ways that connect their heritage or skin color to the mascot qua mascot. One might counter with the Notre Dame "Fighting Irish" or the Minnesota "Vikings" examples, but the former nickname was self-selected by white people for white people, and the latter is not a "living" culture with present and future well-being at stake as are Native American cultures. Regardless, what we witness in these two posts is the rhetorical inventiveness of irony as a countermand to the pro-mascot position that Native Americans must bear the weight of cultural appropriation. The underlying message to non-Natives is that if mascotting is so grand and noble, "take one for the team" for once.

ALTERNATIVE NAMING   The endgame of most anti-mascotting arguments is, of course, to retire the "R-dskin" name. Posters in this study who disagreed with the Washington team's mascot easily moved to this position. Most comments revolved around a sentiment that went something along the lines of "It's derogatory!!! Just change it already!!! The Marquette 'Golden Eagles' changed their name from the Warriors and they are doing just fine. . . . Just make the change already!!!!!" Given the proliferation and profundity of arguments regarding humanization, homology, and irony (among other rhetorical tactics), some anti-mascot proponents seemed to become exhausted, resorting to simple calls to "change it!"

This was especially clear in one commenter's exasperated plea for the retirement of the "R-dskin" name and mascot. The poster said, "Just change it. Even if you don't feel it's offensive, at this point it is simply distracting fans and players from the sport. . . . Change it to 'warriors' or 'Americans' or something that doesn't point directly to skin color. It's simply dumb that this is taking up space as 'news'?" Mascotting in this instantiation became not just about honoring or disparaging Native Americans but also about wasting time. Whereas pro-mascotters made a similar argument with their "inconsequentiality" strategy because they saw the entire issue as a waste of time, anti-mascotters saw the issue as a closed book. They expressed the idea that to continue mascotting was "simply dumb," and, therefore, to endure with the argument that "R-dskin" is not racist or is honorable is a waste of time. The above commenter even says that change ought to be a fait accompli; why, the poster asks, is the R-dskin controversy even "taking up space as 'news'?"

The trope of alternate naming was typically communicated with compromise in mind. Of all the rhetorical tactics that anti-mascot advocates actuated, the issue of a name change was fairly mild in valence. The overwhelming majority of this type of comment would either begin or end with a tenor of concordance. An emblematic remark suggested, "Maybe it is time to end the controversy and find a suitable replacement mascot because as far back as the 1970's there has been a growing group of people that has been offended by this mascot. In a spirit of everyone getting along and moving forward, I think the name Warriors would be a good compromise. Warriors would be honoring to the Native Americans." In this case, the poster bridged the gap between retiring a Native-saturated mascot and keeping some semblance of Nativeness (i.e., the "warrior" moniker). To be fair, there were calls for complete name changes, as we read above with the suggestion that Marquette University successfully removed any scintilla of Native American imagery.

But, again, this rhetorical tactic overwhelmingly appeared in the form of compromise with pro-mascot positions. The issue was partially about finding a less offensive Native American name that failed to invoke skin color or race. Even among anti-mascotters, "warriors" was seen as at least viable and less offensive in this regard, even though the NCAA forced Marquette University to divest its "Warrior" mascot name. In Marquette's case, simply moving to an innocuous though clearly Native-based word did not let the university off the hook.

TEMPORALITY   One anti-mascot theme that we did not find in the chapter 3 analysis of the debate about the 2013 "Proud to Be" and "Redskins Is a Powerful Name" commercials was the importance of time. In the 2013–2015 comments analyzed in this chapter, however, the notion of temporality was quite common among anti-mascot posters. In a way, pro-mascot commenters argued for the longtime presence of the Washington "R-dskins" name as a warrant for its continued use (see the "Celebration" section above). The comments analyzed below indicate just the opposite: that time has moved on and the "R-dskin" name is no longer acceptable. Perhaps the most direct remark was this: "Yes. Pure and simple. Language evolves over time. It's not okay to say broad, wetback, or chink anymore. It's not okay to say Redskins anymore." One will note the linkage between "R-dskin" and other racial sobriquets. But what stands out the most is the admission that it was once "okay" to say "R-dskins," but now times have changed.

Such a rhetorical move was fortified by temporal connections to Native-U.S. history. Both Native-identified and non-Native commenters delivered history lessons, of sorts, in arguing against the Washington mascot. One wrote, "Red Skins is a term the white people used when there was a bounty on Native skins/scalps, they got $200 for one scalp/skin. Please! Let's not forget what has happened to my People in year[s] past. Please change the name." Here, time matters and history remains electric with corrective potential. As one poster said, "Native Americans pass down stories to preserve their history and heritage, because we don't have much of it left. As tribes were systemically exterminated, so too were their respective cultures." The concern for this poster is that Native cultures will continue to suffer diminution if the "R-dskin" name succeeds in representing an essentialized Native America.

One poster's extended narrative deserves attention for how historical facts are set aside from the typical from-the-hip arguments against the R-dskins mascot. In this anti-mascot advocate's case, the "R-dskins" name contains both historical significance and tinges of familial fear:

But we have our stories, and when my mother was young, her parents shared one about the term "redskins." The story in my family goes that the term dates back to the institutionalized genocide of Native Americans, most notably when the Massachusetts colonial government placed a bounty on their heads. The grisly particulars of that genocide are listed in a 1755 document called the Phips Proclamation, which zeroed in on the Penobscot Indians, a tribe today based in Maine. Spencer Phips, a British politician and then Lieutenant Governor of the Massachusetts Bay Province, issued the call, ordering on behalf of British King George II for, "His Majesty's subjects to Embrace all opportunities of pursuing, captivating, killing and Destroying all and every of the aforesaid Indians." They paid well—50 pounds for adult male scalps; 25 for adult female scalps; and 20 for scalps of boys and girls under age 12. These bloody scalps were known as "redskins." The mascot of the Washington Redskins, if the team desired accuracy, would be a gory, bloodied crown from the head of a butchered Native American.

The poster questions the Washington franchise's claim to honor Native Americans with authentic representations of indigeneity. Moreover, he does so through establishing the temporal link between the historical murder of Native Americans and the contemporary social death that he insinuates might befall Native Americans in the pall of the "R-dskins" name as it continues to be underwritten by, perhaps, a complicit fan base, if not the larger U.S. public.

Randall Lake, in examining Native mythos, claims that Native American narratives are "grounded in time's cycle" and seek "to renew the ties between past and present to enact a future."[41] Indeed, the importance of time to Native lifeways is not lost on the decolonial critique of the R-dskins mascot, as the above comments validate.

OWNERSHIP Another decolonizing rhetorical tactic of the anti-mascot position locates power within ownership. This ethos is exhibited by both Native-identified folks and non-Natives. One might expect to read comments from Native Americans such as the following: "The only opinions that matter are the Native Americans. . . . Why should you make a decision about what offends Native Americans?"; "As a proud member of the Sioux Nation, I have had the terrible experience of being called a redskin. Collectively speaking, we as a people no longer condone this label. Please remove"; and "I'm so tired of non-Natives saying that the name is not offensive. I'm 100% Native American and the word is offensive to us." In these statements, cultural agency and discursive power center on one's tribal affiliation (i.e., Sioux), one's experiential evidence (i.e., of having been called a "r-dskin"), and one's exhaustion at having to argue against a slur that one finds demonstrably and unquestionably offensive. This type of decolonial resistance is personal and speaks to the self-directed calls for change that Native Americans have repeatedly issued to the U.S. government and the U.S. public. The issue of ownership speaks, too, to the *Washington Post* survey. Pro-mascotters might read that and say that nine of ten Native Americans are comfortable with indigenous mascots. Still, that a high number of those respondents could not identify their respective tribal affiliations begs the question of veracity vis-à-vis their self-professed Nativeness. In sum, Native ownership certainly was not a surprising theme found in anti-mascot rhetoric, just as we were not shocked to discover pro-mascot commenters claiming their neocolonial ownership to the R-dskins name as fans.

What was not expected, however, was a twist on non-Native ownership arguments that complicate one's lack of indigeneity with one's devotion to the Washington R-dskins team and its fan culture. For instance, one non-Native fan wrote, "Absolute garbage justification and response. Though I'm a 4th generation Washingtonian and support my home team, I have despised the reference since I was a boy. It is a negative racial reference with a horrific historical context—namely of our country with the true Americans and even the team—the last to integrate in the league. Snyder is concerned with nothing more than 'his' economic enterprise." Another wrote, "Excuses, excuses. The name is racial and it offends Native Americans. . . . I STILL SUPPORT THE TEAM. BUT THE NAME IS WRONG." In these comments, non-Natives in agreement with retiring the R-dskin mascot put their fandom on the line, suggesting that they are fans of the city of Washington and Washington's NFL franchise but not of what they perceive to be a racist representation of Native Americans. Both posters seem frustrated with pretexts and Snyder's continued support of the name; the former even suggests that Snyder is disingenuous in his obstinacy about removing the "R-dskins" moniker. Furthermore, the former commenter locates their ethos in generational and primacy connections to Washington and its franchise, thus compounding that person's space to speak out on the issue. Again, this form of ownership indicates that even among the most diehard R-dskins fans, anti-mascot sentiments still abound. Overall, these cases serve as a lesson and reminder that not all Washington fans are pro-mascot, just as not all Native Americans are anti-mascot in positionality.

COMPARISON TO OTHER NATIVE MASCOTS   Finally, some commenters who oppose the use of the R-dskins mascot suggested that they are not so much "anti-mascot" as "anti-R-dskins" in their remonstrative critique of the Washington team. If one recalls, earlier in this chapter our survey results illustrated how "Braves" ($M = 7.12$; $M = 6.71$) and "Chiefs" ($M = 6.92$; $M = 6.56$), followed by a list of tribal-specific mascot names, registered as the most acceptable and most inoffensive among Native American mascots. Indeed, some of the comments we found in our anti-mascot category of discourse speak to this finding.

Those a bit more comfortable with the generic or tribe-specific Native American mascots wrote comments such as these: "Names of actual tribes, if they do not mind, is very different from using a generic, rude Red Skins"; "Braves, Indians aren't derogatory! People really can't tell the difference? SMH! [shaking my head]"; and "Being a 'Brave' or having our logo is fine. Having a racial slur as the team name is unacceptable." Even though these comments might not garner the label "decolonizing," they do illustrate a few key, critical points. First, these posters insist on Native American agency to decide if their tribe could/would/should be included as a team mascot. Second, they declare the R-dskins mascot to be racist, or at least debilitating, thereby fortifying the vigorous claims of other posters who are constitutionally opposed to Washington's mascot. And, third, at least two mention generic mascots such as "Braves" and "Indians," names that our survey showed are generally accepted by respondents (though their images and rituals are not always so acceptable and inoffensive, as we discuss in chapters 5 and 6). The analysis of this particular quasi anti-mascot theme is vital as we move into examinations of Native American mascots outside of the R-dskins case study.

Implications of a Critical Reading of the R-dskins Mascot

An analysis of pro-mascot and anti-mascot discourse within the R-dskins debate demonstrates a clear divide along what a postcolonial lens might indicate as colonial and decolonial lines. On the one hand, those who defend the R-dskins mascot tend to argue from themes that are entrenched in ideologies of territoriality and possession, along with co-optation and appropriation. Those who resist the Washington franchise's use of the "R-dskins" moniker do so by attempting to decolonize the Native American mascot, calling into question the power dynamics associated with the name itself and Snyder's refusal to relent to a change in mascot. In the end, the self-categorization that underscores the qualitative discourse examined above seems almost unassailable. In other words, the impenetrability and intransigence of arguers appears too inflamed to defuse. How do we decamp; how do those claiming a stake in the controversy move past invective? Clearly, the goal would be reconciliation and comfort for all parties involved. Discovering a solution is not the purpose of this chapter. Rather, we have sought to gauge how a sample of the public feels about the controversy through survey and critical-analytical methodologies. It is part of our purpose, however, to trace some implications of our statistical and qualitative analysis.

First, as Jason Edward Black has written elsewhere, the mascot controversy "demonstrates that we are far from a 'post-racial' condition in this country." [42] This seems pretty assumptive, but we in the United States do not talk much about this concept concerning Native folks. In our specific communities—a city named for an Upper Creek Nation chief (Tuscaloosa, AL) for one of us; a city grounded in the crucible of Cherokee and Lumbee survivance for the other (Charlotte, NC)—we hear that casinos, tax breaks, repatriation acts, diabetes funding, alcoholism education programs, triple citizenship, and college scholarships have solved the centuries-old difficulties for our states' Native American communities precipitated by colonialism. But it is difficult to exorcise these ghosts. As the *National Post* reported on June 22, 2014, "We are a long way from consensus on [mascot] questions, judging by the response to a federal ruling that the 'R-dskins' team name is disparaging and its trademarks should be canceled." [43]

Second, the R-dskins case in particular complicates notions of intent. Often we read sentiments like those from Snyder, who says, "If they think we're demeaning them, if they think we think they are mascots, if we were doing it in any negative way, they are wrong." [44] What the recent R-dskins trademark debacle codifies is the idea that the name can still be disparaging even if the Washington team intends respect. The primary agent's intention of mascot use can be sublimated to the connotative meanings of the particular mascot name and to the colonial contexts from which the mascot name derives. It seems that if a term for Native Americans is defined colloquially, historically, literarily, and culturally as "disparaging," then the public has a right to debate its acceptability and/or offensiveness.

Third, an analysis of the R-dskins example indicates the troublesome ways that Native American authenticity is claimed and ownership is animated in the debates over the mascot name. Controversies abound within Native American groups about who is and can be considered indigenous and trib-ally identified as such. American Indian scholar Eva Marie Garroutte has detailed the conflicting methods for determining one's ethnic ancestry and Native identity, ranging from Dawes-era roll sheets and name logs and blood quantum to family tree lineage and word-of-mouth evidence.[45] This same complication seems to come to bear in the Native American mascot controversy, but particularly with regard to the R-dskins case, as is made clear by the comments analyzed above and by the *Washington Post* poll that rigidly insists that all respondents were Native American. When respondents can self-select—whether through online comments such as those detailed in this chapter or in a "national" poll like the *Washington Post*'s—there is no certainty about who the actual in-group is and what sort of ethos they ought to wield. The ambiguity of Native American identity as agent and, thus, the problematics of determining indigenous agency to decide the efficacy of the Native American mascot will continue into the future as subjects for consideration and debate.

Finally, Native mascotting accentuates the ways that neocolonialization is alive but also the ways that decolonization, too, is thriving. Those who have been tracking the mascotting issue since the 1990s can attest that there has not been this much activism involving professional Native mascots since a 1992 lawsuit was brought against the R-dskins and since 1999, when protesters won the lawsuit only to have the Washington organization win on appeal. Even at the height of the NCAA's retirement of Chief Illiniwek in 2007 and its investigation into the Seminole mascot at FSU between 2005 and 2017, activism seemed to circulate mostly on campuses, in discrete spaces tied to the particular dispute. The current R-dskins controversy has generated wholesale movement organizations, television spots, and protests on a national scale that we have not seen in number or intensity in a very long time. This issue clearly is not ancillary to more material conditions for Native Americans. Rather, it is a part of the overall "circuit of culture" that Stuart Hall argues contains "uncritical acceptance" of the status quo on one side and unbridled commitments to "resistance" on the other.[46] Perhaps there appears a "negotiated acceptance" out there. To be sure, there is no panacea when it comes to the R-dskins controversy. Every legal win begets a cultural loss and vice-versa. Chapter 8 follows up on where the R-dskins case may next unfold given the June 19, 2017, Supreme Court's conclusion in *Tam v. Matal* that the USPTO cannot quash or chill free speech related to ethnically charged naming practices.

5

Deconstructing the Mascot, Part 2

Visual Symbols

Most mascotting debates interrogate either words (names) or actions (rituals), and certainly both areas are worthy of exploration. However, logos are the foremost images that ostensibly straddle such a divide—sometimes including the name within yet often also providing a picture of the mascot that performs a ritual. As such, logos become the blueprint through which moving images and actions are formed.[1] Logos have been studied in some connection to and combination with mascot names and ritual practices by scholars such as Sudie Hofmann and Dana Williams.[2] Nevertheless, this chapter begins by exploring such logos in empirical isolation in order to establish the specific roles such images embody and to discover certain elements embedded that make one logo more or less acceptable or offensive than another.

Data from the same national survey of 1,076 respondents mentioned in chapter 4 rated mascot logos in terms of both acceptability and inoffensiveness, again utilizing an eleven-point scale (0–10) with a higher number representing less problematic logos on acceptability/inoffensiveness measures and lower scores indicating more problematic logos on each of the two scales. In sum, teams would optimally seek to yield the highest score possible on each measure; low scores, in contrast, could represent future public relations difficulties.

While Native American mascots similar to those reported in chapter 4 were incorporated, the sampling was different, because some teams have primary and secondary logos that provide unique opportunities for insights through contrasts while other teams may have problematic names or rituals, but their logos may have no elements of Native American imagery built in, so fewer image-based cases were tested.

At the onset of this form of empirical testing—lest we bury the lead—we begin with the ratings for the Washington R-dskins' logo. The R-dskins logo presents an interesting case, primarily because most controversy has focused on the name of the team with relatively less focus being placed on the logo itself.[3] As shown in chapter 4, the *name* "R-dskins" scored a 4.69 out of a possible score of 10 on acceptability and an equally paltry 4.47 out of 10 on inoffensiveness. Such results could be construed as middling, with almost as many people finding the name acceptable and inoffensive as those who felt the opposite. Given the predominant focus on the name over the logo, one would surmise that image scores on the Washington R-dskins' primary logo would be markedly higher. Figure 5.1 shows the image and scores for the *logo* in this regard.

As highlighted in the two primary measures, acceptability and inoffensiveness, scores for the logos are slightly higher than for the name, but not markedly so to the point that the logo, too, is more likely to be deemed unacceptable and offensive than acceptable and inoffensive. Part of this result is likely the inclusion of the team's name within the image itself; part of it is that given the controversy surrounding the name of the team, anything

Figure 5.1. Washington R-dskins logo. Acceptability score: 4.87; Inoffensiveness score: 4.72

a

Figure 5.2a–b. Cleveland Indians logos. Logo A: Acceptability score: 7.03; Inoffensiveness score: 7.36. Logo B: Acceptability score: 4.28; Inoffensiveness

b   score: 4.06

associated with it is likely to have deflated acceptability and inoffensiveness for a demonstrable segment of the population.

The larger question becomes the impact of an actual Native American face included within the logo itself. One could argue that the inclusion of the face personalizes the mascot, yet whether this is a positive or negative development is highly contestable. A useful, possible correlate for understanding the R-dskins logo and use of facial imagery would be to examine two other logos that were a part of the survey: the primary and secondary logos for Major League Baseball's Cleveland Indians. Cleveland adopted the block "C" as a primary logo in 2016 but also included secondary logos as part of their ancillary marketing plan, including one that still incorporates Chief Wahoo.[4] Owner Paul Dolan justified the decision to keep Chief Wahoo—the name of the Indian within the logo—as a secondary image, saying he had "no plans to get rid of Chief Wahoo, it is part of our history and legacy."[5] Such a decision creates fertile ground for exploring the logo, because one uses only the name that scored in the lower half of acceptability and inoffensiveness rankings (5.80 for acceptability and 5.54 for inoffensiveness) while the other simply fashions a cartoonish, caricatured symbol of an Indian without the name attached to it. Figure 5.2 contains scores for both secondary logos of the Cleveland Indians.

Taken jointly, the results offer a multitude of potential implications. First, the logo with just the words "Cleveland Indians" scored significantly better than the word "Indians" did without imagery in the naming portion of the survey in chapter 4. Meanwhile, the logo with the cartoonish, large-toothed Indian scored significantly lower than the name "Indians" did, with the majority finding the logo problematic—even more so than the Washington R-dskins logo. Thus, one could conclude that the primary issue with the Cleveland Indians is the logo with the face of an Indian, even if the name also appeared problematic to some. In addition, it is also fair to assume that the score for the name "Indians" was seemingly marred by the connection many may have placed with the even more problematic cartoon symbol, as the logo without it received somewhat of a halo effect, presumably from people who preferred the logo with just the name "Cleveland Indians" over the logo with the cartoonish Indian.

Second, one can combine insights from figures 5.1 and 5.2 to begin making conclusions about Native American face logos—whether stoic/non-smiling (as is the case for the Redskins logo) or happy/friendly (as is the case for the Indians secondary logo) as being problematic for a majority of Americans.

Thus, another useful contrast can be offered in the case of MLB's Atlanta Braves. From 1956 to 1989, the team featured a logo with an image of a Native American, Chief Noc-A-Homa—in this case, a face that most interpret as a happy/laughing Indian with a Mohawk and feathers (some would argue for a less happy interpretation of an Indian offering a war chant). From 1990 to the present, Atlanta eliminated the facial imagery, opting for cursive "Braves" imagery—yet with a tomahawk included as well. Figure 5.3 indicates scores for the earlier and present logos for the Atlanta Braves.

As shown in figure 5.3, there is a substantial improvement offered by switching from the laughing Indian to the tomahawk logo. The earlier logo scored even worse than the R-dskins logo on both measures; meanwhile, the newer logo yielded scores roughly equivalent to the scores for the name of the team (7.12 for acceptability and 6.71 for inoffensiveness). The cursive word "Braves" becomes a control variable in this comparison, because it remains largely the same in both logos, meaning that dropping the facial imagery in favor of the tomahawk resulted in the average respondent increasing both scores by two to two and a half points.

However, one could question whether it was entirely the face of the Braves' laughing mascot that was problematic, because it is possible that the feather imagery might have played a role. Enter the contrasting logos of the University of Utah Utes. Until the aforementioned 2005 NCAA ruling, the University of Utah had adopted an Indian in full headdress as part of its logo. As attendant to an agreement with the NCAA, Utah opted for a drum with a block "U" in the center with two feathers to the side.[6] Meanwhile, the university retired an Indian mascot in 1996, replacing it with a red-tailed hawk named "Swoop" that was an embodiment of the mascot (and sometimes logo) for the athletic teams. Thus, figure 5.4 indicates overall scores for three different Utah-based images: the original Utah logo, the new "drum" logo adopted in 2005, and the logo using "Swoop" the mascot.[7]

As one can observe from figure 5.4, there was a clear progression of improvement with images, as the drum with a pair of feathers was viewed as a

Figure 5.3a–b. Atlanta Braves logos. Logo A: Acceptability score: 4.57; Inoffensiveness score: 4.13. Logo B: Acceptability score: 6.80; Inoffensiveness score: 6.89

a

b c

Figure 5.4a–c. University of Utah Utes logos. Logo A: Acceptability score: 5.63; Inoffensiveness score: 5.58. Logo B: Acceptability score: 6.91; Inoffensiveness score: 7.01. Logo C: Acceptability score: 7.43; Inoffensiveness score: 7.49

significant upgrade from the Indian in headdress. Moreover, the red-tailed hawk "Swoop" was deemed significantly more acceptable and inoffensive than the drum with feathers. However, the fact that the headdress-based mascot still yielded higher scores than the previous cases of the Redskins (stoic, red-skinned), Indians (friendly, red-skinned), and Braves (laughing, unshaded skin pigment) could indicate that the Utes' face-based logo, while still not preferable to either of the other two, could benefit somewhat by the two choices within it (stoic, unshaded).

The feather imagery, if pertinent, can be teased out even more directly with the case of the Catawba College Indians, a case in which the NCAA denouncement ultimately ended with the association's approval of keeping the mascot after Catawba College cited support from the remaining Catawba Tribe members in North Carolina. Despite later remonstrations of Native American mascots, specifically from a Catawba chief—who called the specific case of the Redskins a problematic attempt to "characterize Native Americans as savages"—Catawba College has kept its nickname and logo, which features feathers, as outlined in figure 5.5.[8]

Figure 5.5. Catawba Indians. Acceptability score: 6.87; Inoffensiveness score: 6.96

Figure 5.6a–h. (a) University of Illinois Illini. Acceptability score: 5.86; Inoffensiveness score: 5.79; (b) San Diego State University Aztecs. Acceptability score: 5.50; Inoffensiveness score: 5.12; (c) North Dakota State University Fighting Sioux. Acceptability score: 5.49; Inoffensiveness score: 5.34; (d) Midwestern State University Indians. Acceptability score: 5.44; Inoffensiveness score: 5.42; (e) University of Louisiana at Monroe Indians. Acceptability score: 4.27; Inoffensiveness score: 4.09; (f) Alcorn State University Braves. Acceptability score: 4.24; Inoffensiveness score: 3.98; (g) Arkansas State University Indians. Acceptability score: 3.91; Inoffensiveness score: 3.62; (h) Syracuse University Indians. Acceptability score: 3.76; Inoffensiveness score: 3.54

Such scores for Catawba roughly mirror that of the Utah logo featuring the drum with side feathers; both score slightly below 7 on the eleven-point scale, indicating general agreement with acceptability—far less problematic than face-based logos and other cases yet clearly representing problems of both acceptability and offensiveness for some individuals.

Given such nuanced scores on these initial measures, it is worthwhile to examine the scores of other facial or fully human-based Native American logos. Figure 5.6 offers scores from a variety of remaining logos (past and present) that reveal insight into which images were more problematic than others. The logos are presented in order of highest to lowest acceptability score.

By ordering these logos from most to least acceptable, clear threads emerge—particularly when including insights from the previous figures in this chapter. First, none of the logos fared overly well, as even the highest-scoring logo, the University of Illinois Illini, only marginally crosses the mid-point 5.0 barrier, indicating slight agreement that the logo is acceptable. All other Indian face or full-body logos fared even worse than the Illini symbol, seemingly indicating that the embodiment of the mascot was consistently problematic for half or more of the people who viewed them.

Second, the scores indicated a trend that again privileges the visually stoic (and presumably more honorable and authentic) over the unmistakably cartoonish (and presumably less honorable and inauthentic). The notion that one could be mocking Native Americans seemingly comes to the fore more readily in such cartoonish caricatures, with respondents generally being more sensitive to these concerns.

Finally, it appears that the final three lowest-rated images all have similar traits: (1) cartoonish depiction, (2) tomahawk/spear in hand, and (3) angry/warlike disposition. Thus, these images—all of which, it should be noted, have been eliminated and in all three cases have even dropped the "Indians" moniker—seemingly offered the worst of all scenarios: mocking the Native American community (via cartoon-like depictions) while also making them seem inaccessible (via placing them "on the warpath").

Indeed, the image scoring the worst of all Native American logos that were tested was the 1970s-based Syracuse University Indians logo, an embodiment of a Saltine Warrior in caricature. The logo was abandoned by 1980, replaced with "Otto the Orange," and the name "Orangemen" was shifted to just "Orange" in 2004. Betsy English, Syracuse's director of bookstores and trademark licensing, argued it was a strategic branding move: "The use of Orange as a single word and color is crucial. By cleaning it up and getting rid of what's not needed, you make it stronger."[9] Some still sought a return to the previous nickname, yet the highly problematic warrior logo was used to show ties to Native American imagery and thus, it was argued, must stay permanently severed. Mark Keeley evoked the previous cartoonish mascot "on the warpath," concluding, "By changing the name back to Orangemen, even though we've scrubbed away the initial connotation, we would be bringing it right back into the discussion.

Intentional or not, you'd be inviting a whole slew of public concerns, protests and drama that you simply don't need."[10]

Sometimes, teams attempt to bridge divides, opting to include Native American imagery (to please traditionalists) while making such imagery more hidden—or at least less prominent (to please those more sensitive to the Native American dilemma). An example of an attempted bridged gap can be found in the case of Arkansas State University. The institution had boasted the "Indians" name since 1930 (before which they were the "Warriors") and utilized a logo that included an Indian in headdress, albeit less prominently than in the cases mentioned earlier in this chapter. Ultimately the institution adopted a new name, the "Red Wolves," and an accompanying mascot in 2008, with emeritus trustee Jim Pickens arguing that "the new mascot and imagery will serve to broaden and unify our base as together we strive for continued excellence in all aspects of our students' experience at Arkansas State University."[11] Figure 5.7 offers scores on both the old and current Arkansas State University logo.

Thus, while the previous logo included the mascot in a somewhat covert manner—likely bolstering its score by at least a full point if not more when compared to other facial/headdress-based logos—the decision to move to the red wolf, an endangered species that once was found in Arkansas, seemingly yielded as close to uniform praise as one can likely find in today's contemporary debate-oriented era.

Relating to the notion about which forms of imagery were more or less problematic than others, some of the aforementioned logos have examined faces versus full-body depictions, coupled feathers versus headdresses, action versus passivity, and happy demeanor versus angry demeanor. However, another form of logo endemic to Native American mascot imagery involves the use of the tomahawk, which is explored in the next chapter in the form of the ritual known as the Florida State University tomahawk chop. With the cases under discussion in this chapter, the tomahawk was not directly tested but, rather, two forms of the arrowhead were assessed, one less familiar to a

a

b

Figure 5.7a–b. (a) Arkansas State Indians. Acceptability score: 6.41; Inoffensiveness score: 6.38; (b) Arkansas State Red Wolves. Acceptability score: 8.24; Inoffensiveness score: 8.31

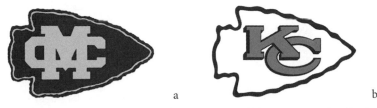

Figure 5.8a–b. (a) Mississippi College Choctaws. Acceptability score: 7.30; Inoffensiveness score: 7.51; (b) Kansas City Chiefs. Acceptability score: 7.36; Inoffensiveness score: 7.15

general population (the Mississippi College Choctaws) and one well known to American sports fans, the logo of the NFL's Kansas City Chiefs. Figure 5.8 illustrates the scores for both of these arrowhead-based logos.

As shown in the comparison offered in figure 5.8, there was no significant difference in the acceptability of each of these two arrowhead logos. The logo of the Mississippi College Choctaws, though, was significantly less likely to be considered offensive when compared to the logo of the Kansas City Chiefs, albeit not by an immense margin. Thus, it appears that familiarity of the Chiefs logo did not hinder its perceived acceptability yet somehow did hinder the perceived inoffensiveness, leading one to wonder whether there were other elements beyond logo that could affect scores regarding the Kansas City Chiefs logo in general. For instance, the name "Chief" was found to be more acceptable than inoffensive within chapter 4's analyses, and the same bifurcation is found with the team's logo as well.

Beyond the tomahawk, a comparable yet distinctly different form of image is the spear, most known in American athletic contexts within the context of FSU's Seminoles. Given the logo that FSU incorporates as primary imagery—one using an Indian war-painted head—and the key secondary logo—one based on the spear, the case of FSU provides another useful glimpse into comparative mascot logo acceptability and inoffensiveness. Figure 5.9 shows scores for both logos of the FSU Seminoles.

Figure 5.9a–b. Florida State University Seminoles logos. Logo A: Acceptability score: 5.42; Inoffensiveness score: 5.29; Logo B: Acceptability score: 6.98; Inoffensiveness score: 6.94

Figure 5.10. Florida State University 2014 logo update. Acceptability score: 5.22; Inoffensiveness score: 5.17

In this instance, we again find the face-based logo as significantly more problematic than even another logo still directly possessing Native American imagery. Indeed, the FSU logo utilizing the war-painted face scored among the most splintering of public sentiments, with a high standard deviation and a generally lower mean than most other images. Such a finding is also interesting given that the demeanor of the face in the logo is difficult to determine; one could witness the closed eye and open mouth as an angry image, while another could see the image as cartoonish and inauthentic via the placement of the words "Florida State" on the feather. Regardless, the spear (albeit one not shown in a hand or in any form of action) appeared to be more acceptable and inoffensive to the majority of survey respondents. Interestingly, the FSU primary logo (with Chief Osceola's head) was leaked as being "updated" in 2014; many waited for the logo to be revealed in hopes of adopting a less problematic logo than the previous primary logo of the war-painted head. However, the updated logo was only slightly changed, as shown in figure 5.10.

Allan Brettman indicated that the new logo caused considerable uproar from the Florida State community, including more than five thousand online posts.[12] However, the primary concern seemed to be that even this change was seen as too severe, not that the logo should have been replaced entirely. As such, FSU issued a statement noting that the action was taken after two years of consultation with Nike, one of the team's sponsors, and that more changes were coming. The logo in figure 5.10 remains the primary FSU logo at the time of this writing, even though it scored lower than either of the other two logos in our survey, seemingly stirring distaste from traditionalists who embraced the other logo while doing little to satiate dissenters who had argued for wholesale alterations.

Figure 5.11 offers yet another nuanced angle to the logo debate, presenting scores for schools that have changed either their mascot name, their logo, or both to outline whether such decisions yielded better acceptability or inoffensiveness scores. Such comparisons are important because they allow for a sense of the type of improvement that can be offered when switching from

Figure 5.11a–f. (a) Midwestern State University Mustangs. Acceptability score: 8.79; Inoffensiveness score: 8.80; (b) Indiana University of Pennsylvania Crimson Hawks. Acceptability score: 8.65; Inoffensiveness score: 8.55; (c) University of Louisiana–Monroe Warhawks. Acceptability score: 8.34; Inoffensiveness score: 8.42; (d) Alcorn State University Braves. Acceptability score: 8.13; Inoffensiveness score: 8.43; (e) Central Michigan University Chippewas. Acceptability score: 7.97; Inoffensiveness score: 8.21; (f) Southeastern Oklahoma State University Savage Storm. Acceptability score: 7.50; Inoffensiveness score: 7.52

previously contested or debated logos. Logos in figure 5.11 are presented from highest to lowest scores on acceptability measures. Thus, one can witness many logo rehabilitation projects that are rendered in figure 5.11. For instance, Alcorn State University retained the nickname "Braves" but nearly doubled acceptability and more than doubled inoffensiveness scores by moving away from all Native American imagery and adopting a simple block "A" with the word "Alcorn" integrated into it. Such movement represents noticeable, yet deliberate, steps away from debatably repugnant mascot names and imagery of its past, as Alcorn State began with the nickname "Scalping Braves" many decades ago.[13]

Similarly, the Southeastern Oklahoma State University Savage Storm seemingly takes another step away from the notion of "Savages" that was found even more offensive than "Redskins" in chapter 4, in the logo incorporating "Bolt," a character created in response to the NCAA letter denouncing the previous "Savages" name. On Southeastern Oklahoma University's website, Bolt is introduced in an interesting manner in that the university notes how the NCAA "forced" the decision to change from "Savages"—ultimately to "Savage Storm"—while also then embracing a two-year process that included a mascot committee, naming competitions, and logo design deliberations that ultimately resulted in the logo represented in figure 5.11.[14] In general, the figure shows that rehabilitating potentially contestable Native American mascot logos is relatively easy to do—or at least has a high rate of success based on the significantly higher scores for each of the updated logos.

Another interesting contrast was highlighted in figure 5.12, arising from a 2015 proposed update to the National Hockey League's (NHL's) Chicago Blackhawks' logo.[15] At the time of this writing, the new logo had been endorsed by Quebec's First Nations chief but had not been adopted. The reluctance for the shift may stem from some media entities that argue the Blackhawks' current logo represents a Native American logo done right, with the *Hockey News* naming it the best NHL logo of all thirty teams because, "unlike the Washington Football Club, the Blackhawks name and logo respectfully honors a great Native American chief."[16]

Figure 5.12. Proposed and current Chicago Blackhawks logo. Proposed logo: Acceptability: 7.95; Inoffensiveness: 8.01. Current logo: Acceptability: 5.22; Inoffensiveness: 5.15

Both the current and proposed logo were assessed, with the proposed logo being significantly more preferred by the sample on both measures. Subsequently, one can conclude that even with face-based logos deemed more acceptable, friendly, and accurate to their Native American roots, the general U.S. population will offer noteworthy concerns about its usage.

Finally, the survey also examined two logos that are sometimes used as comparative cases for Native American mascots: the Notre Dame Fighting Irish and the Boston Celtics. Figure 5.13 offers ratings on both measures for the Fighting Irish and Celtics.

Thus, while chapter 4 revealed that the names "Fighting Irish" and "Celtics" were substantially less problematic than every single Native American name that was tested, the images for these two teams do not enjoy similar separation from the acceptability of other Native American mascot logos. While respondents found these two logos to be more acceptable and less offensive than the vast majority of Native American logos, each logo scored below teams with Native American mascot logos that do not feature faces or full bodies. Thus, while the Fighting Irish and Celtics each feature logos with full-bodied figures as a part of them, neither logo was seen as nearly as problematic as the face-based or full-bodied Native American images outlined earlier in the chapter. Moreover, the Fighting Irish logo was substantially less acceptable (likely because of the metonym of a leprechaun) and more offensive than the Celtics logo, seemingly undergirding the same notion as before: a threatening face or full-body image will be judged less kindly than a friendlier, passively posed face or full-body image.

Overall, the empirical results of the logo survey offer a useful contrast with the naming results of chapter 4. Some schools and teams seem to be suffering from logo issues even more than names (as was the case for one of the Cleveland Indians' logos), while other teams seemingly have problems with both names and logos (such as the Washington R-dskins), deepening

a   b

Figure 5.13a–b. (a) Notre Dame Fighting Irish. Acceptability score: 6.66; Inoffensiveness score: 6.55; (b) Boston Celtics. Acceptability score: 7.08; Inoffensiveness score: 7.03

entrenched public perceptions of a potentially offensive mascotting practice. Perhaps one of the most useful insights is the hierarchy that ostensibly unfolded where images of Native American people were generally found less acceptable and more offensive than some of the items incorporated within Native American cultures and histories. Indeed, logos offer a multifaceted mechanism for exploring what elements are subsumed within the Native American mascot debate, with case studies likely providing even greater insight from humanistic perspectives.

Positioning Native American Images in American Culture

To this point, this chapter has revealed a number of empirical findings concerning public interpretations of Native American mascot logos. As noted, logos—the *visual* emblems of R-dskins, Indians, Braves, Chiefs, and the like— bridge the more textually based mascot *name* and the highly performative *ritual* aspects of a mascot. Sport studies and American Indian studies scholars, such as James V. Fenelon, C. Richard King, Cornel Pewewardy, Charles F. Springwood, and Ellen Staurowksy, have long examined the impact and reach of visuality in the Native American mascotting idiom.[17] These studies have nearly all attended to an "Indian" face or head as central to a logo. With scant exception, academics writing about the Native American mascot agree with Staurowsky that face and head logos, due to their ocular and visceral ties to human sentience, conflate the generic, stylized indigeneity stitched on a jersey or screen-printed on a T-shirt with the lived experiences of Native Americans actually dwelling in our communities. She argues, "The assertion that American Indian sport imagery renders 'Indians' invisible appears on the surface to be paradoxical or just plain wrong. However . . . the mass marketing of ahistorical, essentialized, contextless Indian images (befeathered, fighting, warring images) used as material markers of sport commodities create a distance in the minds of consumers, students, and the general public between 'real' versus 'fabricated' Indians."[18] Such markers are foundational tools of neocolonial logics.

Peculiarly, the overtly visible logo renders imperceptible Native heritage; logos, along with names and rituals, can come to eclipse how a public understands Native American pasts, presents, and futures if the images are ubiquitous, recurring, and left without challenge. Michael Dorris puts the matter bluntly, agreeing with other anti-mascotters that "war-bonneted apparitions pasted to football helmets or baseball caps act as opaque, impermeable curtains, solid walls of white noise that for many citizens block or distort all vision of the nearly 2 million native [*sic*] Americans living today."[19] Indeed, mascot logos can act as a prism through which indigenous heritage and customs are ogled as fanciful and ultimately squared away in settler-colonial logics of conquest.

The results from our survey of 1,076 respondents confirm the public's discomfort with face and head logos, in particular, when appended to Native American mascot names. In the cases where we presented viewers with a team name and then a combination of a team name and a Native American face or head, scores of acceptability and inoffensiveness were higher when the mascot name appeared alone. Moreover, we found that cartoonish depictions of Native American faces and heads (i.e., the Cleveland Indians' Chief Wahoo and the Atlanta Braves' Chief Noc-A-Homa) scored worse than faces and heads that were rendered more stoic or serious in appearance (i.e., FSU's Chief Osceola, the University of Illinois's Chief Illiniwek, and even the Washington R-dskins' chief). Our survey found that such discomfort is also experienced when Native emblems other than the face or head are used. However, our focus is on the latter because of the popularity of faces and heads as a common design practice in Native American mascotting culture.

In chapter 4 we discussed how the Atlanta Braves' name was the most acceptable and most inoffensive among all mascot names presented to respondents. When we gauged the simple script "Atlanta Braves" name as a logo with a small tomahawk under its name, respondents ranked it at $M = 6.80$ for acceptability and $M = 6.89$ for inoffensiveness, slightly lower than the name rating offered in chapter 4 but not immensely so. When the vintage Chief Noc-A-Homa face was added to the scripted "Atlanta Braves" logo, those numbers dipped to $M = 4.57$ and $M = 4.13$, respectively. Thus, the "Braves" name was stable, but the chief's face reduced the palatability of the mascot overall.

The disparity between a faceless logo and one peopled with a caricature was even more starkly noticeable in the Cleveland Indians example. The Cleveland logo with just the team name yielded ratings of $M = 7.03$ and $M = 7.36$ for acceptability and inoffensiveness. Once Chief Wahoo was added to the logo, though, those numbers dropped substantially to $M = 4.28$ and $M = 4.06$, respectively. Of all the mascot logos presented to respondents, Chief Wahoo was patently the least acceptable and least inoffensive. It remains no wonder that Scott Freng and Cynthia Willis-Esqueda opted to study Cleveland's mascot when they tested how Native American logos can trigger prejudice: "We examined the Chief Wahoo image because it is arguably the most objectionable American Indian mascot."[20] The survey results potentially allow these authors to remove the word "arguably" from their assertion, at least strictly based on the logo. Cleveland indubitably seems to be suffering from a logo issue more than a naming issue with regard to its Native American mascot.

This portion of chapter 5 investigates the case of Cleveland's Chief Wahoo (hereafter "Wahoo"), one of the most contested visual emblems in the entirety of the Native American mascotting corpus. Often referred to as "Little Red Sambo," Cleveland's grinning caricature has long been controversial; in fact, Cleveland's MLB team has relegated him to secondary-logo status behind their primary Block-C adornment currently found on players' and fans' game day jerseys and caps. Protested since the 1970s by Native American and non-Native anti-mascot activists, Wahoo and his slow journey toward retirement constitute a fascinating study of veiled negotiation. That is, the Cleveland franchise likely has a sense that Wahoo is problematic. The National Congress of American Indians points out: "Among the remaining professional teams with harmful mascots, actions by the MLB's Atlanta Braves and Cleveland Indians to subtly alter their logos and team branding in an attempt to mitigate harm while keeping established brand identity, indicates that management in these businesses understand the negative social impact of their brands."[21] Lending credence to this claim, current Cleveland Indians team owner, Paul Dolan, met with MLB commissioner Rob Manfred in January 2017 to discuss the perniciousness of Wahoo's visage to many Native Americans. Manfred reported, "Paul has been fantastic about engaging in conversation."[22]

Wahoo is approached in the analysis that follows through a rhetorical-critical lens that, as with the R-dskins example in chapter 4, navigates through a postcolonial framework. The Wahoo logo, related images involving Wahoo, and counter-visuals challenging Wahoo are examined from 2014 to 2016, the time period during which the Cleveland franchise remanded Wahoo to secondary logo and when Cleveland made an extended run in the 2016 playoffs, a weeks-long stretch that actually witnessed the return of Wahoo as the primary logo throughout the American League Championship Series (ALCS) and the World Series. This section develops by offering a summary of the Cleveland Indians' and Wahoo's context before then tendering a colonial critique of Wahoo as a mascot logo, bearing in mind that mascotting is, as we have suggested heretofore, neocolonial in practice—or, as Staurowsky contends, Native American images have been "lifted from American Indian culture and heritage, without permission or acknowledgement, by corporate entities, professional sports franchises, and educational institutions whose power structures are predominantly and often entirely white."[23] Next, we advance a decolonial treatment of anti-Wahoo activists, suggesting that their rhetorical resistance is meant to "recapture popular notions of what it means to be Native American" as they decolonize Wahoo's meaning.[24] Finally, we add a concluding thought about the Cleveland Indians mascot tableau.

Case Study: The Cleveland Indians' and Chief Wahoo's Context

The Cleveland Indians mascot name and Wahoo have a long and disquieted past whose roots were thought to be located in a narrative dating to 1914 and yet were discovered to be otherwise in 1998. For nearly a century the Cleveland franchise's mascot origin story began with a former player named Louis Sockalexis, a Penobscot Indian, who played on the Cleveland Spiders baseball team in the late nineteenth century.[25] Sockalexis apparently had a breakout first year before petering out through a lackluster twenty-eight games over the next two years. As he departed the city on the Cuyahoga River, a fresh team arrived in town thanks to a new franchise grant from the American League. For the next fourteen years Cleveland's team names oscillated among the "Blues" to the "Broncos" to the "Naps" (named for big-time player Napoleon Lajoie). When Lajoie left in 1914, the team clearly needed a new name; here is where Sockalexis returns and the mystery builds.

For the greater part of the twentieth century, Cleveland fans and baseball enthusiasts believed that the "Indian" mascot name had come from a grassroots space. Staurowsky writes that team press releases claimed "the renaming of the franchise was conducted through a contest run by a local newspaper with the winning entry, 'Indians,' allegedly chosen to honor" Sockalexis.[26] Much of the "honoring" trope associated with the Cleveland team revering its Native American mascot has been umbilically tied to Sockalexis as a nomenclated resource and synecdochal inspiration for decades. He was, after all, said to be the first Native-identified baseball player in America and, seemingly, he offered a story steeped in ethos and safety. Interestingly, however, newspaper articles from the *Cleveland Leader, Cleveland News, Cleveland Plain-Dealer,* and *Cleveland Press* from September 1914 to March 1915 tell a different story. Staurowsky analyzed Cleveland-area archives in 1998 and exposed holistically, for the first time, the larger Sockalexis narrative as a smoke screen for justifying the "Indians" mascot, especially during the late twentieth century, when more and more Native Americans began staging protests at old Jacobs Field (now Progressive Field). Instead she found that sportswriters had chosen the "Indians" name in 1915, not to honor Native Americans, but because the popularity of the Boston Braves indigenous mascot was so impressive and pervasive that Cleveland desired a similarly ennobled, yet bellicose, symbol for its team. Part of this rhetorical choice, of course, involved the high profit yields enjoyed by the Boston Braves franchise due in part to its popular Native-oriented mascot. The chances are likely that Cleveland's franchise was also looking to cash in on the esteem and attractiveness of Native American mascots in American sporting culture at that time in the early twentieth century.

Staurowsky's discovery might seem innocuous at first blush, but narrative fidelity makes a world of difference when it comes to contested ground, especially concerning contexts of ethnic respect and story lines of racial disrepute. That she revealed how fans were not responsible for choosing the mascot to honor an historical Native American "removes the cloak of authority from Cleveland's story and reveals several problems" such as those related to public trust, factual veracity, and—the clincher—Native authenticity.[27] Ostensibly, professional sports organizations and universities claim to revere the spirit, strength, fortitude, and survival of Native Americans by choosing to symbolize their communities with a Native mascot. For much of the pro-mascot commentary examined to this point, heritage rhetoric—or the "Celebration" theme—was the strongest argument for maintaining the mascot. In most cases this claim was open and closed for those defending the Native American mascot, whether it be the R-dskins, the Illini, or the Seminoles. Cleveland franchise owner Paul Dolan confirmed this obduracy by noting that he had "no plans to get rid of Chief Wahoo, it is a part of our history and legacy," and that "I look on the Indian as positive. I have a warm, affectionate attitude toward Wahoo."[28] When a time-tested and heartfelt narrative that underscores an entire community falters due to critical archivism, problems are sure to mount. In other words, if the "Indians" name is meant to trigger memories of honor and a venerated past—and those memories and pasts are no longer as they once were—a community's present and future both need to be recast. Such a moment of revision typically offers an opportune time for those wishing to change the terms of the narrative itself.

The origin of Wahoo is equally questionable. The common story line is that former Cleveland owner Bill Veeck hired a teenager named Walter Goldbach in 1947 to sketch an Indian mascot to be used on uniforms and caps. The story outwardly circulated at peak moments in the 1970s during generative anti-mascotting protests and in certain years, such as 1995 and 1997, when the Indians' appearances at the World Series brought ever more attention to—and thus protests of—the team on a national stage. Goldbach is, of course, a clever

Figure 5.14. Cleveland's "Little Indian."

agent for the Wahoo myth, for who would expect a seventeen-year-old kid to intentionally design a mascot that offends an honorable group like Native Americans? According to journalist Bobby Mueller, however, "The truth is that a similar caricature had been used frequently for at least 15 years before Veeck asked Goldbach to design the image. The *Cleveland Plain-Dealer* had images of a stereotyped Indian. . . . It became known as 'The Little Indian'. . . and there's no doubting the resemblance to Chief Wahoo."[29] A glance at the Little Indian in figure 5.14, indeed, illustrates some similarities in caricature style between him and Chief Wahoo. There does not seem to be as much public consternation over Wahoo's complicated origin story as there was with the obfuscation about the "Indians" mascot name rooted in Sockalexis.

Regardless, the legitimacy of both the mascot name and Wahoo continue to be questioned. Yet, Staurowsky writes, "There can be little doubt that the club's 'Indian' identity has been absorbed into the collective consciousness of a considerable portion of the Cleveland populace, forming a shared tradition and common rallying point for many Clevelanders."[30] Thus, the team's mascotting practices are mired in a discursive borderland. Team and fan identities are currently predicated on exploded myths from nearly a century ago, and as they veer into the future with clear changes to Wahoo's presence on the horizon, restitching that identity becomes no easy, uncontestable task. This is part of the danger of hazarding into unverified historical narratives as the Cleveland Indians' marketing department did throughout the twentieth century.

Speaking of changes to the Cleveland Indian mascot and the Wahoo caricature, requests for change have been sought since the 1970s. For instance, the year 1971 marked the 175th anniversary of the city of Cleveland's founding, and groups like the Committee of 500 Years of Dignity and Resistance formed and used the occasion to protest the Cleveland mascot. The group and others have gathered at each new season's opening day since that time to demonstrate against the Cleveland Indians mascot.

Protest culture reached a peak in the 1990s as Cleveland played against the Atlanta Braves in the 1995 World Series, hosted the MLB All-Star game in 1997, faced the Florida Marlins in the 1997 World Series, and squared off against the powerhouse New York Yankees in the 1998 ALCS. As with the summits of R-dskins protest detailed in chapter 4, anti-mascotters in Cleveland comparably relied on the team's national media attention to actuate protest efforts. One scholar in attendance during the 1995 World Series that featured two teams with Native American mascots—the Atlanta Braves and the Cleveland Indians—described the scene for anti-mascot protesters:

> Fans who attended games at the 1995 World Series of baseball in Atlanta were confronted with a striking image on a billboard across from Atlanta's Fulton County Stadium. Macon Morehouse explains that this billboard depicted "a peace pipe broken in half by a 3-dimensional tomahawk" accompanied by a slogan reading "THERE WILL BE NO PEACE-PIPE SMOKING IN ATLANTA. INDIANS BEWARE." Fans by the thousands marched by this billboard daily, on their way into the ballpark to watch their "Braves" take on the visiting Cleveland "Indians." For the fans, the billboard was nothing more than a comment on the competitive spirit of their hometown team. For the groups of Native American protesters who gathered outside the stadium during each game, however, the billboard served as a poignant reminder of how readily mainstream American culture appropriates and romanticizes their heritage and symbols.[31]

The irony of the "INDIANS BEWARE" mandate was not lost on those Native American protesters gathered to resist the racialist undercurrents associated with the mascot names "Braves" and "Indians." The foreboding was palpable and the ferocious tenor was resonant.

Tensions at the Cleveland Indians protest events have definitively teetered on the violent, with both pro-mascotters and anti-mascotters arrested throughout the 1990s. Some arrests of Native activists were later remanded when Cleveland authorities were shown to have violated the anti-mascotters' rights to free expression.[32] The on-the-ground conflicts during such protest events motivated the National Coalition on Racism in Sports and Media, in part, to increase its activism, as symbolized in a 1999 essay by founder and nationally renowned anti-mascot advocate Charlene Teters. She wrote, "This war, no longer on battlefields, is now being fought in courtrooms, corporation boardrooms, and classrooms over the appropriation of Native names, spiritual and cultural symbols by professional sports, Hollywood, schools, and universities. The issue for us is the right to self-identification and self-determination."[33] This seemed to be a moment where folks like Teters and Morningstar Institute founder Suzan Shown Harjo, among others, moved between activism outside of stadiums such as Jacobs Field to delivering testimony before U.S. Senate committees on race relations and lodging legal complaints on a sizable scale against professional sports teams boasting a Native American mascot.

One of those efforts occurred in 2000 when the Penobscot Indian Nation called for the Cleveland franchise to retire Wahoo. The group noted that Wahoo was "an offensive, degrading, and racist stereotype that firmly places Indian people in the past, separate from our contemporary cultural existence."[34] Nothing concrete ever came of the Penobscot resolution, but the episode motivated similar efforts to begin chipping away at the "heritage"-tinged and the "this is how it's always been"–entrenched arguments of Wahoo backers. Some Native American activists looked into filing a slew of cases, from Fourteenth Amendment violations and First Amendment protections to trademark breaches and antitrust exemptions. Meanwhile, civil rights advocates kept pressing the U.S. Commission on Civil Rights, the NCAI, and the National Association for the Advancement of Colored People to intercede whenever possible. And, of course, just as Bob Costas refused to utter the word "R-dskins" during the October 2013 game between Washington and the Dallas Cowboys, so, too, did sports journalists resist the use of the Wahoo logo and Indian name. On this point the Native American Journalist Association issued directives to newspapers in 2003 to cease the circulation of Wahoo's grinning and grotesque visage. A number of West Coast and Midwest newspapers agreed to stop lending credence to the Cleveland Indian mascot by disseminating images of Wahoo.[35] The high-water mark of journalistic recognition of Wahoo's problematics came in October 2016 when Toronto broadcaster Jerry Horwath refused to use the term "Indians" during his coverage of the Toronto Blue Jays and Cleveland Indians ALCS games. He told reporters, "For the rest of my career I will not say 'Indian' or 'Brave' and if I was in the NFL I would not say 'Redskins.'"[36] Moreover, he said he had not uttered a mascot name deemed offensive to Native Americans since 1992; such repudiation could be a sign of increased journalistic support to remove Wahoo. The issue of journalistic resistance is taken up in detail in chapter 8.

In terms of what Wahoo's status is at the time of this writing, he is indeed in a liminal space. In 2009, at the behest of former team president Mark Shapiro, who confessed to being disturbed by Wahoo, the team excised Wahoo from their road caps. In 2013 the chief disappeared altogether from batting helmets. In early 2014 sportswriters reported that the Cleveland franchise was working universally, albeit gradually, to phase out Wahoo by relegating him to a second option as a logo. In other words, his red face and beaked nose would occasionally titivate ball caps, but the Block-C would remain the singular uniform logo and the primary cap logo. The Block-C eventually became the new default logo for players and for fans during the 2015 season and well into the 2016 year. However, Wahoo made a return during the playoffs in early fall of 2016. Suddenly, Sam Allard wrote, "Chief Wahoo is on a hot streak. Though the franchise hasn't offered any explanation for why the Indians have worn Chief Wahoo caps in every one of their postseason games in 2016, the results at the cash register are clear: the three top-selling caps in the team shop bear the Wahoo image."[37] There has been no information from the franchise as to why Wahoo reemerged during the team's 2016 World Series run.

Certainly, though, journalists such as Mueller suggest that with the 2019 All-Star Game heading to Cleveland, MLB commissioner Rob Manfred might be ready to insist on Wahoo's retirement sooner rather than later. As discussed earlier, Manfred met with Paul Dolan in January 2017, noting, "I want those conversations [with Dolan] to continue, and I think we'll produce a result that will be good for the Indians and good for baseball."[38] Dolan insists, though, that he has no interest in retiring Wahoo. In the end, any modicum of resolution remains a mystery. And while it does, the slow pace of retention or removal continues to nurture speculation and catalyze debate. As Paul Lukas argues, "Indians officials have compounded matters by engaging in a slow but unmistakable campaign of de-emphasizing Wahoo, while refusing to acknowledge that that's what they're doing, resulting in a leadership vacuum that pro- and anti-Wahoo forces are both anxious to fill."[39]

What follows is a rhetorical-critical analysis of the Wahoo logo and some attendant images containing his likeness through a neocolonial lens. Thereafter, a number of visual counter-narratives are offered as examples of how anti-mascotters maneuver to decolonize Wahoo, an infamous figure Fenelon deems "among the strongest stereotypical logos of major sports teams."[40]

Analysis of Chief Wahoo and the Cleveland Indian Mascot

NEOCOLONIAL CRITIQUES OF CHIEF WAHOO

The ways in which Wahoo comes to visually represent Native Americans— and the fashion in which fans use his image, indicating the state of indigenous respect—might best be regarded as neocolonial in orientation. Susan Silbey argues in such contemporary, postmodern settler-colonial logics that the "control of land or political organization of nation-states is less important than power over consciousness and consumption."[41] Instead what we are interested in exploring are the visual symbols themselves as they serve as superstructures for informing the use (and often misuse) of Native Americans and the accouterments that constitute their varied lifeways. Thus, any visual rhetorical analysis in this vein attends to how symbols mean and matter as replications of past material conditions of colonization. As Jason Edward Black writes, "Rationalizations of colonialism involve the symbolic, as both generative precursor to and extension of the material realm, and the ways that these symbolic structures function has been labeled 'neocolonization.'"[42] We know, of course, that symbols matter. It makes sense, therefore, to assume they communicate power dynamics in the process of their visual "mattering."

The Wahoo logo is one of the most circulated Native American mascots in professional sports, both historically and contemporarily. Freng and Willis-Esqueda admit that when they performed research on racism tied to Native representations, they "selected Chief Wahoo because previous research used the image, and the symbol is a highly publicized icon in the debate over American Indian mascots."[43] As figure 5.15 illustrates, Wahoo is cartoonish in form and style. Of the logo's description, Fenelon writes, "The grinning caricature depicts a Native American 'Indian' nearly always painted bright red with overly huge front teeth, shifty eyes, and headband with a feather

Figure 5.15. The current Chief Wahoo.

protruding from behind."[44] We add to this visual description that Wahoo's gaze looks askance, as if plotting to charge at those in his line of vision. His triangular-shaped eyes—emblematic of essentialized tepee imagery—are angular, sharp. Combined with a winced or strained smile through ridiculously oversized teeth, Wahoo's face is to many, to put it plainly and candidly, creepy. Is he a "smiling Native," a stereotype of assimilationist Native Americans who often sold out their nations to the benefit of the U.S. government (akin to grossly circulated images of "happy slaves," who were said to be complicit to, or even satisfied with, American slavery)? Is he savagely planning to hit the warpath? Why is he not shown in profile or frontal view? Most Native American mascots' face and head logos appear in these ways; it is indeed rare to observe a Native American mascot caricature whose face is positioned so dubiously, as if he is neither trustworthy nor stoic. These latter two qualities are also elided in Wahoo's case, because his cartoonish face, a unique mascotting design, make him laughable rather than admirable.

While some teams, even the Washington R-dskins, work into their Native American logos Native faces that resemble people, even when the imagery, such as a feather or bonnet or war paint, can appear somewhat trite and reductive, Wahoo is different. He could easily fit in comfortably with a Peanuts character in the Sunday comics section of any given newspaper. Some have argued that he fails to echo any sense of human beingness at all. Perhaps this is at least partly why some question Wahoo as "an unambiguous racial icon meant to symbolize stereotypical and usually negative images of Native people as 'wild' but 'friendly' savages."[45] His mysteries as a caricature call for attention and beg questions of both authenticity and the potential for harm by way of his cartoonishness itself. Staurowsky frets that the "facially shallow imagery of American Indians that resides in the recesses of the American subconscious exempts the populace from accountability for genocide."[46] Whereas one might possibly read across Chief Osceola's sun-battered face, marked with wrinkles of worry and resolve, the reality of removal or termination—as a visual enthymeme—there is no such realism confirmed in a caricatured mascot face. Instead, the smiling Indian obviates the austerity of Native American experiences.

To the question of whether Wahoo represents a bellicose "Indian" ready to take the playing field as a surrogate for the battlefield, one might read fans' actuation of the logo as an affirmative sign. The image in figure 5.16 approximates a muscular image of Wahoo, with added arms and torso, literally busting out of his shirt. A number of placards include textual descriptors about his warrior-like behavior. In one image from the 2014–2016 era,

Figure 5.16. An image of Chief Wahoo as bellicose. (Photo by Arturo Pardavila III)

the Wahoo placard states simply yet tellingly, "Scalp N.Y."[47] There remains little pondering about how the fan views Wahoo's character. He is clearly violent, stereotypically so, as Native Americans are often homogenized as immemorially taking scalps from their opponents. Natives' so-called brutishness was apparently a powerful inventional resource for the Cleveland franchise. Journalist David Leonhardt reports, "The ugliness of the logo is no accident. When Cleveland chose the name in 1915, it had the worst stereotypes in mind: 'Indians on the warpath all the time. And eager for scalps to dangle at their belts,' according to a 1915 newspaper article."[48] Such imagery connects with the "savage Indian" stereotype discussed in chapters 1 and 2. The other image reads, "I'm about to go wild!" as if Wahoo's bestial ethos is poised to be on the loose.[49] In slangish parlance, Wahoo is on the cusp of being "off the reservation," an analog for roguely breaking with normative comportment and turning instead to vileness or insane behavior.

With the Cleveland franchise's successful run in 2016, going all the way to the World Series, the baseball world witnessed more ubiquitous images of "Indians" fans doing what Philip J. Deloria calls "playing Indian."[50] This is the time-worn tradition of non-Native people donning feathers, war paint, moccasins, leather fringes, and headdresses to affirm and justify their honoring of Native American cultures. From colonial revolutionaries dressing as "Indians" and engaging in the Boston Tea Party protest, to the Woodcraft Indian Movement's and the Boy Scouts' obsession with Natives as models of woodsmen—from Sal Mineo (a Sicilian American) playing White Bull in Disney's 1958 film *Tonka*, to a white student at FSU channeling Chief Osceola atop an Appaloosa horse—playing Indian has been alive and well since the dusk of the Indian Wars, when most Native Americans were safely held on reservations or assimilated (or soon-to-be) as "urban Indians." Non-Natives, writes Deloria, have historically "returned to the Indian, reinterpreting the intuitive dilemmas surrounding Indianness to meet the circumstances of their times" over and over again.[51]

Indeed, many Cleveland fans dress as Wahoo conspicuously. Figure 5.17 shows a young man in red-face with his eyes outlined in the recognizable

Figure 5.17. A Cleveland fan "playing Indian." (Andrew Schwartz/Stockimo/Alamy Stock Photo)

triangular shapes of Wahoo. His smile is painted on in grandiose white blocks outlining his own mouth. The only difference between him and Wahoo is that the fan has replaced the single feather of a brave with the headdress bonnet of a Native American chief. In an accompanying photo in this pictorial series, a caricatured sign with the hypermasculine torso and bust of Wahoo reads, "Not in my tepee," as if that particular fan embodies Wahoo and has staked ownership of the stadium as a cipher for the reservation.[52] To be sure, a tepee used to stand in the bleachers behind centerfield. Both the dressing-as-Wahoo performance and the feigned agency of ownership speak to the colonial ideology of possession discussed theoretically in chapter 2 and made electric in the pro-mascotting commenters' sentiments in chapter 4. Now, however, such ownership has moved toward the symbols of Native Americans, especially related to home, hearth, and cultural space—this is the quintessence of neocolonization. Such a territorial action is steeped in supremacy or certainly in access, comfort, and power. "For whites and those who have internalized the value system of the dominant culture," writes Staurowsky, "these images are not only a reflection of the 'other,' the 'Indian'; these images are also a reflection of the invisible forces of white privilege."[53]

In a related image, three seemingly white-presenting fans pose together, two in full chieftain headdresses—a sacred symbol of *earned* reverence and pride over the expanse of a Native leader's lifetime—and one as Wahoo in full-out red face paint, mouth and eye makeup, and a single brave's feather.[54] Seeing them smile without compunction (to be fair, who knows what they are thinking even if their actions belie any serious thought about Native American lifeways?), one wonders if their "Indian" fandom has become so complete that they cannot separate lived Native American experiences from the imagined community that Wahoo elicits. Leonhardt contends that fans "have been looking at Chief Wahoo for so long that many of us have become inured to the logo. We're aware that it has become controversial and probably understand that it's offensive. But then we go back to watching the game."[55] Such return to "normal living" without reflexive thought outside of, say, reading another report of the Wahoo controversy when a peak moment of protest garners news coverage, smacks of neocoloniality. That is, when as a member of a privileged group or dominant public, one can remove their Indianness without worry about the lived experience of cultural traumas and oppression that some Native Americans experience, mindfulness has been clouded by what the Wahoo logo underwrites, sanctions, and verifies: that Native Americans are not people in the shadow and pall of the Cleveland Indians' infamous chief and his smiling red face.

DECOLONIAL INTERVENTIONS INTO CLEVELAND'S "INDIAN"

We next move on to a reading of counterimages as rhetorics of decolonization. As a reminder, decolonization often takes the form of correctively
re-suturing the colonial narratives that are circulated as a dominant public
continues its symbolic conquest over Native Americans. Linda Tuhiwai Smith
opines that for Native Americans "the critique of history is not unfamil-
iar, although it has now been claimed by postmodern theories. The idea of
contested stories and multiple discourses about the past, by different communities, is closely linked to politics of everyday contemporary indigenous
life." It is entirely part and parcel to the "fabric of communities" that value
decolonization as a rhetorical tactic.[56] Anti-Wahoo protesters juxatapose, or
detourn, the Cleveland team's logo as a form of resistance, demonstrating how
Wahoo, in particular, diminishes indigenous character and inculcates misrepresentations of Native Americans as a marginalized and often-harmed group.

Some anti-Wahoo protesters seek to negate the "Celebration" theme
discussed in chapter 4 by repacking what "respect" and "honor" actually
mean to them. As figure 5.18 exemplifies, the word "mascot" is aligned with
racism in the immediate context of Native representation and in the larger
context of race relations. The antithesis of the mascot-as-racism is "peace,"

Figure 5.18. Respect vs. honoring Wahoo. (miker/Shutterstock.com)

Figure 5.19. Protest button resisting the use of Chief Wahoo's image. (Designed by David Jakupca)

as emblemized by the protesters' peace sign. Furthermore, the disassociation of "honor" from the Native American mascot becomes even more robust when we see the demonstrative demands of the activists to "stop" and to "end" Native mascotting practices. Clearly, "honor" and the mascot cannot coexist.

Figure 5.19 shows a "People Not Mascots" button. The simple expression speaks to the anti-mascot theme of "Humanization." Jacqueline Keeler, cofounder of Eradicating Offensive Native Mascotry, argues, "We want to finally make red face unacceptable, just as black and yellow faces are unacceptable."[57] Literally crossing out Wahoo on the button and figuratively retiring him from public landscapes of indigenous meaning avows and clarifies the need to push back at the way caricatured mascot logos dehumanize Native Americans.

One popular image juxtaposes a portrait of Chief Joseph (Nez Perce) with an image of Chief Wahoo. The combination of the portraits functions to exhibit how, though the Cleveland franchise attempts to overlay Wahoo with authentic Native Americans, the respective figures' captioned descriptors could not be further in cultural distance from each other.[58] Kristy Blackhorse, cofounder of Eradicating Offense Native Mascotry, has said of the team's and fans' insistence that Wahoo represents *all* Native Americans in such a stock and standard way that "it gives people a false idea of who we are as a people. It's hurtful to us when you look at Chief Wahoo."[59] Thus, the National Coalition on Racism in Sports and Media, who produced the image, crafted dialectical terms that are offset against each other: "dignified versus disgraceful"; "honorable versus shameful"; "respectable versus racist." The valences attached to both sides need not be articulated, because it remains quite clear where these anti-mascotters see their own cultural icons as foiled to the Cleveland Indians' caricatured champion.

Another decolonial rhetoric involves animating temporality as resistance. Indigenist theorist Duane Champagne writes, "The emphasis on decolonization models creates greater consciousness of the effects of colonization on culture, thought, and institutions."[60] Indeed, as one protester wrote on a sign, "Chief Wahoo is offensive. LEARN Native American HISTORY."[61] The emphasis on history, emblazed with uppercase script, suggests that part of decolonization involves teaching about the past. Ostensibly, as Jackson Miller has written, "Protests can be viewed as a performative struggle for identity because they constitute an attempt" by Native Americans to refashion who they are, and they ought to be understood as human beings and not insignias or playthings.[62] The swath of human history might suggest a representation and lived experience of Native Americans that differs significantly from the stories that the Cleveland franchise attaches to its mascot, especially Wahoo. In the same way that those opposed to the R-dskin mascot remarked in chapter 4 that "Temporality" retained importance to their anti-mascot position, so, too, do those resisting the Wahoo logo ground their arguments in what they deem corrective historical narratives related to the Native-U.S. relationship.

Another way that anti-mascotters decolonize is through what we discovered and labeled in chapters 3 and 4 as the "Homology" argument. That is, folks seeking to retire the Wahoo logo compare—in shape, form, and substance—the red-faced chief to similar constructions of otherness. This decolonizing rhetoric might best be labeled *detournement*, which is "about repurposing the rhetoric of those in power in order to drain the original language of its oppressive assaults in the service of propping up the disempowered."[63] In an image archived with the Newberry Library, a cartoon Wahoo is placed alongside similarly absurd "African," "Hispanic," and "Asian" caricatures.[64] The cartoonist seems to argue that the caricatures are indiscernible. A blight on one is a blight on the others. For example, the blackfaced character with a visage featuring nothing but the "whites of his eyes and teeth" and the Hispanic figure with a sombrero—racist stereotypes, all—would never be acceptable. Therefore, an intimation exists that Wahoo ought not be tolerable either. The visual argument of this image echoes the "Homology" theme discussed in chapter 4's assessment of anti-mascot rhetoric. That is, there remains a sense that if one would not use a racial epithet, say the N-word, to an African American's face, then one should not use a related slur to a Native American's face. The same goes for visuals. One would not point to an Aunt Jemima syrup bottle or an Uncle Ben's rice box and tell an African American, "See, that's you!" Following the visual analogy, one ought not point to a pouch of Redman chewing tobacco or Chief Wahoo and similarly tell a Native American, "There you are!"

Of this genre of visual detournement as a form of mascotting resistance, Leonhardt proposes that it is "worth pausing to think about what the equivalents might be for other ethnic groups—for minorities less marginalized than Native Americans. They're horrific. Imagine the Philadelphia Blacks, featuring a logo with exaggerated lips and similar big teeth. Or the San Francisco Chinamen, featuring slanted eyes and a pointy hat. . . . Or the New York Jews, with a short mascot who had a large, crooked nose and wore a yarmulke."[65] Even a diehard Cleveland Indians fan, Keith Good, considered the racial homologies when ultimately deciding to stop donning the Wahoo logo. He told a reporter, "I first remember hearing about the Wahoo controversy during the 1995 World Series because it was the Braves against the Indians, and there was all this talk about how it was two Native American mascots. At the time I thought it was a stupid thing to get upset about. Of course, I was very young then. But in the past few years, I've started to look at the other side of it. One of the turning points for me was when I saw those caps comparing Indians to other ethnic stereotypes."[66] In Good's account, we actually witness the power of both homology *and* temporality as anti-mascot themes. The argument goes that there may have been a time when Wahoo was acceptable; however, times—therein, motivating attitudes—change.

Detournement intersects starkly with parody in figure 5.20, wherein an anti-Wahoo group named A Tribe Called Red designed a T-shirt featuring a reverse of the Wahoo caricature. In the design, a white-identified logo replaces Wahoo and the name "Caucasians" replaces "Indians." Interestingly, the parody gained a co-signature from a national sports media personality known for his progressive views on cultural politics. "The idea of race serving as the name of a franchise is preposterous at its core, something ESPN's Bomani Jones showcased earlier this year when he wore a T-shirt modeled after the Indians' logo, with 'Caucasian' replacing the word 'Cleveland,' and a smiling blond man replacing Chief Wahoo."[67] The decolonial power of this image is that it turns the exoticized gaze of the settler-colonialist back on itself. No longer is the Native American caricature ogled and co-opted. Instead, the absurdity of the white mascot is brought to the forefront of a critique of Native American mascotting practices. That the logo also contains a dollar sign, perhaps signifying how the Cleveland Indians make money from their caricatured Wahoo logo, adds an additional piercing of the team's

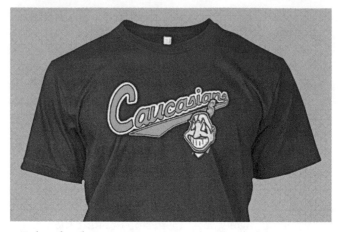

Figure 5.20. T-shirt that detourns Native mascots by way of a "Caucasians" mascot.

neocolonial veil. Likely calculated both to raise social consciousness and to offend, the Caucasians parody dually serves the purpose of visual resistance and performance inasmuch as an anti-mascot advocate could or would wear the T-shirt publicly.

Finally, one of the more unique ways that anti-mascot activists have de-colonized the Wahoo logo between 2014 and 2016 is through a practice called "de-chiefing" wherein Cleveland fans remove their Wahoo patches from jerseys and baseball caps (see fig. 5.21). A type of performative or bodily protest, this practice punctuates the legitimacy of anti-Wahoo sentiments by grounding true and dedicated fans as the central agents of change. Journalist Paul Lukas explains this rhetorical move, brilliantly outlining how "this is the 'de-Chiefing' phenomenon, a form of silent protest by a small but growing number of Indians fans who love their team but are opposed to the Wahoo logo, which they view as an offensive caricature. They say they're not accusing pro-Wahoo fans of being racists or telling them what they should or shouldn't wear. They've simply made a decision not to wear the Chief themselves."[68] This bodily performance is qualitatively more powerful than a R-dskins fan who might refuse to say the word "r-dskin" in that de-chiefing, as a visual demonstration, remains more conspicuous to the public. De-chiefing rep-resents an active protest, while a fan of a team boasting a Native American mascot refusing to utter a word engages in passive resistance. The practice of de-chiefing, in other words, is bold in its outward presence, its visible agency, and its rhetorical demonstrability.

The origin of de-chiefing goes back to 2014 when fan Dennis Brown tweeted pictures of his jerseys with noticeably grayed places where Wahoo

Figure 5.21. A "de-Chiefed" Cleveland baseball hat.

had been wrested away from the fabric. Soon, a Twitter account called @ DeChiefWahoo appeared and a number of fans began posting similar pictures. Come to find out, fans had been de-chiefing for quite some time. The action of removing a logo leaves a muted silhouette behind. As Brown writes, "So the night before we left [for the last game], I depatched [my jersey]. I wanted to leave a shadow, or whatever, on the sleeve, to show that I'd made a conscious choice to remove it."[69] The shadow is a material emblem of desires to remove the physical Wahoo from Cleveland fandom. Concomitantly, the shadow is a metaphor for how Wahoo has left only traces of Native American heritage in the wake of his *over*shadowing of authentic indigenous symbols and lifeways. Such a decolonial move is pregnant with rhetorical inventiveness and encapsulates well how anti-Wahoo activists articulate the harmful impact of Wahoo on Native Americans. In the end, de-chiefing proves that one can still be a fan of a team but find its mascot offensive, thus reducing the uncertainties and anxieties of cognitive dissonance.

A Parting Comment about Chief Wahoo and the Cleveland Indians

Whether one agrees or disagrees with the inoffensiveness and appropriateness of the visual Wahoo, or the Cleveland franchise's mascot name overall, there is one fact that stands sentry over the "Indians" controversy. That is, since 1963, "when the Dallas Texans relocated and became the Kansas City Chiefs, no professional teams have established new mascots that use racial stereotypes in their names and imagery. Additionally, some professional teams, such as the National Basketball Association's (NBA) Golden State Warriors have changed their logo, removing the headdress to reduce the use of negative stereotypes."[70] Those who oppose Wahoo—or the Washington "R-dskins" mascot name and logo, for that matter—enthymematically know why this is the case. We presume that mascotting, as a debilitating logic of neocolonialism, is disputed by such professional sports franchises. For those in favor of Wahoo and his contemporaries, such a fact might foment pause. One could potentially lose oneself in cognitive dissonance by pondering the question "If Native American mascots are said to honor Native Americans so much, why have we not seen new 'Indians' enter the sporting arena for over five decades?"

As for the Cleveland Indians' case, despite decolonial critiques on the one hand and even admissions from some fans that Wahoo can be problematic—evidenced even more emphatically by the Cleveland franchise's own gradual remanding of Wahoo to the wayside along with the 2017 decision by Topps baseball cards to eliminate Wahoo from all future Cleveland cards—a great number of Indians fans have refused to accept change.[71] Whether this is based on one's baseball fandom and family tradition or one's inability to break out of the notion of "playing Indian" is for another study to determine. To be sure, however, the situation is in an odd and conflicted state of flux. Staurowsky concludes:

> Although Cleveland has occasionally tempered its representation of certain "Indian" aspects of the organization, as seen in the elimination of the tepee once located in center field and the retirement of the famous neon Chief Wahoo sign that was mounted for many years at the entrance to the stadium, protests registered over the years by numerous American Indian groups have failed to fundamentally weaken the connection between "Indian" identity, the franchise, Cleveland fans, and others tied to the Cleveland and baseball communities.[72]

In the face of Freng and Willis-Esqueda's findings that demonstrated how "exposure to Chief Wahoo triggered negative American Indian stereotypes," it might be worthwhile for us as a reasonable and responsible public to continue the conversation about what, how, and why Wahoo means for Native American communities and what can be done to reconcile likely harm.[73]

6

Deconstructing the Mascot, Part 3

Rituals and Performances

The names and images examined in chapters 4 and 5 precipitate an ultimate and predictable endgame for Native American mascotting: the enactment of rituals. After all, if a team is invested in a name and possesses set images used to promote the brand surrounding that name, it is somewhat inevitable that such images, representations, and performances will come to life in the form of dances, ceremonies, chants, and gestures that we collectively address within this chapter as rituals. Such rituals make altering a mascot a truly Herculean effort, because a ritual creates a *performance* of what it means to be a team or school's fan. Enacted fandom is inherently more difficult to change than cognitive perceptions of fandom.

Performed for many generations dating back to events such as the University of North Dakota "Pow Wow" of the 1930s, rituals are employed within all levels of sport fandom as a mechanism for moving one from passivity to action—seemingly part and parcel of being an identified fan.[1] When that involves the University of Alabama performing an "Elephant Stomp" led by "Big Al," the elephant mascot, few problems arise. However, in the case of Native American mascots, such enactments present layers of problematic history tinged with settler-colonialism, hegemonic masculinity, and other elements of dominant culture.[2]

Thus, to explore this third and final form of mascot deconstruction, the data from the same national survey data of 1,076 respondents outlined in the previous two chapters was again utilized. Rituals were assessed by embedding short video clips (found on YouTube) of noteworthy Native American rituals as part of athletic events. Clips ranged from fifteen to thirty-five seconds and were viewed in their entirety. Respondents rated mascotting rituals in terms of both acceptability and inoffensiveness, again using an eleven-point scale (0–10), with a higher number representing logos that were less problematic in terms of acceptability/inoffensiveness measures and lower scores indicating logos that were more problematic on each of the two scales. The lower the number, the more offensive, unacceptable, and generally problematic the respondents found the ritual to be.

The first ritual tested involved the "tomahawk chop," most inextricably tied to the Atlanta Braves, particularly in their consistent playoff runs of the 1990s but with origins within other Native American mascotting practices. L. V. Anderson notes that the tomahawk chop action most likely originated with Florida State University, connected to imagery that seemingly was not formally enacted until decades later:

> Florida State University adopted the Seminole as its symbol in 1947, and early depictions were of a Native American holding a tomahawk, the type of hatchet used by Colonial-era Native Americans and white colonists. It's not clear exactly when Florida State fans began doing the tomahawk chop—a rhythmic extension and contraction of the forearm, with the palm open, to mimic the action of chopping—but a former FSU president once claimed that it was invented by the FSU marching band in the early 1980s.[3]

The practice of the tomahawk chop continues in various forms with a multitude of mascots; it seemingly transcends any one nickname within the Native American mascotting palette. Recent efforts persist toward banning such practices; however, the ritual remains entrenched within many of the most mainstream Native American team practices.[4] As such, the survey first offered respondents the opportunity to view a video clip of Atlanta Braves fans performing the tomahawk chop at a baseball game that resulted in middling scores, indicating a fairly problematic practice for roughly half of the population surveyed. Interestingly, while the acceptability of the practice was rated a 5.35, the inoffensiveness was substantially lower (4.60), suggesting that respondents were significantly more likely to view the practice as "offensive" than "unacceptable," revealing an interesting juxtaposition.

A telling contrast is provided in the Kansas City Chiefs' "Chiefs Nation" war chant, which was also part of the ritual video-clip survey. Video of the war chant features an amalgam of rituals, including people performing the tomahawk chop while chanting the same war chant of the FSU Seminoles. Respondents rendered nearly identical assessments of this chant when compared to the Atlanta Braves' tomahawk chop (Acceptability Score: $M = 5.45$; Inoffensiveness Score: $M = 4.67$), showing that the combination of song with a chopping motion seems to lead to slightly above midpoint scores on acceptability and slightly below midpoint scores on inoffensiveness.

Another mainstream ritual within the Native American mascotting experience involves the fight song for the NFL's Washington Redskins. Originating in the 1930s, the song has become a standard practice at every game for many decades.[5] The singing of the song is often considered integral to being a true Redskins fan, with lyrics that fans know by heart:

> Hail to the Redskins!
> Hail victory!
> Braves on the warpath!
> Fight for old D.C.!
>
> Run or pass and score—We want a lot more!
> Beat 'em, Swamp 'em, Touchdown!—Let the points soar!
> Fight on, fight on 'til you have won
> Sons of Wash-ing-ton. Rah! Rah! Rah!
>
> Hail to the Redskins!
> Hail victory!
> Braves on the warpath!
> Fight for old D.C.!

The video clip of people singing the song was included in the survey, with one of the strongest bifurcations between acceptability and inoffensiveness found in the entire survey. Respondents rated the acceptability of the singing of the song far higher ($M= 6.81$) than their feelings about the name or logo, yet their feelings about the perceived inoffensiveness of the song was right in the middle of the scale ($M = 5.00$). Thus, it appeared that respondents believed the practice of the song could be entrenched and seemingly "grandfathered" into the consciousness without its ultimately being something that lacks an offensive element, again harkening to nodes of colonialism within that distinction.

Two rituals used by the FSU Seminoles were incorporated in the study in an effort to compare and contrast elements of the rituals embedded within their mascotting practices. The first ritual employed a video clip from an FSU pep session in which the "Marching Chiefs"—decked in Native American attire—performed the school fight song; the second advanced the formal entrance ritual at a Seminole football game, consisting of a student dressed in Native American garb as Chief Osceola, who enters on his Appaloosa horse, Renegade, with a flaming spear while the entire stadium participates in the Seminole War Chant. The pinnacle of this ritual occurs when the flaming spear is planted into the football field. The former ritual is not overtly Native American, with the obvious exception of the attire of the "Marching Chiefs"; the latter is much more entrenched in multifaceted Native American elements, from the attire and the chant to the feather-laden flaming spear and horse. Moreover, the second ritual is presumably amplified by having over one hundred thousand people participating in the chant itself. The name "Seminoles" is endorsed by the Seminole Tribe of Florida; the sense of approval surrounding the war chant ritual is much less settled, arising from a homecoming committee brainstorm of 1962 by non–Native American Bill Durham and implemented sixteen years later upon approval from football head coach Bobby Bowden and the STF.[6]

The two FSU rituals were assessed, with both yielding relatively middling results on both core measures. The "Marching Chiefs" ritual was marginally better on both (Acceptability Score: M = 5.80; Inoffensiveness Score: M = 4.81), with the war chant registering as slightly more problematic (Acceptability Score: M = 5.12; Inoffensiveness Score: M = 4.67). Given that there is a great deal more layering to the second ritual, it could be assumed that the presence of any primary Native American imagery causes a demonstrable segment of the population to become more skittish on its presence, with a considerably smaller proportion of the population, thus, finding such problems to be amplified through additional elements such as the Appaloosa horse and flaming spear.

The next contrasting pair of rituals involved two songs linked to fan practices for the Cleveland Indians. The first was "Indian Fever," a song with the following lyrics:

> Indian Fever!
> Catching fire with everyone!
> Indian Fever!
> You can be part of the fun!
> You're the winner at every game.
> That's where the excitement begins!
> Catch Indian Fever—be a believer!
> With the Cleveland Indians!

The second was "Let's Go Tribe," a song with the following lyrics:

> Hey! Hey! Hey! Let's Go Tribe!
> Hey! Hey! Hey! Let's Go Tribe!
> C'mon!
> It's Tribe Time now.

C'mon!
It's Tribe Time now.
Are you ready to rock?
Are you ready to scream and shout?
Crank up the noise.
It's game time now!
Hey! Hey! Hey! Let's Go Tribe!
Hey! Hey! Hey! Let's Go Tribe!

Neither overtly mentions any Native American practices, but the first references the team with the word "Indian," while the latter focuses attention on the word "Tribe."

Interestingly, a significant contrast was found within these two songs on acceptability but not on offensiveness. "Indian Fever" had an acceptability score more than a full point lower than "Let's Go Tribe" (M = 5.64 vs. M = 6.67); however, in terms of inoffensiveness, both received scores below the midpoint of 5.0 (M = 4.73 for "Indian Fever" and M = 4.91 for "Let's Go Tribe"). Consequently, the two songs—similar in all other meaningful ways—contrastingly highlight that the American public seems to have more problem with the word "Indian" than the word "Tribe," with the song containing the word "Indian" yielding acceptability scores that are quite similar to the acceptability of the same name found in chapter 4 (M = 5.80).

Another variation worthy of examination within this empirical portion of the ritualistic performance of mascotting occurs with the Alcorn State University Braves. As witnessed in chapters 4 and 5, Alcorn State maintains the Native American moniker, yet their name, "Braves," was found to be the most acceptable of all Native American names listed in chapter 4, and their modern logo, tested in chapter 5, received one of the highest scores found on image-oriented measures. However, the ritual embedded within their fight song, "Cherokee," yielded the most bifurcated result between acceptability and inoffensiveness. The song, which features a stop in the music for fans to repeatedly "squawk," was shown in the video clip largely from a fan perspective, with the marching band being part of the video but with the predominant focus centered on fan involvement with the song. Ultimately, the song received a substantially higher score on acceptability (M = 7.12) with a much more middling score (M = 5.02) on inoffensiveness. If there is a ritual that can seemingly be both somewhat offensive and yet dubbed ultimately acceptable, the performance of Alcorn State's "Cherokee" appears to be that case.

Finally, the eliminated ritual surrounding the University of Illinois's Chief Illiniwek was assessed to gain a sense of whether the elimination of the Chief (and his accompanying "Crazy Dance") truly represented a case of dropping the most offensive practices first—a low-hanging fruit, so to speak. Respondents viewed a performance of Chief Illiniwek in full Native American dress and performing his dance at a football game. Indeed, respondents found considerable problems with the performance on both measures (Acceptability Score: $M = 4.46$; Inoffensiveness Score: $M = 4.65$). Perhaps such a result is a remnant of some respondents knowing the Chief was eliminated, leading some to think the dance must indeed be unacceptable and offensive. However, the large majority of respondents were unlikely to know details of the Chief Illiniwek debate, making the core finding of less than midpoint acceptance to be one with considerable veracity.

Beyond these overall ratings, a telling mechanism for understanding how respondents felt about rituals was again to segment out non–sports fans (less than 7 on an eleven-point scale indicating overall level of sport fandom) and sports fans (7 or higher on the sport fandom scale). Table 6.1 offers results segmented between these two groups.

As table 6.1 shows, sports fans tended to be more lenient about these ritualistic practices than were non–sports fans, but the scores were not as bifurcated as the differences between the two groups regarding naming practices reported in chapter 4. Perhaps more intriguing was that ANOVA tests resulted in no significant differences between non–sports fans and sports fans on measures of inoffensiveness but yielded four significant differences between the two groups pertaining to perceived acceptability. More specifically, the tomahawk chop, the Chiefs Nation war chant, the FSU war chant, and the dance of University of Illinois's Chief Illiniwek were all more likely to be labeled acceptable by sports fans than by non–sports fans. Quite intriguingly, this implies that there is agreement among fans and non-fans regarding

Table 6.1: Ratings of Native American Rituals by Sport Fan Identification

Ritual	Acceptability (M)		Inoffensiveness (M)	
	Non-Fan	Fan	Non-Fan	Fan
Tomahawk Chop	5.05	5.63	4.36	4.85
Chiefs Nation	5.16	5.72	4.56	4.79
Hail to the Redskins	6.82	6.79	5.05	4.99
FSU Marching Chiefs	5.75	5.84	4.71	4.92
FSU War Chant	4.75	5.46	4.50	4.84
Indian Fever	5.51	5.76	4.57	4.90
Let's Go Tribe	6.61	6.71	4.84	5.01
Alcorn State	7.17	7.09	5.09	4.98
Chief Illiniwek	4.20	4.72	4.48	4.83

the offensiveness of Native American rituals yet considerable disagreement about whether these rituals are acceptable, implying that sports fans are more likely to simply allow more Native American borderline-offensive rituals to remain part of the sports fandom landscape.

Such results again highlight the degree to which Native American mascotting rituals are endemic within the larger performances one exhibits by being a sports fan. It should be noted that the overwhelming majority of the respondents were not likely to be fans of these specific teams; given the national sample, the chances of significantly focusing on any one fan base are slim. Thus, such sympathy rendered by sports fans likely arises due to the leeway of performing sports fandom, regardless of whether a fan is a part of a Native American mascotting fan base.

Positioning Native American Rituals in American Culture

Rituals tied to Native American mascotting practices sanction vital spaces where fans of collegiate and professional sports teams can layer their personal and social identities over and through their selected "Indian" mascot. Rituals enable fans to perform and to do so together, often in unison, or to watch others perform a collectively treasured brand of Native American "identity." In many ways, mascotting rituals are religious or border on religious experience, as evidenced by the mass "worship" at NFL stadiums and National Association of Stock Car Auto Racing (NASCAR) tracks on any given Sunday (a sacred day unto itself in Christian communities). While congregating at these grand temples of sport, there are saintly figures (one's team's players and drivers) and sinner-devils (anyone on the opposing team). People pray for their team to make the extra point or to stretch the fuel mileage to cross the finish line and grab the checkered flag. People dress alike, chant the same songs, shout the same slogans (i.e., "Keep pounding!"), and employ gestures.[7] As an aside, the NFL is the most popular sport organization in ratings, and for many years throughout the late 1990s and into the 2010s, NASCAR was a close second.

Daniel A. Grano writes that within such sporting contexts "particular theological images, tropes, or objects can come to represent or condense the complex social relations that constitute a conjecture." He continues that things like rituals "become theological, in this sense, when they represent the act of making experiences sensible by interpreting back and forth between immanence and transcendence, the material and the metaphysical."[8] Indeed, immanent and material components of Native American mascotting rituals exist. For instance, fans congregate and engage in fellowship in a place of worship (the stadium) and don common apparel (T-shirts, jerseys, hats) that bonds them together based on their faith in a team. Mascots—say, in the form of a figure like Chief Osceola—lead the congregation in songs and inspirational renditions of customs with which all in attendance are familiar and even perform themselves in time with the sonic, the kinetic, and the visceral. Metaphysically and spatially, rituals introduce fans into the community or, depending on how many seasons in the sun (or rain or snow) one has weathered, confirm and legitimize anew one's personal and social location in said community.

Results of our survey of 1,076 respondents statistically indicate that most people found a practice like the tomahawk chop, made popular by both FSU and then magnified by the Atlanta Braves organization, more offensive than unacceptable. Part of this finding might be explained by the sheer throngs of fans—many, if not most, non-Native—moving and vocalizing in uniformity in the video clips we showed respondents. Indeed, it is one thing to read a mascot name or to see a logo appended to the name in a vacuum; it is quite another to observe thousands of people animating such mascot culture with their bodies. Perhaps respondents' worries about offensiveness hail from the conspicuous lack of Native-identified people present in a milieu in which they are said to be recognized, honored, and even emulated by masses of team adherents. Or, perhaps still, seeing names, logos, and rituals merge into a performance itself concretizes the oddities of fans embodying a racialized mascot. That is, one is not witnessing an isolated mascot name in the newspaper or seeing a mascot logo on someone's car flag. Rather, the observer recognizes that mascot support is plural and abundant. There exists a visuality that connects with the sensory, especially when it comes to something like the dress code for fans of teams with Native American mascots. Often the most offensive wellspring of mascotting culture is the seeming offensiveness of taking on the role of a Native American by donning what appears to be genericized and feigned displays of indigeneity. These dress codes are seen on people themselves and they are performed for onlookers. Again, this type of public show differs from a R-dskins or FSU Seminole pennant on someone's bedroom wall.

In his now classic article "Plotting the Assassination of Little Red Sambo," Roberto Rodriguez takes readers on a poignant mind-walk through a scenario of racial mascotting via rituals. Here is his inducement to reconsider Native American mascot practices:

Imagine, if you will, a tall, thin Black man dressed in Hollywood-inspired African warrior attire, bearing a scowling countenance, and brandishing a spear. Now imagine this character being used as the mascot of a college sport team—the Blackskins. At half time, a White cheerleader dressed in full costume and Blackface might portray a Blackskin and run up and down the sidelines high stepping in a mock African war dance. His antics are imitated by spectators in the stands who stab at the air with their crudely fashioned lances, growling and screaming like fierce animals. Then, imagine all of this broadcast weekly to a nationwide television audience. . . . Sadly, for Native Americans across the country, there is nothing imaginary about this indignation.[9]

Clearly maneuvering from the "Homology" theme of anti-mascot rhetoric, Rodriguez overlays Black myths with Native myths to raise a narrativized rhetorical question about whether we ought to be engaging in such spectacularization of Native Americans. Clearly, we do not experience Black cultures on display in these forms and fashions. Why, then, intimates Rodriguez, do some ritual practices "stick" and persist? Even more ontologically, why do they exist at all? Do they separate bandwagon fans from authentic fans in order to prove in-group status?

This portion of chapter 6, does not aim to answer these questions. However, the analysis that follows presents a rhetorical-critical reading of the neocolonial logics of performance by locating Native American mascotting rituals in the arena of "playing Indian." This concept merges the dominant public with marginalized indigenous nations to the point of the latter's cloudy representativeness. Ellen Staurowsky writes, "As a consequence, things sacred to Indians, such as wearing of eagle feathers, religious chanting, and dancing, assume qualities of the dispossessors, who regard these things as fun and harmless activities to be engaged in *en masse* at the ball park. Thus, as the symbols metamorphose from the religious to the frivolous, the collective acts of imitation create symbolism that has an Indian façade but a racialized-ethnocentric value structure and meaning."[10]

To punctuate the importance of ritual in Native American mascotting culture, the analysis that follows attends to fanfare at FSU during its game-day rituals. One of the nation's powerhouse NCAA football teams, the FSU Seminoles attract both a generational and loyal fan base and enjoy privileged circulation of their mascot through widespread print, televisual, and online media coverage. The choice of FSU as a case study versus another university thus seems clear. As an example of collegiate mascotting, FSU is the largest and most popular school—perhaps almost rivaled by the University of Illinois Illini and the University of Utah Utes—that engages in an array of performative

Native American mascot platforms at its games. FSU's football team has won three national championships, including one as recent as 2014 with a flashy, media-attractive, Heisman Trophy–winning quarterback (Jameis Winston). The football program's popularity, success, and ubiquity combined with the multilayered mascot performances at FSU means that its rituals are consumed by the masses in prominent ways. As for why we chose to address a collegiate case versus a professional sports team's ritualistic practices (i.e., the Atlanta Braves' tomahawk chop), we reason that collegiate culture differs from professional sports culture in enmeshment. As Jason Edward Black argued in a previous study, "University culture was chosen . . . because college identity is earned through immersion in two to four years of university culture, which pervades the classroom, workplace, home, and recreational spheres such as sports. Upon matriculation at, say, Central Michigan, an individual is a 'Chippewa.' A fan of Washington's professional football team is a Redskins *fan* as opposed to a 'Redskin.'"[11] This decision is not meant to be blithe or unmindful. Rather, it is critically attuned to the importance of fan immersion in a team culture that carries weight not just in proximity to the community but in nominalization and nomenclature as well. When one of us receives periodic correspondence from our alma mater's booster club, it sometimes begins with "Dear Seminole." Without the collocation of the word "fan" (that might follow such a salutation if the letter simply came from an NHL team's ticket renewal office: "Dear Blackhawks Fan"), one's identity is linguistically hinged on the Native American name. One's identity is also subsequently culturally tied to the qualities for which a mascot is said to stand regarding one's alma mater.

Moving forward in this chapter, we build a contextual outline of Native American mascotting rituals at FSU before delving into a neocolonial analysis of those rituals themselves, including an assessment of the Seminole War Chant and the tomahawk chop, Chief Osceola's ritual entrance into Doak Campbell Stadium, the Marching Chiefs' performances, and the way FSU fans adorn themselves in stylized Native American clothing.

Case Study: Osceola, the War Chant, and Seminole Fanfare at Florida State University

Founded in 1947, FSU is still relatively young compared to other large state institutions of higher education. One of the first actions the school took as it transitioned from its predecessor, the Florida State College for Women, was to create a mascot name, logos, and rituals in order to fasten the student body's identity to the new university. According to lore, the student body voted in

1947 to confirm "Seminoles" as its moniker, with the name winning out over other options such as "Statesmen," "Rebels," "Tarpons," "Fighting Warriors," and "Crackers."[12] Of the vote, FSU University Communications waxes that "the name was selected specifically to honor the indomitable spirit of the Florida Seminoles—those people whom the Seminole Tribe of Florida (STF) refers to as the 'few hundred unconquered Seminole men, women, and children left—all hiding in the swamps and Everglades of South Florida.' FSU's use of the name honors the strength and bravery of these people, who never surrendered and ultimately persevered."[13] In later decades the university and the STF would codify a relationship, but at that generative moment FSU decided on its own to move forward with its mascotting. Staurowsky reminds us that at institutions such as FSU, which has the methodized support of a namesake tribe, "it is notable that in none of these cases did American Indian tribes lobby for this recognition. The engagement of American Indian tribes in these discussions is only after the fact, and well after the fact at that."[14] It is also important to note that "Rebels" and "Crackers" were considered options for the FSU mascot name. Clearly, worries about offending people were not prime among the university's decision making. Even if a contemporary interpretation of these words seems anachronistic, both terms as early as the 1940s connoted certain Dixiecratic politics in one case and caricatures of poor whites in the other, respectively.

In FSU's case it was not until the late 1960s and early 1970s that the STF began investing in working with the university. For the roughly thirty-year period following its inception, however, FSU authorized what its University Communication office admits were cartoonish or caricatured versions of generic Plains Indians symbols. According to FSU, in the early years: "Native American imagery and mascots were heavily influenced by the Hollywood version of the American Indians, and often bore little or no resemblance to the Seminole Indians of Florida. It would take several decades for attitudes to evolve, and for the university to fully appreciate the importance of its symbols. As time passed, however, FSU's mascots adopted more and more aspects of the Florida Seminole tribe, and were presented in a more respectful manner."[15] Along these lines, FSU's first "Seminoles" mascot was named Sammy Seminole, a slapstick character portrayed by a white member of the men's gymnastics team who would flip-flop, tumble, and tom-tom dance his way across the basketball court or lurch among students at pep rallies. Sammy represented the university from 1958 to 1972.

In the time between Sammy's introduction and what would be a quick transition through three other mascots on the way to Chief Osceola in 1978,

FSU introduced a few more rituals related to the Seminole mascot. First, the Marching Chiefs band was founded in 1949 and began its traditions of weaving stereotypically Native percussive beats and spaghetti Western orchestrations into its repertoire, capitalizing on the indigenous theme saturating the university's new mascot identity and the culture it authorized. Moreover, the band incorporated tribal patterns and garnet and gold colors into its uniform trim. Second, homecoming at FSU almost immediately came to be known as "Pow-Wow," named, of course, for annual gatherings that Native nations sponsor to bring their extended families together in order to renew fellowship across tribes and bands.[16] Third, by 1957 the first horses and "Indian riders" appeared during Pow-Wow festivities, paving the way for Chief Osceola and his Appaloosa horse, Renegade, in 1978. Fourth, FSU cheerleaders began wearing uniforms with Seminole patchwork fabric built into the design as a complement to the Marching Chiefs, the Sammy mascot, and the overall cultural fanfare associated with Seminole accoutrement.

As the end of Sammy Seminole's tenure was drawing nigh, FSU introduced yet another cartoonish character named Chief Fullabull, who mostly danced at basketball games. Students were actually aghast at the gross stereotypes inculcated by Fullabull, so the university phased him out in favor of Chief Wampumstompum, who, from what older alums recall, was not much better. He was quickly replaced by yet another mascot named Tahola ("the spirit chief"), who by many accounts lent more fidelity to STF lifeways and appearances. In the end, FSU learned quickly that it was necessary to adjust to changing cultural mores. To its credit, the university helped form the American Indian Fellowship, a group that was influential in reaching out to the STF for input on the Seminole mascot. And by the mid- to late 1970s, FSU was poised to make a change to its mascotting culture. It had become more educated about Native Americans and the STF, specifically. FSU notes that along with their understanding came some changes to their Seminole mascot and fanfare. The university claims that "it became very important to portray the university's namesake with dignity and honor, and to do it with the graces of the Florida Seminole tribe. This attitude culminated in a mutual respect between the two institutions, and further tied their futures to one another."[17]

The year 1978 was an incredible watershed for FSU as it formalized its relationship with the STF. During the first few months of 1978 alum Bill Dunham worked with new football coach Bobby Bowden and his wife, Ann, to start the Chief Osceola and Renegade tradition at football games. When STF chairperson Howard Tommie was approached about his thoughts on the ritual, he granted approval to FSU to adopt the Osceola mascot and insisted that the tribe help create or authenticate any regalia the mascot chief wore onto the field. Chief Osceola and Renegade appeared on the field for the first time in September 1978. The official FSU narrative describes the authenticity of Chief Osceola's outfit, given to the university by the second football game of the season, as such:

> The new costume consisted of a long, multi-colored cotton shirt with a neck-erchief. The headdress was a long sash that hung over the rider's shoulder. The rider carried a long spear, handmade by local doctor Herb Mantooth, adorned with feathers. FSU's 1993 Renegade yearbook states that "not only were the cloak and moccasins authentic, but around the rider's neck hung a unique artifact in Seminole history. This silver necklace sparkled with count-less charms, Spanish coins collected by the Seminole Indians." Later, the head-dress was changed to a shorter cloth headband with a single feather in the back. The wig was added. With the final touches of body paint, the rider's image was complete.[18]

The only thing missing from FSU's new mascot ritual of Chief Osceola riding Renegade onto the field before each game, punctuating the start of football festivities with a forceful jab of a flaming spear into the midfield turf, was a tribally affiliated Seminole person (versus a non-Native FSU Seminole).

One of the anti-mascotters' critiques of the Chief Osceola ritual, then as now, is that a white-identified student has always portrayed the Chief. Nearly twenty iterations of the Chief have come and gone over the years. These per-formers are still handpicked by the Dunham family, receiving a scholarship for their service as long as they maintain a steady 3.0 grade point average and training for two years before debuting at Doak Campbell Stadium. The question of whiteness does not seem to annoy the STF, though the Seminole Nation of Oklahoma (SNO) raises issues with the portrayal. In fact, the SNO has disagreed with the FSU-STF relationship for the veritable entirety of the arrangement between the university and the tribe. Still, current STF chair-person, James Billie, recently defended the "white Osceola." He argued, "The man who portrays Osceola may not be an Indian, but behind the war robes, he must carry Osceola's spirit with him. . . . For he portrays one of the most well-known warriors throughout world history."[19] Clearly accessed here is the "honoring" trope of pro-mascotters, as a white student is able to "play Indian" if he can successfully channel the nobility of the great war chief.

The merging of non-Native and Native identities to honor Osceola can pose dangers. Jackson Miller contends that "the dialectical tension between 'ritual' and 'play,' where 'play' is taken to mean 'make believe' and 'ritual' is taken to mean 'making belief,' is present to some extent in all performative events. . . . The performative tension between ritual and play results from the fact that the lines between the two terms have become altogether blurred."[20] In other words, where does the performance leave the identity of members of the STF and the SNO, and, of course, what does it say to and about the hundreds of thousands of non-Native students and alumni who think they are suddenly and undeniably "Seminole"?

Another sticking point about the relationship between FSU and the STF is that a number of people in both internal and external publics remain skeptical about the benefits extended to the STF in exchange for the university's deployment of Osceola's name and body, along with the use of other symbols of Seminole heritage. True, it is well known that student acceptees hailing from the STF are given scholarships to FSU. But rumors exist that there are more monied ties at stake. Billie has quickly stemmed these rumors, asserting, "Contrary to what many may think, we do not ask FSU for any particular favors in return for using Seminole as their mascot. . . . We stand on our own two feet and we don't ask for any particular favors."[21] Yet individuals such as scholar Carol Spindel have questioned the motives of a tribal chairperson who she describes as a "leader credited with inventing the notion of Indian gaming, who sells his own line of Indian Secret cleaning products, and travels not on horse but in a helicopter."[22]

Of course, FSU's mascot narrative extends beyond the Chief Osceola milieu. The next notable piece of fanfare circulating around mascotting rituals involves the war chant, the tomahawk chop, and the fight song. As the university entered the 1980s, the Marching Chiefs had already been playing an instrumental tune called, quite ominously, "Massacre." The tune might best be known as the melody, beat, and rhythm that is backgrounded as the "whooaaa-ohhh-uhhh-ohhh's" of the war chant are vocalized at football games. The tomahawk chop's origin story is incredibly opaque, with many agents working the channels of "the politics of memory" to claim their version of the story as the most veracious and authentic. With only scant space available here, we dispense with the conflicts and instead settle on the one fact upon which most agree: the tomahawk chop started in 1984 to accompany the war chant. The Palm Beach County Seminole Club offers one of the most succinct descriptions of the chop's genesis: "During [an] exciting game, the Marching Chiefs began to perform the [war chant]. Some students behind the band joined and continued the 'chant' portion after the band ceased playing. The result, which was not very melodic at the time, sounded like chants by American Indians in Western movies. Spirited fans added the 'chopping' motion, a repetitive bending of the arm at the elbow, to symbolize a tomahawk swinging down."[23] FSU's University Communication office confirms this story, reminding the public—in true public relations form—that FSU's version precedes those eventually started by the Atlanta Braves, because "by the time the Atlanta Braves started with it, the chant and the arm motion generally were associated with Florida State's rising football program."[24]

FSU claims that it has always had the support of the STF and that when the relationship has ever needed adjustment, the two parties have always been able to compromise. In perhaps one of the most pronounced and publicly interrogated challenges to the relationship, the NCAA issued a directive in August 2005 asking universities to maintain an "atmosphere of respect for and sensitivity to the dignity of every person."[25] The writing on the wall was clear: institutions claiming Native American mascots were being asked to change names, logos, and rituals. Roughly fourteen schools changed some form or fashion of their mascot. Nineteen schools did not comply and were placed on a watch list. Three notable universities in particular were caught up in the NCAA wrangling over the watch list. Those who did not comply would begin to lose scholarships and would be unable to participate in postseason tournaments. The first was the University of North Dakota, whose defense of their "Fighting Sioux" mascot name and logo wended its way through the federal courts, concluding with a wholesale change of their mascot, in all its forms, to the "Fighting Hawks" in 2014. The second was the University of Illinois, who, after a two-year battle with the NCAA, settled on retiring its mascot, Chief Illiniwek, and his "Crazy Dance" ritual, but managed to retain the "Illini" name based on an argument that it could theoretically represent all citizens of the state of Illinois.[26] The third institution was FSU, which received an exemption based on the approval of the STF.

The exemption led to a firestorm of comments from a number of parties invested in the Native American mascot controversy. Expectedly, the STF released a statement in support of its longtime partner, emphasizing pride as a sentiment: "The Tribal Council further extends an invitation to Florida State University . . . to continue their relationship and collaborate on the development of logos and nicknames that all members of the Seminole Tribe of Florida and officials and students of Florida State University can be proud."[27] FSU effused about a familial connection to the STF: "FSU considers it a great privilege to represent a group of people whose courage and spirit we admire and respect. . . . The Seminoles do not just give a stamp of approval from afar—they are full participants in the activities of the university. Their leaders have publicly stated that they feel the FSU family is part of their family."[28] Oppositely, David Narcomey, member of the SNO general council, expressed revilement. He lamented, "I am deeply appalled, incredulously disappointed. . . . I am nauseated that the NCAA is allowing this 'minstrel show' to carry on this form of racism in the 21st century."[29] Representing the larger anti-mascot position, he was concerned that the continued use of the "Seminole" mascot *still* harmed Native folks even if a singular tribe affirmed the mascot. Billie countermanded with a stern rebuke, exhorting outsiders to "stay out of my territory. This is my place, my home, my university, my mascot, my Tribal members and my extended family."[30] And because the STF is said to have been consulted in everything from the design of Chief Osceola's clothing and the raising of the Appaloosa horses to the spear designs on the apparel fans wear, it is assumed that the NCAA exemption involves Native American mascotting rituals performed at FSU as well.

In the end, the STF-FSU relationship remains strong. The university still refuses to admit it has a mascot, maintaining instead, "FSU does not have a mascot—we have a symbol that we respect and prize. . . . By calling themselves Seminoles, members of the FSU community are engaging in a tradition of tribute for a people whose indomitable spirit is one that is deserving of honor."[31] Perhaps if FSU admitted it had a mascot, it would spark the sense that mascots actively perform playfully and intentionally imitate Native American culture, whereas a symbol is meant to "stand for" something of its own accord. This is the "Celebrating" theme embodied, par excellence. And the STF has professed its renewed faith in and love for its extended family. As Billie wrote in 2013, "Though our Tribal population has recovered, if you consider all the current students and past graduates of FSU, this extended family of Seminole supporters is several hundred thousand strong."[32]

Despite the idyllic union between the tribe and the university, all is not a panacea outside of their bond. That is, some anti-mascot activists worry about one tribe deciding the fates of thousands of other Native Americans. One Native commenter replying to a Facebook story about FSU's exemption disbelievingly queried, "What real right does THIS group of Seminole have to speak for all people who call themselves Seminole? For that matter, the tomahawk chops, the comments on 'scalping,' etc., are all slurs and misrepresentations thrown at ALL Native people—what right does one Seminole government have to encourage behaviors that affect us all?"[33] Scholars such as Danielle Endres have argued that it remains possible for Native Americans to self-colonize. This is not to say that such a practice is their own fault; rather, "one of the goals of colonization is to embed the framework within the minds and actions of the colonized."[34] Native Americans can get caught in the undertow that a veritable ocean of colonization exudes.

The following analysis critically reads some of the rituals at FSU through a neocolonial lens. The austerity of such a venture in the face of the STF's clear approval of FSU's mascot is attenuated by the argument that even what might appear emancipatory on its contemporary surface can still reflect some deeper colonial currents of the past. Raymie McKerrow labels this type of analysis a "critique of freedom."[35] Moreover, as a justification, the respondents to our survey noted some quantitative difficulties in accepting the entirety of FSU's mascotting rituals. The findings therein call us to reflect on FSU's mascot rituals more profoundly.

Analysis of the Rituals at Florida State University

The pervasive Native American rituals staged during FSU's football games clearly fuse non-Native persons with contrived Native personas that the former perform in a lighthearted way at the potential expense of the latter. Despite any one side's claim to honor the other, the fact remains that the Native American part of the dynamic must live—in body, spirit, and mind—with the hot breath of colonial history, the weight of material oppression, and the burden of symbolic stereotypes that are always and ominously present. No matter how "Indian" one thinks one is across the expanse of a few hours of a tailgate and a football game, one can easily leave their "Indianness" behind to pursue the more "serious" aspects of personal and social life beyond the stadium's gates. For Native Americans, indigeneity is not the equivalent of costume play, or *cosplay*—activated in safe, fun, and comfortable spaces. Rather, indigeneity is *lived* experience, all day, every day, until the final whisper of one's vapor. Part of the difficulty of "playing Indian," even on a metaphorical playground that some other "Indians" say is okay in which to dwell, is that one's non-Native fantasy colludes with someone else's reality. Miller argues that the "ritual/play dialectic is evident in the tension between viewing Native American cultures as ritualistic, spiritual, full of sacred objects, dress, and so forth, while simultaneously seeing these same cultures as 'playful' in light of 'the Euro-American prioritizing of the rational over the mythical.'"[36] The question that many anti-mascotters pose to those who partake in ritualized mascot play is "If performing Indianness honors and helps Native Americans, how does *your* performance make their lives any better?"

Not to ignore mascot names and logos, but most anti-mascotters willingly admit that the ritualistic aspects of mascotting are more problematic than any other representational form, because those claiming Native identity via the mascot must employ their bodies in—and wrap their hearts around—the performance itself. Rituals are active and demand commitment, while wearing a Wahoo hat or drinking from a R-dskins coffee mug is much more passive. Returning to Miller again, he talked with Native peoples about the presence and impact of rituals. What he found confirms the impulse to interrogate these Native American mascot rituals:

> While the names and symbols that sports teams adopt are upsetting to many protesters, the primary concern is how those symbols get used or embodied. Tim Giago, a leader of the protest movement, explains: "It's not so much the fact that a team is named after a race of people or the color of people's skin"; instead, what protesters find offensive are the "sham rituals and ridiculous impersonations that become part of those rituals." . . . Bob Roach, a Lakota Sioux activist, echoes this concern when he states, "We're upset with the antics of the fans, the ridiculous costumes and antics supposedly copying Native Americans."[37]

The common denominator between these two respondents is the notion of "antics" that manifest in impersonations, whether it is performance by way of clothing, face paint, songs, chants, or other bodily actions. With this in mind, antics at FSU are addressed next.

One of us is an FSU alum and recalls, fondly and vividly, the scene depicted in figure 6.1. The image presents a snapshot of the tomahawk chop, the ultimate ritual at FSU that involves fans in a direct, bodily way. Whereas the visual displays of Chief Osceola and the Marching Chiefs, discussed below, represent rituals in their own right, the tomahawk chop performed while harmonizing the war chant with one hundred thousand other Florida State Seminoles fans is about as embedded as one can get in performing one's "Indianness" at FSU.

The chop itself seems innocuous at first, and, to be honest, one can get absorbed in the absolute awe of thousands of people moving in unison, bonded by a love for community. However, delving a strata or two deeper, the point of the chop is to engage in violence. First, we are speaking of a tomahawk, a blunt weapon historically used in Native warfare. Can it be used as a hammer, a fulcrum, a wood splitter, a hunting tool, or a cooking implement? Yes. Was it designed for those purposes, though? Probably not. Second, the tomahawk chop requires employing one's body to emulate cutting, puncturing, penetrating. Ironically, even though an actual hatchet does not appear in folks' hands—though some buy inflatable tomahawks on the way to Doak

Figure 6.1. FSU fans engaging in the Seminole War Chant. (Ruth Peterkin/Shutterstock.com)

Campbell Stadium—it is the body itself that is the weapon, perhaps making the gesture seem even too personal. Third, though there is no personal, material enemy standing in one's way, the point of the tomahawk chop is to use one's body to perform Indianness in the service of intimidating the opposing team.

If the last point seems overdone, consider what the tomahawk chop necessitates as entailments and accessories. We are speaking of the war chant. The mere name connotes a bit of the articulation's critique as violent, a punch line leaked too soon. This chant involves the unmistakable "whooaaaa-oohhhh-uhhh-ohhh" that readers have most likely seen or, maybe, experienced for themselves. What might sometimes be forgotten is that the war chant replicates a call to war essentializing all Native Americans as if whoops and hollers—in the crucible of battle—were similar for all Native nations. Regardless, the war chant requires that one participate in a ritual steeped in bellicosity. Taken with the tactile tomahawk chop, the verbal war chant interlaces with the body to double down on a performance of savagery.

The twin bedfellows of the chop and the chant might seem somewhat benign in isolation, if not for three additional not-insignificant points. First, the song that the Marching Chiefs play in the background as fans whack away and make raw their voices is called "Massacre." The instrumentation is a rough approximation of a Hollywood Western movie soundtrack: tom-toms, the brass section doing its best to rally the warriors with a high/low melody, pregnant pauses in between loud bursts of drumbeats. The idea of participating in a ritual involving a "massacre" seems considerably dubious. Moreover, it adds an auditory dimension: in the offing, a ritual performer in an FSU game-day context imitates hitting someone with a tomahawk (tactile), while screaming something called a war chant (oral), while concomitantly listening to—and getting riled by—a song called "Massacre" (auditory). The second point that challenges the supposedly nonthreatening ritual is that all of these performative components circulate around violent images of Native Americans situated in the past, located in the Indian Wars (spoiler: the wars ended around 1890 with the Wounded Knee *massacre* inflicted by the U.S. government [emphasis intended]). Finally, there is a better-than-not chance that those engaging in violence and remanding Native Americans back to a violent past are not Native Americans themselves.

The reading of the tomahawk chop and the war chant to this point garners inspiration from Charles Fruehling Springwood and C. Richard King, who emphasize the problems with stereotyping Native Americans through such ritualistic play. Drawing from Philip Deloria's concept of "playing Indian," they write, "Mimicking the indigenous, colonized 'other' through imaginary play—as well as literature, in television, and throughout other media—has stereotyped American Indian people as bellicose, wild, brave, pristine, and even animalistic."[38] Miller concurs, pointing us to why a number of Native Americans find practices like those rituals performed at FSU to be distasteful, even if the STF consecrates the practice for its own community. He proffers, "Protesters particularly object to the emphasis on the war-like nature of the Native American, as well as to the notion that Native Americans are somehow extinct. [Some take] issue with the cries and pretend scalpings. . . . Protesters also object strongly to the way in which the symbols serve to condemn Native Americans to the past."[39] In other words, the "Indianness" that mascotters perform is not one rooted in Native American presents and futures and is certainly not emblematic of their lived behavior and action; they do not run around with tomahawks, war-whooping on their way to a massacre any more than non-Natives do. Still, in the entanglement that is fantasy and reality, Native Americans *become* the practice in which non-Natives at FSU engage.

The FSU fight song wedges itself into this tableau right along these lines as well. We will not address the song type ("fight song"), for it is a generic word that almost any and every team—Native American mascot involved or not—includes in its assignation of fandom. However, we do present the FSU fight song lyrics:

You got to fight, fight, fight for FSU!
You got to scalp 'em, Seminoles.
You got to win, win, win, win this game, and roll down and make those
    goals.
For FSU is on the warpath now, and at the battle's end she's great.
So fight, fight, fight, for victory.
The Seminoles of Florida State.
Florida State! Florida State! Florida State!
Wooooooooooooooo![40]

Made electric here is the discursive enclosure that borders the lyrics' content: war. The "fight" mentioned in the song admittedly pertains to the action on the field. But given the Native American fanfare and the violence of the chop and the chant, performers of the ritual are right back to typecasting Native Americans as bellicose relics. The notion of fighting is absolutely punctuated by expressions such as "FSU is on the *warpath* now" on its way to "the *battle*'s end." And, lest we forget the song's earliest charge: "You gotta *scalp* 'em, Seminoles." In addition to dwelling in an indubitably heinous Native American stereotype (scalping), the song calls to the performers as "Seminoles," as if pro-mascotters own the identity. The final salvo is to complete the circuit of one's Native identity and ownership by war-whooping at the end the song. This, of course, speaks to the "Ownership" theme that we discussed in chapters 3 and 4.

One of the less fan-active but visibly stimulating rituals at FSU is Chief Osceola's grand entrance before a football game. (See fig. 6.2.) There is no doubt that the regality of this fanfare is impressive. With "Massacre" playing in the background and with the Marching Chiefs in full formation as infinitely abreast as waves out at sea, Osceola appears aloft on his muscular black and white Appaloosa, Renegade, in complete regalia, including war paint. Brandished in his hand is a body-length spear with garnet and gold feathers at one end and a glistening arrowhead at the other. The feather end is lit on fire just as the Chief careens around a goalpost and enters onto the field with a nudge to Renegade's flank. The band is playing, Renegade is braying and bucking, and Osceola rides stoically, breaking his poise only to occasionally raise his spear, gesturing to the audience to partake in a battle whose embers are kindling into a blaze the more the band plays and the more Osceola strikes up the audience. Then the war chant starts; next the tomahawk chop commences. Within the expanse of roughly five minutes, every sense is ignited and every pulse seems spiked with even more electricity as tension builds. One hundred thousand voices scream in pitch, and one hundred thousand right arms hinge and unhinge in metronomic concord. The tautness of anticipation ultimately leads to Osceola steeling himself one more time with a visible exhalation and taking one last half dip around a goalpost before charging Renegade full-out to midfield. As they reach the freshly painted Osceola logo at the fifty-yard line, a snapped tug of the reins brings Renegade up on his hind quarters, his front legs batting away as if he is boxing for his life in the twelfth round. Osceola raises his spear to full mast. Time is suspended for a moment as in a slow blink, horse, chief, and enflamed wood are caught by inertia and slam down to the earth together. "Thump!" goes the spear and "Hmmppphh!" exhale one hundred thousand voices, whose guttural syncopation is almost too otherworldly to believe. The spear quivers in the ground, forming a perfect ninety-degree angle as Osceola and Renegade circle its entry point once before bolting to the edge of the field. Osceola has indeed made his grand entrance.

Lest we wax too effusive, this ritual's pageantry has been confirmed by both insiders and outsiders as just *that* extraordinary. Journalist Jim Joanos reminds us that "recently, Florida State University's 'Osceola and Renegade'

Figure 6.2. Chief Osceola making his grand entrance. (Ruth Peterkin/Shutterstock.com)

rider and horse performance was voted the best college football pregame tradition in the country. In a poll conducted over the Internet by ESPN SportsNation and EA Sports, this FSU tradition won out overwhelmingly over the others in the competition."[41] Although the ritual is splendorous, and despite the fact that Osceola "wears accurate (and tribe-approved) period dress and rides an appaloosa horse named Renegade," all is not uncontested and utopian when it comes to the ritual.[42]

In the case of Chief Osceola's ride, he performs what Brenda Farnell calls feigned "fancy dancing," a riff on an actual dance genre performed at contemporary Native American pow-wows. In the parlance of mascotting rituals, "fancy dancing" means performing distortions for the non-Native, giving the audience what they want to see. Regrettably, Farnell argues, "The dancing Indian body that signified wild, savage, spontaneous, hypersexual, warlike, heathen passions—the dark and dangerous antithesis of all things civilized and Christian—[is] nevertheless simultaneously pregnant with fascination for the projected wildness and sexuality of the New World Order."[43] For all the historical sturdiness and resistive ethos surrounding Chief Osceola, who lived from 1804 to 1836 and was "unconquered" on his own—departing his mortal coil only by governmental duplicity—he may not be taken seriously in the pregame context. Absent from his performance are *why* he is stoic, *how* he comported himself to the battle field/field of play during the Seminole Wars in the swamps of Florida, *what* he had to deal with as a leader and man, and *who* he had to face down in those moments *when* he felt compelled to swipe two fingers dipped in war paint under his deep-set eyes. The lived Osceola is gone, replaced by a facsimile whose vibrancy is lost in the carbon copy of time. Carol Spindel even jokes that Osceola is a sham unto himself: "The mascot looks like a Lakota who got lost in an Apache dressing room riding a Nez Perce horse. But a spokesperson for the Seminole Tribe of Florida maintains that the issue [of stereotyped inauthenticity] simply doesn't apply to his tribe. Florida State's Indian imagery, he responds, is nothing like Chief Noc-A-Homa, the smiling dumb Cleveland Indian, or the Washington Redskins."[44] When it boils down to the utility of his presence, Chief Osceola is a racialized hype man for the much bigger show to follow: the game itself, the moneymaker.

Some anti-mascotters communicate their ire that, in the pinnacle offense, Osceola is played by a white-identified student. One commenter on a Facebook news story about FSU's exemption granted by the NCAA wrote, "Meanwhile the university maintains a minstrel show. A non-native student dresses in 'authentic gear' (never mind the Seminole people not using war horses in swamps) and paints his face red. Meanwhile, the band plays a non-native drumbeat and the fans make war whoops. Yep, the students really are honoring the legacy when they paint themselves, dress in headgear which is sacred items to natives (sound familiar R******* 'fans'?)" Another remarked, "And then there is the white guy dressed as an Indian carrying a spear who races a horse around the arena making moves of violence with the spear. . . . To those of us who resent this cheap imitation of what it is to be Indian, it is annoying and yes, revolting."[45] These comments indicate that some see the performance as a sham, one underwritten by the STF, but a sham nonetheless, somehow protected by the dictates of expected ritual—the plight of the "dancing Indian" and the burden that FSU's version of Osceola must bear.

The Marching Chiefs are a longtime staple at FSU, representing an incredible point of pride for many students, alums, and FSU Seminoles fans. We have already discussed the musical performance of the band—namely, their repetition of "Massacre" during the war chant and tomahawk chop. Here, we are interested in their bodily performances. Unlike Osceola, the band does not enter our lines of sight as ritual-dwellers in full Seminole garb. At best, the band uniforms sport an arrowhead on the back center of the shirt, occasionally a small Osceola patch on the left breast of the shirt, and various combinations of garnet and gold flourishes (see fig. 6.3).

Figure 6.3. Chief Osceola and the Marching Chiefs in action. (Ruth Peterkin/Shutterstock.com)

The drum majors, however, occasionally dance around the field. Such movements are par for the course for band leaders, but the drum majors at FSU actually *embody* a "Native look," for lack of a better term, and when combined with the stark and sharp—and sometimes erratic—moves in which drum majors engage, they could be construed as "dancing Indians" as well. The oddest aspect of the "dancing Indian" is that Native American dances were all but banned at the turn of the twentieth century. At that point, the Ghost Dance was long gone and the Sun Dance was punishable with a prison sentence should a Bureau of Indian Affairs agent or law enforcement official catch one engaged in such a spiritual conversation with the Great Spirit. Farnell reports what cruel irony it was that the U.S. government attempted to control and suppress these "dynamically embodied forms of expressive culture within reservation communities [while] colonial constructions of dancing Indians began to proliferate off reservations—that is, in Wild West shows and expositions and especially on American university campuses. The colonialist message was clear: dancing for the entertainment of a White audience was acceptable, but dancing for spiritual and cultural purposes on the reservation was not."[46] To be clear, Native American dancing was not considered with understanding and tolerance by the U.S. government and the American public through most of the eighteenth, nineteenth, and early twentieth centuries. By the 1880s to 1920s, however, dancing was *only* permitted under the watchful eye of whites *for* white communities' consumption, whether through Wild West shows, on the theater stage, or during mascotting rituals.

Thus, when we witness the mascot ritual of non-Natives dressed as Native Americans dancing, the colonial logic in play is communicated in three ways. First, such a practice colludes white bodies and Native spaces. Second, in a similar vein, it demonstrates that whites can embrace the privilege of dancing, even in spite of the historical limitations set up for Native Americans by non-Natives over time. Third, it obscures the historical fact that Native Americans faced this kind of spiritual persecution at all—that is, at one point in the nineteenth and twentieth centuries, the government outlawed certain Native American dances such as the Sun Dance. Instead, as we enter into, experience, and move away from the dancing drum major in Native American attire at a football game, we assume not only that such disjointed and sometimes asymmetrical dancing styles are authentically Native but also that we all can own the practice. Again, these kind of settler-colonial dynamics punctuate the neocolonial undercurrent of FSU's ritual performances.

We come now to one of the more idiomatic ritual performances undertaken amid FSU's Seminole fanfare. In chapter 5 we analyzed the practice of Cleveland Indians fans painting their faces while donning headdresses, feathers, headbands, and other accoutrements when attending games. A similar type of performance takes place at Doak Campbell Stadium as well. FSU fans go "all out" to perform their "Indianness," all in a desire to prove true fandom and decisive in-group status.

This ultimate form of "playing Indian," wherein one's corporeal body *becomes* Native in spectacularized fashion, works from several neocolonizing themes ranging from ownership to appropriation. Ultimately, dressing up, or what we might call "cosplaying," is meant as a fantastical exercise for the individual who assumes an alternate identity. In the context of non-Native persons "playing" a Native persona, the lived experiences of Native Americans are occluded from any serious discussion. "The accumulated effect of this metamorphosis," writes Staurowsky, "is the delivery of limiting impressions of Native peoples as fictional, near-mythic fighting figures or exotics whose customs and practices are viewed as comical or quaint rather than deserving of reverence." Public reception is also a factor, she continues, because "this impression expands exponentially through the sheer amount and magnitude of exposure these images receive."[47] And, indeed, the images of young fans, most dressed very scantily (women) or shirtless (men), are circulated and exposed quite often in the sports media for their garishness, if for nothing else.

Notice that in figure 6.4 fans have misappropriated the Native war paint and feathers and have even worn Native bandanas and headdresses. You may see, in particular, that fans have painted their faces and bodies with red paint and have made lines and other designs against the garnet red of their war paint. We use "misappropriated" mindfully because these fans have taken incredibly spiritual and revered symbolic gestures, such as adorning oneself in paint and the display of eagle feathers, and have sported them for the sake of, well, sports. This is an apt example of how "mascots, logos, and rituals serv[e] to exclude contemporary Native Americans from full citizenship by treating them as signs rather than as speakers, or caricatures rather than as players and consumers, commodities rather than citizens."[48] The use of headwear such as bonnets and bandanas was not always a part of Seminole culture; it likely would have posed some problems of survival to crouch and slink around the swamps of Payne's Prairie and the flats of the Everglades in a headdress containing a few scores of eagle feathers to weigh one down and make one highly visible to enemies. Such use of the headdress is not just about "playing Indian" from the safe confines of one's impermanent and adaptive "Seminole-ness"; it is also about old-fashioned ignorance and a lack of respect for Native American lifeways.

Figure 6.4. FSU fans "playing Indian" at a game. (Ruth Peterkin/Shutterstock.com)

So egregious did the practice of wearing headdresses at FSU football games become that in May 2016 the Student Government Association passed a resolution insisting that FSU "does not condone the wearing of headdresses because it inaccurately depicts the culture of the Seminole Tribe."[49] However, the resolution has no legal teeth due to First Amendment complications, thus it is only a suggested and informal rule. Despite the resolution flying easily through the Student Government Association chambers, the succeeding 2016 football season still brought to the fore its share of chieftain headdresses. But because whiteness can sanction such performances of "Indianness" without recourse, there is not much FSU can do aside from increasing the way it critically educates its students and fans about Seminole culture and Native American veneration. Alternatively, FSU could excise such rituals altogether by *not* assuming a Seminole mascot, thus making moot the certainty that some fans will wear headdresses or don war paint and feathers.

In the end, the notion of fans painting themselves and performing their version of manufactured Native American identity smacks of colonizing contours. Ostensibly, these fans can simply strip off and tear away their playful "Indianness" and fade right back into the more privileged spaces of their personal and social lives. Or as Staurowsky summarizes, "This assumption of Indianness, this presumption of Indianness on the part of non-American

Indians, relies on an understanding that the status conferred by mascots is imbued with benefits of being American Indian without every suffering the price exacted by the U.S. government and society at large."[50] Dressing up as a Seminole does not an Indian make, but it does a colonizer suggest.

A Word about Seminole Performances

At the end of the day, Native American mascot rituals, such as those performed at FSU, seem less about an exercise of respect for indigenous people or about conferring egalitarian spaces for any number of the hundreds of Native tribes in North America and more about commodified team identity. There are some implications related to this claim that rituals obfuscate the realities and lifeways of Native Americans.

First, such mascotting rituals permit fans a chance to transform Native Americans and their images, religious symbols, histories, faces, clothing, traumas, arts, and cultural practices into the fulfillment of some fantasy. That we do not perform in blackface or yellow-face in our public culture should be evocative of the reasons we might reconsider Native American ritual performances. Such a notion reflects the long-standing colonial ideologies of possession and territoriality, which translate contemporarily into neocolonial logics of appropriation and commodification. Until pro-mascotters come to grips with the way their rituals of "playing Indian" are really about themselves, as opposed to Native Americans, such mindlessness will only further sanction fans' acceptability of appropriation and commodification.

Second, any way one slices it, the Native American collegiate mascot, in particular, exists for the colonial host's pleasure. And that pleasure tends to elide Native American presents and presence; mascots stand in for, rather than represent, indigenous peoples. As Black once wrote, "Florida State University creates the FSU Seminole and traditions like the 'Tomahawk Chop' to provide university constituents with some semblance of their 'Indianness.' Soon, constituents—as well as the public that sees national championship football games and mascot fanfare exhibited there—cannot think of the Seminole tribe without bringing to mind the garnet and gold glitz of Chief Osceola and the FSU Seminoles."[51] Concealed or perhaps unnoticed in the process are the triumphs and tragedies—the resolute indigenous equipment for living—that remains so necessary for Native American survival in a neocolonial age.

All of this is not to say that mascotting rituals erase Indianness altogether inasmuch as grossly devised policies such as removal, allotment, reorganization, and termination did not "kill off" indigenous people in entire and wholesale ways.[52] Rather, Native American cultures are understood, through rituals such as the tomahawk chop or Chief Illiniwek's now gone "Crazy Dance," as something *other* than Native American. That *other* involves the tokenizing of Native Americans and their symbols and heritage for the pleasure, play, and whimsy of, and ultimate misuse by, non-Natives for non-Natives under the purviews of franchises or universities owned or administrated by non-Natives—all so that these non-Natives can feel "Indian" before retiring in repose to their safe, colonially uncomplicated non-Native lives after the game. These rituals are indeed a "game" within the game.

7

What Is Lost?

The Perceived Stakes of Recent and Potential Mascot Removals

Thus far, this book has established the fervent and passionate contours of both sides of the Native American mascot debate. Some have attempted to end the debate by arguing that the stakes of these debates are too unimportant to warrant attention; others have quelled more robust deliberation, arguing the inverse: that the use of Native American mascots is so abhorrent that any alternative argument should be squelched by the sheer mass of the offensiveness of such names, images, and rituals.[1] This chapter seeks to explore such presumed stakes (or lack thereof) within localized discussions of two similar cases that are nonetheless polar sides of decision making: surveying University of Illinois fans about the removal of Chief Illiniwek and contrasting those responses to Florida State University fans and the current stance to keep Chief Osceola.

The Retirement of Chief Illiniwek

To start our journey into determining what could be lost when and if Native American mascots are eliminated, we opted to explore a relatively recent case of mascot retirement, Illinois's 2007 decision to discontinue the use of Chief Illiniwek. To be clear, many within the Illinois community would not call this a "mascot" retirement but rather a "symbol" that was eliminated, yet the Chief clearly functioned in a manner that was very similar to that of mascots for other universities. Chief Illiniwek would perform rituals—found to be problematic in many previous scholarly investigations—to amplify crowd enthusiasm (in this case, including a routine called the "Crazy Dance,"

Table 7.1: Illinois Fan Sentiments (0 = Strongly Disagree; 10 = Strongly Agree)

I am very aware of debates surrounding Native American mascots.	8.84
In 2007, I felt the decision to retire Chief Illiniwek was the correct decision.	4.42
In 2016, I feel the decision to retire Chief Illiniwek was the correct decision.	5.70
My fandom changed when Chief Illiniwek was retired.	1.94

largely viewed by the lay public as having ties to the Native American tribe but not historically rooted in the heritage of any Sioux nation).[2] Nevertheless, the Chief was popular with fans, akin to a mascot in being available for fan pictures and other interactions. After the chair of the University of Illinois Board of Trustees, Lawrence Eppley, announced the retirement of the Chief in 2007, some fans resisted, creating a "Council of Chiefs" who would arrive at games in similar regalia.[3] In 2016 Illinois announced it would form a task force to create what they argued would be a "first" mascot, as they regarded Chief Illiniwek as a "symbol."[4]

To assess overall sentiments from Illinois fans nearly one decade after the decision, we surveyed ninety-two self-identified Illinois fans. They completed a short survey that mostly asked open-response questions but also contained some questions in which they could indicate their agreement (or lack thereof) on a scale from 0 to 10. Table 7.1 indicates how these fans responded to key questions.

First, fans consider themselves well-aware of the issues surrounding the use of Native American mascots, showing they are much better informed than the general public, whose responses are offered in chapters 4–6. Second, Illinois fans are still fairly split on whether the retirement of Chief Illiniwek was the right decision but have moved more toward agreeing with the decision over the course of the nine years since the retirement was enacted (moving from 4.42 in 2007 to 5.70 in 2016). Finally, fans were very open in indicating that, by and large, their fandom has not shifted as a result of the retirement of the Chief (just a 1.94 on the notion of their fandom changing after the 2007 decision).

QUALITATIVE RESPONSES ABOUT CHIEF ILLINIWEK

When mining the comments provided by the fans, there is a bit more nuance in the responses than the numbers reveal. For instance, many fans felt it was the "right" call but that it was not necessarily the use of the Chief that was "wrong" in any formal manner. Consider one respondent's sentiments: "At the time of his retirement, I thought it was just political correctness run amok, instigated by White liberals, as opposed to any genuine offense taken by Native Americans. Now, however, I realize the Chief and his performances were cultural misappropriation and offensive, albeit unintentionally." Many others indicated that while the decision was justified, the manner in which it was made was problematic, viewing the action as less an attempt to do what is right and more an attempt by Illinois to do what it "had to do" given the political pressure. The belief that the university decision was less a moral one and more a pragmatic one was echoed in responses such as this: "I was proud of the University for making the right decision, although disappointed they essentially made it under duress. A mascot doesn't make the school. I don't understand the people who said they stopped being fans after the University retired the Chief."

However, the largest trend among respondents who believed that Illinois made the right decision was that they were ready to move on from it (e.g., "I expect the majority of fans like me would rather quickly forget all about the controversy"). One fan lamented the vacuum that the retirement of the Chief caused, all while admitting it needed to happen, indicating that "the symbol was used at the expense of a minority. A public, state-funded University should be a welcome environment for all walks of life. Honestly, I just wish the school had a new mascot. Anything. Just something to rally behind." All of these statements provide interesting spurs to the overall feelings that many expressed succinctly, which were "I did agree that Chief Illiniwek could be seen as offensive and it was overdue to be changed" and "I believe that the Chief should have been retired, and my fandom has not changed since the retirement."

It is also fair to note that some fans did feel the retirement of Chief Illiniwek changed what they felt was the core of their fandom (e.g., "The loss of the Chief looms heavy on game day. Something is missing"). Some described their feelings in a matter-of-fact orientation (e.g., "I was and am a supporter of Chief, and want to see him back on the sidelines of Illinois games"), while others used much more dramatic characterizations of their fandom shift (e.g., "I felt as though a part of the University and myself died with the dismissal of the Chief").

There was also a demonstrable portion of the sample who reported that although their feelings toward the Illini (largely as embodied by its sports teams) had not changed, their sentiments about the university as a whole had been altered, in some cases irreparably. These fans perceived the Chief as "strong" and, in contrast, the administration as "weak" in not embracing this strength. Consider the following comments:

- The administration was weak in dealing with this issue. I took a step back until there were administration changes made.

- Felt like a slap in the face from the university administration. They refused to stand their ground for the iconic mascot.
- My lack of support for the decision was based on the fact that outside groups were forcing a change based on biased opinion.
- I have the [same feelings for the team] but my feelings toward the University itself definitely changed to become more negative and un- trustworthy.

These types of comments were also justified by the notion of the Chief as a symbol more than a formalized mascot. While some believed this was a symbol worth keeping (e.g., "Chief Illiniwek was a symbol. One that, I be- lieve, was very tastefully done and supervised"), others used this denotation as a way to mitigate any perceived loss (e.g., "Chief is just a symbol"; "The use of a symbol does not define my loyalty to my alma mater"). Most who embraced the conception of the Chief as a symbol still argued that it was not at the heart of why they loved the university (e.g., "I had always been a fan of the Chief as a kid and into my teens but that symbol wasn't the reason for my fandom").

The sense of history that was lost seemed to be the most frequent area of lament. For many, the rituals they were embracing were not overtly Native American–oriented by-products of decades of consistent fandom and game attendance. Consider the comment from one fan: "I love my school and was aware the Chief was a manufactured and inauthentic representation. But I also grew up going to games and cheering for the Chief and the music before I even became a student, so it was bittersweet when it was over. Local people really cannot get over it, and the university or community really needs to take a stance against these 'fake Chiefs' that run around at games and events, which cheapens the representation even more."

Finally, there was an interesting thread from many respondents indicating that the debate surrounding Native American mascots—and the use of Chief Illiniwek—was useful for encouraging people to explore Native American cultures (e.g., "I don't buy that it was created to honor anybody, although it may have grown to do more to educate and honor than it was conceived to do. However, its presence at a football or basketball [game] has little to do with my fandom"). Many were concerned that the loss of the Chief could result in a loss of the richness of Native American heritage people uncovered when attempting to become more informed about the debate surrounding Chief Illiniwek, an argument known as "false benevolence" for those advocating for mascot elimination. Consider the various robust lines of argument that could be debated within the following comment:

Native American mascots could be used to educate students. By locking these symbols in closets, we aren't learning or fighting for Native American rights. We're closing the door on an opportunity to learn. The professor leading the way on this campus for getting rid of Chief isn't helping the cause of raising awareness for Native American rights, he's hurting it. What he provides is a temporary fix, but in ten years there will be no memory of Chief on campus; how will we remember and honor the history and culture of Native Americans?

Or in this more personalized, yet similar, sentiment from a respondent: "Chief is the only reason I've come across in my life that peaks [*sic*] my interest in learning more about Native American culture and history. Not just the history of those tribes and federations that lived in this state, but ones across the country. I still believe that Chief can be a symbol that continues to educate students on Native American history." For more on this neocolonial ideology, see the analysis in chapters 2, 3, and 4.

These types of comments could be seen as overlapping with people's senses of where to draw the line on offensiveness, as some felt it was the aliveness of the human mascot/symbol that was the core of the problem (e.g., "I think if the U of I would have just had the Chief logo, which I've always loved just from an aesthetic standpoint, and not had the live representation of it we might still have it today"), while others thought the lack of political correctness of the Chief was a way of separating the symbol/mascot from formally attempting to emulate Native American tribal elements:

I do get embarrassed by some fans proclamations and cluelessness surrounding the Chief. People complain that the different ideals of Chief aren't completely representative of traditional Native American rituals. His dance isn't of the correct tribe, the clothes he wears are of a different tribe. In reality, wouldn't it be more offensive if he did wear a traditional Chief outfit? Wouldn't it be more offensive if he learned a traditional and authentic war dance? Those were rituals deeply embedded into the spiritual lives of Native Americans. For him to wear those things to excite a crowd for a football game would be far more offensive.

In sum, it is fair to conclude that debates continue within the Illinois fan base, but these debates seemingly are less about whether the Chief should return (most are either resigned to or happy to know the Chief will not be reinstated) and are instead more focused on determining what role the Chief actually played in the history of their school, focusing, one could argue, on the postmortem analysis of the 2007 decision more than wanting to revisit or overturn it.

Illinois Fans and Native American Mascots as a Whole: Calling Out Florida State

Illinois fans were also surveyed about their attitudes about Native American mascots as a whole. Many noted that it is the manner of the representation that is most crucial to making this distinction rather than outlining lists of correct or incorrect names (e.g., "When they are portrayed as cartoonish or bafoonish [sic] that is wrong. I believe if it is done respectfully, it can be OK"). The most frequent mascot that these fans felt should be banned was the R-dskins, but these same people felt there still should be room for Native American mascots in certain areas under specific circumstances: "The symbols like Chief Illiniwek at Illinois or the Chicago Blackhawks are done with a reverence and respect for the peoples they are representing, not unlike the U.S. putting a president's face or profile on a coin or paper money. I do, however, see the issue with the live (typically non–Native American) person dancing at halftime." The localized defense of these two mascots, in particular, makes sense given that these respondents resided in the state of Illinois, which boasts both the Illini and Blackhawks.

The notion that intent matters (e.g., "doesn't mean any harm") was tinged with ancillary comments about how there needs to be room for difference of opinion, seemingly trying to deflate the reality that teams and schools ultimately have to override some segment of public opinions to either retain or remove a Native American mascot: "It's confusing. There are graphic depictions and live action depictions of Native Americans at different schools. Are both offensive? Is there no First Amendment right to interpretation? Or do they cross a line, like a blackface depiction of an African American, that we no longer tolerate or endorse?" Many of these same respondents also offered a call for some level of consensus-driven discussion (e.g., "If the PC crowd was more flexible and the Meatball crowd more educated on the issue, there may be a common ground").

However, the most common response from Illinois fans when asked about Native American mascots as a whole was to employ a disassociation strategy by pinpointing other schools and teams that should follow suit while placing Illinois as a perceived leader in the need to remove other offensive mascots. While some of the respondents went beyond Native American mascots to the inevitable slippery-slope arguments (e.g., "Native Americans are not a cartoon, [but] I suppose the same can be said for all historic mascots including Spartans for Michigan State, Running Rebels of Ole Miss, and the obvious Fighting Irish of Notre Dame"), and others tried to use any other mascot as an argument for inclusion of the Chief (e.g., "Wake Forest Demon Deacons: for Christians across this country, this should be offensive. A Deacon is a leadership position in a local Church. Taking something inherently Christian and tagging 'Demon' onto the front for intimidation could also be labeled as offensive"), most addressed other Native American names, images, and rituals, with a specific focus on one school's mascot: the FSU Seminoles. This underscores why FSU was such an ideal exemplar for investigation in chapter 6.

Perhaps the comparisons to FSU were natural or even media-driven, because the team had recently won a national title in football (in 2014), and for many FSU is viewed as the most egregiously problematic mascot currently present in the Football Bowl Subdivision (FBS), placed on the same NCAA "watch list" as Illinois and many others. However, the sheer number of comments directly pointing to problems and hypocrisy perceived between Illinois's use of Chief Illiniwek and FSU's use of Chief Osceola was very significant. Some of these comments came in the context of people having some reluctance to retire Chief Illiniwek, such as the response from a person who noted they were dismayed by Illinois's decision: "The real hot button issue at Illinois was the live action Chief actor's dance, which was not authentic, and like the Seminole warrior of FSU, was portrayed by a non–Native American. The Illiniwek mascot only appeared at halftime, performed a dance and left the field. It was deemed 'hostile and abusive' and retired. Yet the Seminole warrior continues his mock war entrance and flaming spear attack at every home FSU game. Not deemed hostile and abusive enough, apparently." These people thought that in the comparison of offenses, Illinois was less guilty than FSU (e.g., "the Seminoles mascot riding a horse and throwing a flaming spear at midfield is a more violent and disrespectful representation of the Native American lifestyle but somehow that's acceptable").

However, far more people used FSU as an argument for why there should be a blanket ban on Native American mascots: "The initial disappointment in the Chief retirement in 2007 was not that change had to happen, but that the same change would not happen at other universities [e.g., Florida State] connected enough to buy off their critics and dodge the issue. If the issue is a civil rights issue, replacement of a Native American symbol/mascot should be mandatory." The argument was offered for Illinois to be the presumed tipping point for the removal of all Native American mascots at the college level: "If the Chief was banned by the NCAA, all Native American mascots should be as well. It is patently absurd that the NCAA has not instituted a blanket ban on Native American mascots. That Illinois' use of Chief Illiniwek was, according to the NCAA, 'hostile and abusive' while FSU's mascot—usually a White, middle class male—continues to plant a spear at midfield each Saturday is equal parts intellectually irreconcilable and capricious."

There were particularly many comments about the well-documented relationship between FSU and the Seminole Tribe of Florida.[5] Still, most of these comments seemingly framed the relationship as a marriage of convenience to assuage any dissenters of the Seminole mascot (e.g., "Just because the Seminole tribe receives money and gives their approval, Chief Osceola can ride onto the field with a burning spear and emphatically joust it into the 50-yard line?"). Respondents also noted that there should be a distinction between "relationship" and "financial relationship" that seemingly leads to more approval from the STF than would be presumed to be otherwise. We noted this relationship distinction in chapter 6. One fan even tied this relationship to the lack of the possibility of one for his preferred school:

> I'm aware the Seminole nation has "sanctioned" FSU's activity. However, there exists a significant and indeed well-documented financial motivation for its support. The Illini nation, having very few remaining descendants (resettled in Oklahoma), has neither the robustness nor enduring culture to be approached by the University of Illinois for its approval. Herein lies the most basic reason for a blanket ban. It's simply unacceptable that FSU can buy the Seminole nation's support while the Universities of Illinois and North Dakota are treated as pariahs.

To summarize the sentiment from these many fans who drew direct comparisons to FSU, one comment seemingly encapsulates the group's beliefs: "It seems like they should all go, including Florida State, regardless of whether some portion of the tribe endorses it. It's either disrespectful and demeaning or it's not, and money shouldn't make it any more palatable."

Sentiments from Tallahassee:
The Lack of Retirement of Chief Osceola

Given the direct comparisons from the Illinois fans, attaining data from FSU fans seemed to be in order. A total of 147 self-identified FSU fans completed the survey, which asked largely the same questions yet with adaptations, since the fans were not responding to the removal of their mascot/symbol, Chief Osceola. Table 7.2 reports their scores on the numeric measures.

As was the case with the Illinois fan responses, overarching insights can be gleaned from these initial numbers. For instance, FSU fans self-reported a

Table 7.2: Florida State Fan Sentiments (0 = Strongly Disagree; 10 = Strongly Agree)

I am very aware of debates surrounding Native American mascots.	8.86
I believe Chief Osceola should remain the FSU mascot.	8.93
I believe the rituals surrounding Chief Osceola are acceptable.	8.57
My fandom would change if Chief Osceola were retired.	3.73

high level of awareness of the debates surrounding Native American mascots (8.86), mirroring the levels self-reported by Illinois fans (8.84). However, other scores seemed to offer a much more resistant picture about a potential removal of Chief Osceola than how Illinois fans felt about the actual removal of Chief Illiniwek. In this case, a clear, overwhelming majority felt the use of Chief Osceola was acceptable (8.57), with even higher scores offered for sentiments about whether the Chief should remain (8.93). While a relatively low mean was offered when asked whether retiring the Chief would shift their fandom, FSU fans were far more likely (3.73) to believe their fandom would change than Illinois fans reported the removal actually did cause a change (1.94).

QUALITATIVE RESPONSES ABOUT CHIEF OSCEOLA

Delving into the open-ended remarks, it was clear that many FSU fans felt that the exemption the NCAA granted for their Seminole mascotry was based on several binaries, such as having a relationship with a tribe versus no relationship with a tribe and also a core element of naming: mascot versus symbol. Those two binaries appear inextricably linked for some respondents, with one suggesting that FSU was different from other cases of Native American mascots because of these core elements: "Mascots such as 'Redskins' and 'Indians' should be changed because they do not honor the people and traditions associated with those words—and no relationship exists with a particular people group. Osceola is NOT a mascot. He's a symbol." Some attempted to operationalize the difference between symbol and mascot (e.g., "Chief Osceola is not a 'mascot' and doesn't participate in mascot hijinks and mascot marketing"). The feeling of having Chief Osceola as a symbol agreed upon by the STF seemingly negates, and is presumed to end, the debate for some fans. Consider this response: "Chief Osceola is not a mascot. FSU calls it by the more appropriate word, symbol. The Seminole Tribe of Florida actually designs the clothing and approves of the usage of Chief Osceola at FSU. Chief Osceola is not used in any other way than the pre-kickoff ritual at FSU football games. This question has no relevance in this survey because a change of the symbol of the University is not at risk."

I am a supporter of Florida State University, not the symbol it chooses to represent itself." Yet, while some respondents tried to make a clear demarcation between the notion of a mascot and a symbol, others inevitably used the two interchangeably, tacitly acknowledging that they find a fair amount of similarity between the two terms: "The Chief is considered a symbol for the University. It's an honor. Along those lines . . . why would a team/school have a mascot/symbol that they're not proud to be and call themselves? As far as I'm concerned, most every name/mascot/symbol for a team/school is an honor." Thus, it is fair to conclude that those who invoked the notion of Chief Osceola being a symbol were attempting to lessen presumed offensiveness or to mitigate the stakes involved (e.g., "At the end of the day, it is just a symbol").

The conception of "symbol" versus "mascot" begs the question, Symbol of what? Responses also seemed to indicate that while Chief Osceola—and conceptions of the Seminole more generally defined—are imbued within Native American cultures and understandings, a fair number of respondents felt the issue had less to do with Native American issues and more to do with a national debate regarding political correctness, as highlighted throughout this book. Many responses as to whether fandom would change if Chief Osceola were retired neglected Native American issues entirely in their argument For example: "The reason as to why my respect or admiration would decrease is due to this issue largely being a result of the recent culture shift from 'America: land of the free, home of the brave' to 'America: home of the hypersensitive, easily offended and generally ignorant.'"

Thus, it appears the Native American mascot debate was seen by many as largely hijacked by the culture wars that have argumentative poles of liberal/conservative more than pro-mascot/anti-mascot. Rich Lowry made this case for the conservative side, arguing that liberals "fabricate outrage" about the issue.[6] As one respondent succinctly noted, the debate is about much broader issues now, making it "not all about the mascot." Below is a series of comments we received that place emphasis on the politics of the issue more than ethical senses of acceptable/unacceptable or right/wrong when considering Native American mascot eliminations or alterations:

- I would be upset and annoyed that the pressures from liberal media and those that have no relations to the issue cause its change.
- I would be disappointed that the administration caved in to pressure applied by those who don't truly know the history of FSU and the Seminole Tribe.

- I'd still be an FSU fan but I would be pissed off at society for letting
  political correctness destroy everything. Thankfully the Seminole
  Tribe fully supports FSU.
- I couldn't support a University that gives in to politically correctness.
- If the Seminole Tribe is okay with Chief Osceola, but FSU capitulated
  to the PC folks anyway, I would lose respect for the school.
- I would be disappointed that FSU and the Seminole Tribe of Florida
  ceased a long-standing tradition that honors the warrior spirit of a
  great people in favor of political correctness.
- [My fandom wouldn't change], but I'd be disappointed the University
  gave in to this bullshit.

In sum, it appears there was a larger sense of the hypersensitive workings
of modern politics. Debates over Native American mascots have been percolating for decades, yet one person who was seemingly oblivious to these
prior debates offered this question: "Why is this just now coming up? Did we
all decide to have a moral compass in 2015–2016?" The sense of present day
being a key cornerstone in any debate seemingly is embedded in the notion
that to win or lose amounts to a victory or defeat for the political red team
or blue team most likely to embrace their side of the argument.

Much was also made of the NCAA's so-called Florida State exemption,
meaning the STF had endorsed the use of both the name and the appropriation of Chief Osceola, which should end the discussion.[7] No one mentioned
the contrary views of the Seminole Nation of Oklahoma (a much larger constituency) and its 2013 stance to condemn "the use of all American Indian
sport-team mascots in the public school system, by college and university
level and by professional sports teams."[8] However, respondents were specific
in claiming the endorsement not of all national Seminole tribes but of the STF
specifically, lending a considerable amount of authority to that relationship.
Many noted that not only was the special relationship key to the acceptability
of the mascot (one suggested that this should be a "case by case situation"),
but that the lack of the endorsement would change their stances considerably. Here is a sample of these thoughts:

- If FSU lost support from the Seminole tribe on this issue, I would
  then favor a change. Mascots themselves are a tricky business.
- FSU has the backing of the Seminole tribe. . . . If they didn't I would
  change my mind on the mascot[;] I wouldn't support it. They are Native American so if most of them don't have an issue with it non Native Americans really shouldn't have an opinion on it to be honest.

- Since FSU has the support of the Seminole Tribe of Florida and they are consulted on almost everything that is done, I see no reason to change.
- [The use of the mascot] should remain in perpetuity, unless the Seminole Tribe of Florida were convinced otherwise.
- People need to keep their nose out of FSU's business with the Seminole tribe of Florida.
- FSU's situation is unique because they have the permission of the Seminole Tribe of Florida.

Consequently, the notion of not only an endorsement but also an interaction with the STF is argued to trump all other opinions, including that of other Seminoles outside of the state. In doing so, the name and the use of Chief Osceola become normalized and accepted by fans within the in-group. One respondent directly noted, "Chief Osceola was a cooperative project between FSU and the Florida Seminole Tribe and to this date participated hand-in-hand with the university." This perceived interactivity with the STF was crucial, with one citing evidence of a dialogue by noting that the use of Lady 'Nole was eliminated at FSU after the STF argued it was inauthentic, a distinction outlined in Deloria's book *Playing Indian*.[9] However, by treating the FSU case as unique, some fans were able to condemn other usages of arguably similar mascots by noting not only the endorsement but also the specificity of the moniker of "Seminole" (as opposed to a more generalized "Indian" or "Brave"). One respondent negotiated the FSU situation in comparison to others in the following way: "I think that the political correctness of Native American mascot usage varies. Most general terms (Indians, Redmen, Braves, Redskins, etc.) with cartoon caricatures are stereotypically offensive. A tribute to a specific tribe (Seminoles, Sioux, Chippewas, etc.) that is endorsed and embraced by said entity should be allowed to remain as a school's mascot."

In the end, the majority of FSU fans were recalcitrant in their stance against any possible shift in the use of the nickname or of Chief Osceola yet fairly confident that their fandom would not change demonstrably—at least after they were given some time to adjust. As one person noted, "Syracuse switched from 'Orangemen' to 'Orange' several years ago, and that didn't affect anyone's fandom." Nevertheless, many others felt that either some dimension would be eliminated (e.g., "If the Yankees don't wear pinstripes, they're still the Yankees, but they aren't the uniforms you fell in love with when you became a fan") or that time would be needed to adjust to a new normal for their fandom (e.g., "It'd take a while, but I'd get over it"; "It certainly would feel like something I'm proud of is missing").

A final note from the generalized feeling about the FSU symbol/mascot is that many people feel pride in having gained a deeper understanding of a culture about which they believe they otherwise would have known little. For instance: "I am very proud of our connection with the Seminole Tribe [and] their resistance of the U.S. Government's removal efforts. Having Chief Osceola as our mascot adds another level of pride for me that a tiger, bird, etc. would not. By having Osceola represent us, I get to feel pride over our athletic teams but also over a real group of people who accomplished something remarkable."

There was ample sentiment that while some people could misunderstand the name or use of Chief Osceola, there were others committed to making the mascot a passion of understanding and that to eliminate it would mean that their efforts to embrace the mascot in a noble way were for naught. Consider this extended passage from what appears to be an FSU fan who has spent considerable time in contemplating the issue:

> I have no doubt that before my time, the choice of the Seminole name probably had little noble purpose, and the deep meaning I described did not exist in the beginning. I'm sure there are many old photographs and program covers that are cringe-worthy today. And those can and should be condemned. But by the early 1990s, that deep reverence for what it meant for FSU to call themselves the Seminoles was already well in place. And I have been proud to see how it's been continuously deepened and improved over recent decades, with further involvement of the Seminole Indians, and increased authenticity improvements to the Chief Osceola tradition. Changing the name Seminoles and retiring Chief Osceola would affect my fandom, because it's not just a tradition to cling to. It's not like redefining a logo or new uniforms, which people get grumpy about, but ultimately don't matter. In this case, the Florida State Seminoles are one of a handful of sports nicknames that are deeper than a reference to some local geography or incident. I like to think with FSU, the name, in a small but real way, makes the team. Constantly striving to live up to the spirit of being a Seminole is an essential part of the Florida State program, and is bigger than wins or losses. FSU didn't "invent" the Seminoles, but instead tries to carry on their legacy, and a change to that would affect my fandom.

The Case of Florida State—In Comparison to Other Mascots

When asked to compare the use of Chief Osceola to other Native American mascot debates, one common response was defensiveness against even drawing comparisons at all. One strategy was to negate (e.g., "Why this remains an issue is beyond my understanding"), yet others were concerned with any equating of FSU with other issues. As one wrote, "I think this question could be a trap. The use of the term 'Redskins' is derogatory and degrading in reference to a subset of the human race. However[,] FSU's use of Chief Osceola and the tribe name 'Seminoles' is all approved for use by the Seminole Tribe of the state or Florida."

Few felt that all current Native American mascots were appropriate as a whole, offering distinctions within such negotiations ("Some nicknames are patently offensive; others are not"). One fan indicated that they found FSU's current practices to be acceptable, (e.g., "I do not agree with students or fans dressing up in stereotypical 'Indian dress' or the widespread use of 'scalp 'em'"), while others again offered the mitigation of some formal agreement with the related tribe (e.g., "Depends if the tribe they are using as a mascot have an issue with it"). Such a comment connects the aforementioned problems with a lack of direct equivalency, with cases such as the Illinois mascot, and with the lack of a specific constituency from which to draw an endorsement for generalized terms such as "R-dskin" or "Indian." While some would invoke the 2016 survey that nine of ten Native Americans are not offended by even the "R-dskins" name, others would argue that the survey response of "does not bother me" is semantically divergent from finding the use of such mascots "acceptable."[10]

Slippery-slope arguments were also common (e.g., "If they change this one then they will start changing other mascots. It's no different than Fighting Irish or Ragin' Cajuns"), but considerably more common was the attempt to elide any potential unacceptability of the FSU case against other cases deemed considerably leaning toward the unacceptable side of the spectrum, including the following:

- "Seminoles" isn't nearly as offensive as "Redskins" or "Orangemen" are. Or if there were a team called the "Savages." With those names, I get why people would want a change.
- Use of the proper name of Native Americans (Seminole, Apache, Cherokee) is acceptable with blessing from the Tribal Leaders. The professional team in Washington is not acceptable. There a distinct difference on use of proper name versus derogatory words. Indians is also a negative term because Native Americans will tell you they are not from India.
- Derogatory names, though, are not acceptable as in the case of the team in D.C.

A final strategy was to diminish the issue entirely in the same manners outlined in the YouTube comment streams of chapter 3, noting that regardless of existing uses, they could be considerably worse. For instance, one person argued, "As long as it isn't blatantly offensive, I don't know why people care so much. It's not like there's a team out there called the 'Black Faces' and sporting a Confederate Flag as their logo"). Other times it was difficult to discern whether responses about these types of extreme cases were offered as serious commentary or tongue-in-cheek satire, such as one fan who claimed they would be "absolutely thrilled if there was a collegiate team with a generic 'White person' mascot who was depicted as having characteristics such as bravery, strength and leadership."

Conclusion

When combining these two surveys of contrasting—yet in many ways similar—college football fan bases, the overarching notion of resistance is evident. This is so, however, in a way that often has less to do with Native Americans and more to do with politics, societal pressures, and the differences between what is intended and what is perceived through Native American names, images, and rituals. What is also clear is that what fans saw in Chief Illiniwek and still witness in Chief Osceola is seen as part of their fandom but is not so essential as to warrant dramatic downgrades in their fandom if such a symbol were eliminated. Finally, these fan bases seemed to know considerably more about the issue than one may expect from a general population that is not as heavily invested in the debate. However, whether such knowledge hails from Native American history or Native American mascotting culture is central to the overarching controversy. Whether such endeavors to know more about Native Americans warrant the continuation of potentially problematic mascots should be part and parcel of the modern Native American mascot debate.

8

W(h)ither the Mascot?

Pathways through the Logics
of Native American Mascotting

To this point, we have interrogated and outlined the silhouettes of the Native American mascot controversy. Examining the three main mascotting tableaus of the textual (naming), the visual (logos), and the performative (rituals), we have attempted to ply the *whats* and *hows* of the debate.

We began by framing an analysis of the three primary milieus of mascotting practices in the United States with the aid of two theoretical arcs: self-categorization and postcolonialism. Self-categorization allows scholars to assess the ways that people define their in-groups, particularly as they clash with other groups articulated as threats or antagonists. Self-categorization, the focus of chapter 1, can be linked to sport culture, as fans of one in-group or camp tend to be appositioned to other out-groups who fail to share team identities, including traditions, history, and overall fan culture. Each successive analytical chapter began by polling sports fans and non-fans alike about their perceptions of Native American mascots in terms of their acceptability and appropriateness and offensiveness and inappropriateness. That data was then used to help us analyze textual, visual, and performative case studies through a postcolonial lens.

As chapter 2 positioned this latter lens, postcolonialism is a dual process by which scholars identify and critique colonial machinations at play in a colonized context (i.e., the relationship between the United States and Native American communities over time) and analyze the ways that rhetors, or colonized voices themselves, call into question, demystify, and attempt to suture the wounds that colonization leaves in its wake. We framed the practice of mascotting as a neocolonial tradition, employing both data gleaned from our survey and individual case studies to demonstrate the neocolonial logics at work in mascotting and the fashion in which Native Americans have resisted the mascot through decolonization.

Chapter 3 attended to a preliminary and contemporary case study from 2013—the clash between the Washington R-dskins franchise and the Change the Mascot organization over the R-dskins mascot via competing national advertisements. We analyzed public responses to these advertisements in order to ascertain themes of self-categorization and typologies of both neocolonialism and decolonization. These themes helped us to analyze the resultant textual, visual, and ritualistic elements of mascotting in chapters 4, 5, and 6, respectively. The chapter concluded by surmising that the most vigorous lesson that can be drawn from an examination of these public comments— both for and against a Washington mascot change—is that there is far more being contested in this cultural geography than merely a nickname, logo, or ritual alone. Rather, there is a mélange of culture that is both implicated in and affected by a potential change to Native American mascotting practices. This singular example of the R-dskins controversy was used as an insignia of the cases to follow.

Speaking of cases, chapter 4 represented the first of our three core analytical chapters, this one specifically concentrating on Native American mascot names. Conclusions drawn from our empirical survey spotlighted the differences between assorted kinds, types, and contexts of Native American names. Through our analysis of the R-dskins advertisements in chapter 3, we found that the controversy is often constructed as one side that is against the use of all Native American mascots versus another that is agreeable to the status quo in all contexts and cultural environments; as we noted, that simply was not the case in the survey. For instance, the gap between the name "Braves" and some of the names scoring the lowest on our survey's scale (e.g., "Redskins" and "Savages") was as wide as the gap between "Braves" and most any other mainstream mascot name. Thus, we argue that distinctions among Native American mascot names must be understood.

The chapter then proceeded with a Washington R-dskins case from October 2013, when the controversy reached a zenith during the Change the Mascot group's magnified resistance to the Washington team name, all the way to July 2015, when a U.S. Federal Court denied the Washington team its trademark appeals. Our analysis of public comments appended to news stories was grounded in both self-categorization as a theory that underscored the vitriol of in-groups and out-groups and in postcolonialism, which explored the public discourse surrounding the R-dskins news coverage as one entrenched in colonial logics and decolonial responses.

We concluded in that chapter that pro-mascot and anti-mascot discourse within the R-dskins case substantiates a clear divide along neocolonial and decolonial lines. That is, for those who defend the mascot, arguments involve themes pivoted in ideologies of territoriality and possession as well as co-optation and appropriation. Resistance to the "R-dskins" moniker involved attempts to decolonize the mascot by calling into question the cultural power tied to the name and the Washington franchise owner's repudiation of any and all calls to change the mascot. In the end, Native mascotting—as emblemized by the R-dskins case—heightens the ways that neocolonization flourishes, but as a study in resistance it also illuminates how such power is attenuated through decolonizing rhetorical tactics.

Chapter 5 centered the visual landscape of Native American mascotting as its primary topic. The goal of the chapter's survey portion was to assess logos in empirical isolation in order to establish the specific roles that such images embody and to discover certain embedded elements that make one logo more or less acceptable or offensive than another. The survey data indicated that schools and teams seem to experience more difficulties with logos than names (especially the Cleveland "Indians"), while other teams, such as the Washington R-dskins, face problems with *both* logos and names. The double complications of a mascot like the R-dskins confirms an intensification of deep-rooted public perceptions of offensive mascotting logics. Ultimately, logos offer a multifaceted mechanism for exploring what elements are subsumed within the Native American mascot debate.

We coupled the survey data in chapter 5, yet again, with a critical reading of a case study. The case here centered on the Cleveland Indians mascot, most dramatically represented by the caricatured and infamous Chief Wahoo, to show how logos present even more complications across the topography of Native American mascotting than names alone. With the aid of Native-centered postcolonial and decolonial scholars, such as Glen Sean Couthard, Danielle Endres, and James Fenelon, we argued that the conspicuously visible and starkly circulated logo renders Native heritage unintelligible. In other words, logos help obfuscate how a public understands Native American temporality (pasts, presents, and futures). This is especially the case when visuals are made to be ubiquitous, habitual, and unimpeded. Exploring the rhetorical-visual dimensions of Chief Wahoo, we offered a postcolonial critique of how his image was used by the team to relate the Cleveland franchise's narrative and how fans channeled their fandom into visual "play" of Wahoo's visage and symbolism. We concluded by advancing a decolonial reading of activists who resisted Wahoo and, in turn, detourned the way that Native Americans are best understood as more multifaceted than the condensed narrative in which Wahoo features and through which the Cleveland Indians broker their so-called Native identity.

The volume's last core analytical piece, chapter 6, attended to rituals associated with Native American mascotting. Data from the survey was again accessed; this time rituals were appraised by looking at short YouTube clips of significant and pervasive Native American mascotting rituals that have been part of athletic events in both collegiate and professional sports contexts. As with our study of names and logos, respondents rated performances based on acceptability and inoffensiveness, again utilizing an eleven-point scale (0–10) with a higher number representing less problematic rituals on acceptability/inoffensiveness measures and lower scores indicating more problematic rituals on each of the two scales. The lower the number, the more offensive, unacceptable, and generally problematic respondents found the ritual to be. We specifically tested Florida State University's tomahawk chop, the Kansas City Chiefs' Nation war chant, the FSU war chant, and the dance of University of Illinois's Chief Illiniwek. The overall results we obtained emphasize the degree to which Native American rituals are endemic within the larger performances sports fans exhibit as a part of their identities tied to the team (or school).

The chapter then moved on to an analysis of mascotting rituals at FSU in terms of the performative aspects of Native American mascotting practices. We located FSU's ritual performances within the backdrop of "playing Indian." This concept involves fans embodying their own form of Nativeness through taking on the names, symbols, and practices of Native Americans by way of cultural surrogacy. To emphasize the importance of ritual in Native American mascotting practices, the postcolonial analysis explored "playing Indian" fanfare at FSU during its game-day rituals. Specifically, our neocolonial treatment of those rituals included an assessment of the Seminole War Chant and the tomahawk chop, Chief Osceola's ritual entrance into Doak Campbell Stadium, the Marching Chiefs band performances, and FSU fans donning stereotypically stylized Native American clothing. Ultimately we argued that rituals, as exemplified in FSU's game-day context, appear to be less focused on respect for Native Americans and about liberated spaces for indigenous people and far more about fan ownership of Native identity through their own surrogacy and "play."

Finally, chapter 7 explored the perceived stakes of the Native American mascot controversy. Using empirical surveys, we assessed these stakes through localized discussions of two related cases that nevertheless represent divergent stances of opinion formation and behavior. That is, we surveyed

Illinois fans about the removal of Chief Illiniwek and juxtaposed those responses to those of FSU fans and their fight to retain Chief Osceola. We found that the resistance University of Illinois fans felt a decade earlier had somewhat dissipated and that Florida State fans fervently believe that any change to current practices will result in long-held continual resistance and dissonance.

As we combined these two similar yet contrasting cases, we found, of course, that many fans expressed resistance to mascot changes. However, this resistance to changing the status quo had less to do with Native American culture and representation and much more to do with political processes, so-called political correctness, social anxieties, and the conflation of what is symbolically intended and received through mascots in terms of names, visuals, and rituals. As we also reported, fans saw in Chief Illiniwek (and continue to view in Chief Osceola) a challenge to their fan identity, but it would not merit a demotion of their fandom should the mascot be abolished. In other words, the stakes of removing mascots in terms of fandom are not that high, thus signaling that mascot changes are both acceptable and possible, according to fans at FSU and Illinois.

Cultural Impacts of Native American Mascotting Logics

Whether one agrees or disagrees with the findings of our quantitative analysis or the tone and valence of our more decolonial critical treatments of mascotting case studies, one common denominator stands out above all others and ought to be shared among all people settling into the plural points along the "keep/remove" spectrum: mascots both *mean* and *matter*. Because of this reality, the mascot controversy is not going away anytime soon, even if all Native American mascots were to be removed.

To be sure, those who subscribe to the status quo—namely, that mascot names, logos, and rituals are protected practices—have attempted to close the debate by claiming inconsequentiality. As we explored through the R-dskins case studies, inconsequentiality represents the "just get over it" argument on the part of pro-mascotters. Common discourse associated with this position runs the gamut from dismissals such as "there are more important issues to deal with" and "just stop, seriously stop; the world has a lot more to worry about" to political critiques in the vein of "it's too bad our government spends more time forcing sports teams to change their names." If Native American mascots were *not* debated in the public sphere, *not* considered in corporate sports advertising decisions, *not* contemplated at all levels of the federal court system, *not* defended with vitriol by sports franchises and universities, and *not* protested by both Native and non-Native folks alike, inconsequentiality would be a viable response. In that case, the issue might face symbolic removal and termination, thus eternally quashing any question about the mascot's efficacy. As a result, fait accompli would be the controversy's watchword. However, that is not the case.

Protests have not weakened, as evidenced by the establishment of the Change the Mascot organization and the *Blackhorse* case against the Washington R-dskins in 2013 that has wended its way through the federal courts. Cleveland Indians fans have continued to "de-chief" since the 2014 Twitter campaign that later catalyzed offline as fans protested with their bodily performances of redacted apparel. Even those who were previously pro-mascot have realized what the mascot means for the lived realities of Native Americans. As one University of Illinois fan noted, "At the time of [Illiniwek's] retirement, I thought it was political correctness run amok . . . as opposed to any genuine offense taken by Native Americans. Now, however, I realize the Chief and his performances were cultural misappropriation and offensive, albeit unintentionally."

For many anti-mascot protesters, specifically those involved in the R-dskins milieu, the issue is neither fleeting nor unpopular merely because a 2016 poll reported that 90 percent of Native Americans asked did not care about the issue. For instance, working from discussions with the Washington NFL franchise as early as 1972, R-dskins protesters have asserted that the debate is no flash in the political correctness pan: "There is a feeling that this is a new issue with us. It's nothing new. It's just that no one was listening."[1] More to the point of en masse Native American support for retiring the name and imagery associated with the R-dskins, an amicus curiae to the *Blackhorse* case reminded the federal courts that "as is plainly demonstrated by the descriptions of the Native American organizations [nearly thirty] participating in this brief, the Native Americans who find the term 'Redsk*ns' disparaging are not a 'small group of radicals,' nor is the Native American community 'deeply divided' on the issue." To the contrary, the group argued, the "vast majority of Native Americans find the term 'Redsk*ns' . . . to be deeply offensive and disparaging."[2]

Following suit, such resistance to mascotting has inevitably prompted powerful pro-mascotters to address the issue (including seeking Supreme Court writs of certiorari) in forthright fashion, even if these folks have simply retrenched their position, as R-dskins owner Daniel Snyder did in a May 2013 interview with *USA Today*: "We will never change the name of the team."[3] (To date, Snyder has not released a statement in the wake of the 2017 Supreme Court case; see below.) The point here is if the Native American mascot debate did not *mean* and *matter*, why are our publics—Native and non-Native, corporate and community-centered, pro-mascot and anti-mascot, vernacular and institutional, pop cultural and political/legal—so invested in the controversy? Given what we have uncovered in this book, we agree with the Associated Press that "we are a long way from consensus on [mascot] questions."[4]

The mascot controversy is neither a relic to be remembered as an asterisk in the annals of sports history and fandom culture nor is it a footnote kicked to the sentence's end, a page to be turned, or a chapter closed. Rather, we insist that the issue remains electric and as relevant and ardent as ever. Furthermore, given our analysis throughout this book, we contend that the status quo does not leave many viable paths to attain respect for Native Americans and does not genuinely offer sports franchises, universities, and their attendant fans and alumni many benefits that a changed mascot could not also provide.

On the latter point, there is really nothing much lost when (or if) Native American mascot names, logos, and rituals are retired. Chapter 7 indicates that fandom, as an example, would not change in noticeable ways, as substantiated by an Illinois fan base that seems as dedicated as ever a decade after retiring Chief Illiniwek. Teams would not lose revenue in the sense that fans would still continue to "show up" regardless of a change (in fact, a move to change names and logos would likely reactivate the sale of merchandise, because fans would want to supplement their collection of team accouterment). For instance, on a scale of 1 to 10, some 92 respondents at the University of Illinois rated a possible change in their fandom at 1.94 in light of Chief Illiniwek's retirement. This is low. In 2007, however, 4.42 of these fans agreed with retirement. Nine years later, the number crept *up* to 5.70, but perhaps even more noteworthy was that those who still disagree with the decision generally did not find any difference in their loyalty to the school. One fan summarized what may be the dominant sentiments of the "changed" fans, remarking, "I was proud of the University for making the right decision, although disappointed they essentially made it under duress. A mascot doesn't make the school. I don't understand the people who said they stopped being fans after the University retired the Chief."

The argument from those who still miss the mascot, however, tends to be exemplified with this sentiment: "I had always been a fan of the Chief as a kid and into my teens but that symbol wasn't the reason for my fandom."

A related survey of 147 respondents at Florida State University concluded that on a scale from 1 to 10, a change in the "Seminoles" moniker would still not result in any demonstrable change in their fandom ($M = 3.73$). Part of this higher number (than Illinois's respondents) most likely hinges on the *real* relationship solidified between FSU and the Seminole Tribe of Florida and the simultaneous *perceived* closed conclusion about the stability of the Seminole mascot because of that relationship. Many FSU fans would still be a bit frustrated with the university (e.g., "[My fandom wouldn't change], but I'd be disappointed the University gave in to this bullshit"), but it appears that as long as FSU fields a nationally competitive football team, they will have a packed stadium—whether they are the "Seminoles" or the "Swamp Foxes." Again, the mention here of the STF underscores why the change in fandom data point might be higher than it is at Illinois. Even for a mascotting school steeped in perhaps the most legitimized use of Native American imagery, the number of fans who would drop their support of FSU is considerably low, particularly when the FSU surveys seem to indicate that this number would drop even further if actually eliminating Chief Osceola and the rituals surrounding him.

On the former point, the status quo does not discernably help improve the respect offered to Native Americans by a larger U.S. public. As the National Congress of American Indians indicated about a June 19, 2017, Supreme Court decision that will likely allow the Washington franchise to keep its "R-dskins" trademarks:

> This is an issue we have always believed will not be solved in a courtroom, and this ruling does not change some very clear facts. Washington's football team promotes, markets and profits from the use of a word that is not merely offensive—it is a dictionary-defined racial slur designed from the beginning to promote hatred and bigotry against Native Americans. This is a word that was screamed at Native Americans as they were dragged at gunpoint off their lands.[5]

Furthermore, nearly every category of anti-mascot arguments detailed in chapters 3 and 4 (humanization, homology, ironic sentiments, alternative naming, temporality, ownership, and comparison) confirms that the *respect factor* is the one fundamental reagent intersecting the entire universe of the Native American mascot controversy.

Due to the low stakes of change for franchises, universities, and their fans, and because of the palpable benefits of such change for Native Americans, we wish to offer some ways the Native American mascot may diminish in quantity and perhaps in general presence over time. This aim is indeed decolonial in orientation. Of this type of scholarly labor, Raka Shome and Radha Hegde write that such research is "concerned with phenomena and [the] effects and affects of colonialism" through "not only . . . the framework of dominance but also . . . that of resistance."[6] We offer these nodes of change out of respect for Native Americans and also with the understanding that such changes are complicated for franchises and universities. We also believe there is common ground to be reached and that a dichotomous or deterministic solution is not required in order to forge the respectful and manageable end of Native American mascotting practices. In sum, we agree with R-dskins fan Paul Kendrick, who insists that being a fan of a team with a Native mascot "means loving our team enough to say that I'm in for the future. I'm in for changing the name for the better."[7]

Before we consider the question of "W(h)ither the Native American Mascot" by responding with avenues for change, we provide an update on a Supreme Court case that has all but ensured Dan Snyder and the Washington R-dskins will be able to retain their mascot name, logo, and, thus, performative rituals. Of course, Snyder's writ of certiorari to the high court is illustrative of how and why the Native American mascot controversy is not inconsequential (as pro-mascotters would have it) but rather is still very much alive. The franchise's adamant defense is proof positive that the issue has a long way yet to go.

Cultural Cloudiness in the 2017 Supreme Court Decision on the R-dskins

At the time of this writing, the U.S. Supreme Court has motivated a major development in the Washington R-dskins' appeal for reinstatement of its trademarks. In terms of the R-dskins' legal saga, we left off in chapter 4 with an outline of how the U.S. Patent and Trademark Office had decided to cancel six of the NFL franchise's trademarks, which they called "disparaging . . . to a substantial composite of Native Americans" based on the Lanham Act.[8] According to Supreme Court justice Samuel Alito, the USPTO's paramount issue was a provision of the Lanham Act, "which we will call 'the disparagement clause.' This provision prohibits the registration of a trademark 'which may disparage . . . persons, living or dead, institutions, beliefs, or national symbols, or bring them into contempt or disrepute.' This clause appeared in the original Lanham Act and has remained the same to this day."[9] The USPTO's cancellation came in spring of 2014 and was followed with a number of appeals from Snyder and the Washington R-dskins, noting that their First Amendment rights had been violated. A federal appeals court agreed with the USPTO in July 2015. In this way the court upheld the prohibition of the R-dskins' name and logos based on the assumed disgrace heaped on Native Americans by the mascot. Snyder and the franchise sought a writ of certiorari to the Supreme Court, and the case was to be considered during the 2016–2017 session. The high court never did hear the R-dskins' case, but another related First Amendment case involving potential cultural disparagement vis-à-vis an ethnically associated trademark was heard and held in the affirmative, likely yielding promise for pro-mascot advocates and, specifically, for the Washington franchise's trademarks.

The case in question, *Matal v. Tam*, involved an Asian American rock band called "The Slants," who had previously defeated a USPTO rescindment of its trademark name. The USPTO had cancelled the trademark because "slants" is a racial epithet used to cast excoriation at people of Asian descent (a stereotyped image of essentialized eye shape). The federal government then asked that the Supreme Court hear the case. The high court added the case to its docket and agreed with the Slants, represented by lead singer Simon Tam, that any annulment of the trademark would violate the First Amendment. Justice Alito wrote the majority opinion, holding the following: "We have said time and again that 'the public expression of ideas may not be prohibited merely because the ideas are themselves offensive to some of their hearers.' . . . For this reason, the disparagement clause cannot be saved by analyzing it as a type of government program in which some content- and speaker-based restrictions are permitted."[10] In challenging the Lanham Act's "disparagement clause," the Supreme Court returned the trademark back to the Slants in the June 19, 2017, decision. Predictably, the R-dskins franchise immediately viewed the case as a victory. And this is likely the result of the ruling in *Tam*.[11]

Interestingly, the Tam case brings to bear a character and credibility element that is *not* present in Snyder's and the Washington franchise's case. That is, the Washington R-dskins are not a group of Native Americans arguing for the use of a Native American name, logo, or performative ritual for themselves as indigenous peoples. In Tam's case, he chose the Slants' "name as an act of re-appropriation—taking a name sometimes used to disparage Asian Americans and owning it as a badge of pride, thereby robbing the slur of its power."[12] Here we have an Asian American appellee re/assuming an ethnic stereotype and racial epithet conjured by the dominant public to decolonize the term itself for the betterment of Asian Americans. Such a resistive rhetorical tactic is similar to African Americans "taking back" the N-word. In nonethnic contexts, this textual protest maneuver also remains akin to women re/appropriating the B-word, the LGBTQ community resituating and using the word "queer," and people with disabilities reclaiming the word "crip." Alito actually used the "ownership" component of the Slants case in his holding. He reasoned, "The band members believe that by taking that slur as a name of their group, they will help to 'reclaim' the term and drain it of its denigrating force."[13] Moreover, Alito continued by writing that the trademark is tied to Asian American identity in particular, therein begging the question of whether Native American identities could commensurably be considered in the decision to assail the Lanham Act's disparagement clause. He contended that Tam "chose this moniker in order to 'reclaim' and 'take ownership' of stereotypes about people of Asian ethnicity. The group 'draws inspiration for its lyrics from childhood slurs and mocking nursery rhymes' and has given its albums names such as 'The Yellow Album' and 'Slanted Eyes, Slanted Hearts.'"[14]

Perhaps in the future the pairing of the Slants case and the R-dskins case will be seen as disproportionate given the differences in the ethos that each agent (Tam and Snyder, respectively) commands with respect to the ethnic case in which they are entrenched. As a vital footnote, Tam himself remarked that "he does not like the Washington team's name."[15] To Tam, the "R-dskins" name is clearly seen as reprehensible even compared to a word like "slants," or, in the least, Tam's cultural ownership of "slants" may be seen as more palatable compared to the Washington franchise, whose leadership—historically and contemporarily—is not Native American.

The current opinion among the media is that the R-dskins and their mascot names, images, and rituals will concurrently be held harmless when it comes to Lanham's disparagement clause. Ostensibly, the assumption is that the trademarks will be returned based on the Slants case. The *Los Angeles Times* reported, "It appears to mean that the Redskins also will be able to continue using their name, even though it offends people,"[16] and *Forbes* writer Darren Heitner wrote, "The Washington Redskins should be able to claw back at federal trademark registrations after the Supreme Court ruling. . . . It is safe to assume that the Washington Redskins will be able to take up its fight for reinstatement of its own registrations and likely succeed in its efforts."[17] The media has speculated in a prospective and future tense. Meanwhile, as we note above, the R-dskins camp has commented in the present tense about the Slants case with certitude that the Washington franchise is in the clear. R-dskins attorney Lisa Blatt told the *Chicago Sun-Times* that "the Team is thrilled with today's unanimous decision as it resolves the Redskins' long-standing dispute with the government. The Supreme Court vindicated the Team's position that the First Amendment blocks the government from denying or cancelling a trademark registration based on the government's opinion."[18] Words like "resolves" and "vindicate[d]" unmistakably signify the sense of a self-evident irreversibility vis-à-vis the R-dskins case. Snyder was reported to have said he was "thrilled" at the decision because it had pulled the team off the hook.[19]

Seemingly, the Washington R-dskins organization believes the *Matal v. Tam* judgment represents a carte blanche license to continue its mascot use. Of course, there is a difference between legal justifications and ethical and even moral justifications. As Dr. Martin Luther King Jr. wrote in his "Letter from a Birmingham Jail" in 1963, there are just and unjust laws. He argued, "I would be the first to advocate obeying just laws. One has not only a legal but also a moral responsibility to obey just laws. Conversely, one has a moral responsibility to disobey unjust laws. . . . An unjust law is a code that is out of harmony with the moral law."[20] If we agree that mascots disrespect and harm Native Americans, perhaps the ruling on the Slants case ought to be reconsidered on the basis of ethical and moralistic grounds—namely, the cherished and understood code that human dignity ought to eclipse any corporation's wish to appropriate indigeneity, legality be damned.

Of course, there are few, if any, utopian remedies in public life, especially when it comes to cultural issues as a whole and First Amendment interpretations in the legal sphere, specifically. To assume exactitude between the Slants and the R-dskins would be premature at best and shambolic at worst. The *Washington Times* reported, "The Washington Redskins aren't in the clear with their team name just yet, even after the Supreme Court ruled."[21] This is so for a number of reasons. The first involves the cultural landscape of the word "r-dskin." We need to recall that the term is still considered deleterious to a great number of Native Americans. For instance, an amicus curiae in the *Blackhorse* case argued:

> Born at a time in our history when the national policy was to seize Indian land and resources, and hunt down Indian people who stood in the way, the term "Redsk[*]n" has been perpetuated through such media as western movies and television. Most often the term is coupled with derogatory adjectives, as "dirty Redsk[*]n" or "pesky 'Redsk[*]n" which is used interchangeably

with the word "savage" to portray misleading and denigrating images of the Native American.[22]

Change the Mascot, the NCAI, and others have vowed to continue pushing on the disparagement clause. The former two argue that "if the NFL wants to live up to its statements about placing importance on equality, then it shouldn't hide behind these rulings, but should act to end this hateful and degrading slur."[23] The rulings, applied to *Tam* but not yet to Snyder's case, will indubitably be challenged by the Native-centered groups at other court levels and, as the above quotation indicates, to the NFL as well.

The second reason that the Washington franchise is not in the clear involves money. David Carter, professor of sports business at the University of Southern California, has pondered the social and business realms the Washington franchise inhabits. He told the *Washington Times*:

> Just because the Redskins may believe they're in the clear or the Cleveland Indians or even some collegiate teams (think) they're in the clear, that doesn't mean that those that do business with the team, including its sponsors, are going to take their foot off the gas if they believe change is really required. A positive legal ruling may not yield beneficial business impacts in and around the sports business world because we've seen heightened sensitivity over the years to this topic.[24]

This type of potential outcome is a result, in many ways, of the NCAI's and the American Indian Movement's public education campaigns and the ongoing presence of anti-mascotting protest over the years. Even in the midst of what appears to be a dismal Supreme Court outcome, the NCAI responded in a press release on June 19, 2017, that activists have "raised awareness about the problems with mascots such as the R-word epithet used by the Washington NFL team, and brought the important issue of mascotization to the forefront of social consciousness."[25] Advertisers are well aware of the choppy waters that must be navigated regarding sponsoring sports teams or universities with Native American mascots. This may be so as consciousness raising has been a fifty-year rhetorical tactic of the anti-mascot set. But even aside from corporate sponsors, fans and university constituents could still have a say about their teams via their economic support. Lawyer Brian LaCorte argues that if, in the future, fans or students "don't like their slogan, mascot, or trademark and/or the marketplace—those tickets or support of the athletic programs of the university in general—I think will still be a driver on what is acceptable and what is not. It will become, I think, a point for the consumer marketplace to define parameters."[26]

Speaking of the future of both the Washington R-dskins and Native American mascots in general, we finalize this chapter with some thoughts on changing mascotting culture in the United States.

W(h)ither the Native American Mascot?

As an ultimate conclusion, we assert that the endgame of the Native American mascot controversy is to stop appropriating and controlling Native names, images, and performances in neocolonial ways that are reflective of long-standing logics such as territoriality, control, and benevolence. Again, as we noted earlier, fandom does not seem to be compromised with the removal of Native American mascots. However, the continued presence and actuation of these mascots underwrite both material and symbolic harm for Native communities. The NCAI reported the following in 2013: "As these stereotypes continue to be perpetuated by national and local media and popular culture, Native youth—the fastest growing segment of the Native population—are at an increased risk of harm, both self-inflicted and by those who are non-Native. NCAI's position to end negative and harmful stereotypes is directly linked to our ongoing efforts to build a healthy and nurturing environment for Native youth to flourish and become the next generation of leaders and Native citizens."[27] This view is supported by the American Psychological Association, the American Sociological Association, and the National Association for the Advancement of Colored People. Even the NCAA—at least in theory—agrees with the argument that mascots can harm, insisting in 2005 that it "objects to institutions using racial, ethnic, national origin references in their intercollegiate athletics programs. . . . As an association, we believe that mascots, nicknames, and images deemed hostile or abusive in terms of race, ethnicity, or national origin should not be visible."[28] Moreover, the state of California has banned the "r-dskins" mascot in public schools, and between 1990 and 2012 more than thirty public schools have changed their Native American mascots. Even more universities and colleges have been added to that list, including Dartmouth, the University of North Dakota, Stanford University, Marquette University, Miami University, Syracuse University, the College of William and Mary, and St. John's University.

More poignant and vital for this book's analysis, respondents to our surveys also revealed trepidation about the impact of Native American mascot names, logos, and rituals on the lived realities of indigenous peoples. The final dénouement to the controversy should be motivated by the question, Given the turmoil—often culturally cataclysmic—related to the Native American mascot debate, why not just change mascotting culture? We answer this query affirmatively by discussing five avenues where change may be possible.

AVENUE #1: LINE OF DECLIVITY

As one may surmise, the lowest-hanging fruit in terms of changing Native American mascotting culture involves the Washington R-dskins. A venomous, colonial term used throughout centuries of Native-European relationships to control the land, labor, bodies, languages, sovereignty, liberties, economies, religions, cultural lifeways, and symbols of indigenous peoples, the word "r-dskins" connotes a history of oppression translating into presents and futures of related difficulties. According to former NCAI executive director Leon Cook, the epithet is one that is endemic to Native concerns. He once wrote, "I have traveled extensively throughout Indian country, met with Native American leaders on dozens of reservations, and talked with Native Americans from all walks of life. I have only rarely encountered a Native American who has expressed disagreement with my understanding that the Washington football team's name is disparaging, discriminatory, and offensive to Native Americans."[29] C. Richard King, the preeminent scholar of the Native American mascot controversy, offers a summary of the word that is exquisite in its brevity: "*Redskins* is a problem."[30] And when the owner of a sports franchise like Larry Dolan, whose Cleveland team mascot is the Indians, actually says, "If we were the Redskins, the day after I owned the team, the name would have been changed," then one need not guess too much at the level of negative valence accorded to the term in our popular and political consciousness.[31]

During an interview with current NCAI executive director, Jacqueline Pata, we confirmed why the R-dskins case is so very important to the larger anti-mascot position. Simply put, as the worst insult to and dastardliest metonymy of indigenous communities, "r-dskins" is a term most Native Americans are eager to remove from popular culture and whose defeat they are poised to parlay into the retirements of other Native American mascots. Pata argued, "The worst offender is the Washington team and its name. We believe that if the name of the worst offender goes away, then the others will follow suit." We call this tactic of mascotting change "the line of declivity." In this instantiation for change, the argument is that as goes the r-dskin mascot, so, too, go others that at first blush might appear more acceptable and less offensive.

The R-dskins mascot, in other words, is the first and most imposing domino to fall that could potentially enact a chain reaction.

The NCAI and others have not given up on the Washington R-dskins cause in the wake of the decision in the Slants case. Despite the Supreme Court's holding on the *Tam* case, Pata cosigned the NCAI's June 19, 2017, press release that read in part, "We are gratified that this Supreme Court case amplified the intensifying public debate over the NFL's support for bigotry against Native Americans. The work of Amanda Blackhorse and other leading activists fighting against the use of the R-word has been tremendously successful and critically important."[32] The line of declivity starts with the R-dskins. From there, if our quantitative data is any indication, the line would next point to "Indians" (perhaps with Cleveland's Major League Baseball team in the crosshairs); then to tribally specific mascots that are unsupported by a Native nation (i.e., "Aztecs," "Illini," "Sioux," "Chippewa," "Choctaws"); then to a mascot like "Seminoles" that is supported by the STF; then to more genericized names and logos such as those boasted by the Kansas City Chiefs and the Atlanta Braves. Recall that earlier fan comments proffered by adherents of FSU, Illinois, and the Cleveland Indians tended to use the R-dskins mascot as a bedeviled foil against which to gauge the more angelic mascots associated with their respective teams. Indeed, without the fall of a team named for what many consider "the N-word for Native Americans," there will likely be no declivity to speak of at all.[33]

AVENUE #2: EDUCATION

The issue of education is another venue through which Native American mascotting culture could ultimately change. Education seems to hold a special place in both the pro-mascotting and anti-mascotting camps. Those who profess to support a Native American mascot have often argued that mascots teach the larger public about Native American history and culture. As one respondent at Illinois wrote in 2016, "Chief [Illiniwek] is the only reason I've come across in my life that peaks my interest in learning more about Native American history. . . . I still believe that Chief can be a symbol that continues to educate students on Native American history." Mascots in this ideation, therefore, are claimed to teach some semblance of authentic Indianness. Typically this pro-mascot argument is coupled with some benevolence. That is, while the Native American mascot "teaches," it also simultaneously remains incumbent upon the pupils to enact the lesson unfurling from that teachable moment in a type of cultural quid pro quo. Brenda Farnell calls this practice "good intentions making our actions moral," the claim that feigned indigenous symbols controlled by sports franchises and universities ought to be protected.[34] In 2007 one commenter wrote on a Save the Chief Facebook page, "If Illiniwek does not keep alive the very thought in people's minds of the Illini, then it will die. . . . We must step into the breech and promote the memory of the Illini. I, for one, will not let the memory of the Illini people die. That memory is our heritage too and that is something no one should be permitted to take from us." Interestingly, as Susan Ryan reminds us, "Asserting what will contribute to the well-being of another . . . is best understood as an exercise of power in itself."[35] The question becomes *who* gets to educate and about, on, and for *whom*.

Education, too, occupies quite a bit of anti-mascot rhetorical aims. In a recent interview, Pata spoke directly of the need for Native Americans to help educate the larger public about indigenous history and lifeways. The mascot controversy, of course, can be massaged into such an opportunity for community pedagogy. Of this social change tactic, we reiterate what Pata said as offered in this book's introduction:

> We always felt that our best strategy is to educate America about who we really are. Educating the common fan, educating the schools, educating the cities, and the other people who care about their home teams. A lot of times, these fans haven't yet considered the breadth of the impacts of the team's mascot, especially on the mental health of Native youth. Once they open themselves up to learning about, for example, the origins and history of the term that the Washington team uses as its name—a racial slur that treats Native peoples as less than human—we find them willing to support our cause.

Recall, too, that many anti-mascotters remarked about the convoluted senses of history from which pro-mascotters reason. In fact, the issue of temporality was spotlighted as a decolonizing logic tendered by those who vehemently resist Native American mascots. For example, one individual at a Cleveland Indians protest rally held a sign that read "Chief Wahoo is offensive. Learn Native American HISTORY." Also, a famous image circulating around the Cleveland Indian milieu presents Chief Joseph (Nez Perce) alongside Chief Wahoo with the words "dignified," "honorable," and "respectful" emblazoned above Chief Joseph and the words "disgraceful," "shameful," and "racist" sublimated under the smiling red face of Wahoo, thereby setting into relief historical Native Americans with caricatured versions.

All of this is to say that education matters in the crucible of the Native American mascot controversy; from a social change perspective, many hang their hopes on the possibility that future generations will learn from the misgivings of their forebears. Pata spoke of posterity in the above quotation, but others do as well. For King, education is one of the principal strides toward retiring Native American mascots. He recently explained that "a good first step might be for state legislatures and school boards to mandate increased mainstreaming of American Indian history. On the other hand, increased emphasis on media literacy and critical thinking will enable students and citizens to make sense of what is being said in a given moment and why it matters, allowing them to assess images, unpack rhetoric, and decipher significance in a more sophisticated and systematic fashion."[36] The undercurrent behind Pata's and King's sentiments is that the dominant public remains mostly mindless, typically thoughtless, and wholly uncritical about Native American culture and, subsequently, punctuate the same lapses when it comes to how Native Americans ought to be represented in responsible ways (versus caricatured in inexcusable fashion).

Teaching becomes decolonial in its aims of laying bare and stripping down gross and anachronistic stereotypes of Native Americans and likewise countering the uncultivated and muddled narratives that the American public tends to craft about Native-U.S. relationships. The optimism of education is made resplendent by Washington R-dskins fan Paul Kendrick. Working through white reflexivity, Kendrick notes the backwardness of a number of R-dskins fans (in particular) and what he predicts education can foment: "There's gonna come a time—I don't know when it is, 20 years, 40 years, whenever—there's gonna come a time when people are gonna look back and say can you believe those idiots thought Redskins was appropriate? . . . That day is coming, because the Redskins will be so far removed from the NFL you're gonna need a microscope to find it. It's here for now, but it won't be for long."[37]

AVENUE #3: ECONOMIC PRESSURE

Another thoroughfare for change appears to revolve around profit-based contexts. It requires precious little exposition to make the claim that sports are vital as a part of the national economy. From ticket and merchandise sales to media contracts, advertising transactions, product endorsements, and local "footprints" (i.e., hotels, restaurants, taxis/Ubers, etc.), sports economies reign near the top of America's financial food chain. The R-dskins franchise alone, reports the *Washington Times*, is "the fifth most valuable team in the NFL at $2.95 billion."[38] It is said that money talks, but it also runs, pitches, catches, tackles, slap-shots, and slides its way into our cultural sports consciousness.

Absent legal success, as we are currently witnessing with the 2017 Supreme Court decision about the "disparagement clause" vis-à-vis ethnic trademarks, some have suggested that economic anxieties are a surefire way to push the effort to retire Native American mascots even further into the public sphere. Journalist Steve Whyno opines, "Supreme Court precedent may help the club in its ongoing legal battle, but the fight over the Redskins moniker will continue in social and business realms. The Redskins, Cleveland Indians with their 'Chief Wahoo' logo and other professional and college organizations featuring Native American nicknames and mascots cannot be censored by the U.S. government, but that doesn't take the pressure off."[39] Whyno is referring to the power of advertisers to back out of team sponsorships based on the latter's use of Native American mascots. What he does not mention—but what can be implied or extended—is the power of the boycott.

The boycott has been a long-standing rhetorical action related to social change overall but especially connected to decoloniality as a rhetorical move. Jill Lane argues that to resist power, one must bother and disrupt typical functions of the status quo. She writes, "The only viable avenue for oppositional practice is to produce calculated 'disturbance' in the rhizomatic or 'liquid' networks of power itself."[40] The expression "liquid" here very clearly may refer to the material realm; in the case of sports economies, we are talking about money. Boycotts have traditionally reaped benefits for social change efforts. This is particularly true for the American labor movement and the black liberation movement (i.e., mainstream civil rights and black power). The tactic of withholding personal capital by redirecting purchasing power away from a target or multiple marks, along with motivating advertisers and cottage corporations to do the same, can certainly impact social and cultural politics.

Though not many contemporary anti-mascotters suggest the boycott as a formidable tactic of social change, the cultural pump is primed for activists to start attracting corporate legitimizers in their campaign to end Native American mascotting practices. After all, according to St. Johns University intellectual property law professor Jeremy Sheff, "While the Supreme Court has essentially shut the door on legal challenges to the Redskins name, 'there can still be social pressure brought to bear.'"[41] Seeking the help of advertisers, thereby relying on and harnessing energy from corporate authorities that have the ears of mascotting franchises or institutions, is one way to engage in boycotts.[42] Another is to boycott those very legitimizers who cosign for mascotting entities by sponsoring their teams. If "X" company, perhaps already sensitive to public controversies surrounding mascots, fears that collusion with mascotters will impact their profit margin, it might reconsider its support of said mascotters.

In the R-dskins' case it appears that Snyder will soon attempt to seek public funding for a new stadium. The arena debate will likely ascend as the next topography across which the "R-dskins" moniker could be challenged. Carter predicts that the likelihood of Snyder "being able to accomplish that in this environment is really slim until or unless he changes the name of the team. I think it's going to boil down to money and what will the trade-offs be."[43] Consequently, even if the Supreme Court links the success of Tam's First Amendment case to the Washington R-dskins' case, cultural and economic pressures could buoy the R-dskins controversy as a hot-button issue for years to come.

AVENUE #4: JOURNALISTIC PROTEST

Working with and against third-party corporate legitimizers is called "coact-ive strategies" of social change.[44] A related coactive strategy for substantially changing Native American mascotting practices involves engaging the sports media in symbolic and material agitation against franchises and universities who peddle in Native American names, imagery, and performances. The sports media are *the* primary channel through which the public experiences sports culture, whether by consuming sporting events (proper) or by learning more about sporting scenes through both on- and off-field news.

We have already discussed Bob Costas's verbal screed against the R-dskins mascot during an October 2013 NFL game between Washington and the Dallas Cowboys. In addition, we have outlined the stand taken by Canadian sportscaster Jerry Horwath, who refused to say "Indians" during Cleveland's 2016 American League Championship Series with the Toronto Blue Jays; Horwath also revealed to the public, "For the rest of my career I will not say 'Indian' or 'Brave' and if I was in the NFL I would not say 'Redskins.'"[45] Others in the sports media have also come forward to insist on some modicum of change. Media outlets and sports reporters associated with the magazines *Slate*, *Mother Jones*, and the *New Republic* have dropped Native American mascots from their lexicon. Newspapers such as the *Oregonian*, the *Portland (ME) Press Herald*, the *Kansas City Star*, the *Lincoln (NE) Journal Star*, and the *St. Cloud Times* have refused to print the word "R-dskins." Following suit, *Sports Illustrated*'s Peter King and *USA Today*'s Christine Brennan will not say or write "R-dskins" in their sports spots and pieces, respectively. And in July 2013, NFL Hall of Famers Darrell Green and Art Monk admitted that a change to the "R-dskins" name "deserves and warrants" further consideration because of its disparaging connotations of and for Native Americans. Notably, both of these former players were a part of Washington's franchise during their careers.[46] Former NFL coach and current football commentator Tony Dungy sides with Green and Monk. Their agreement raises the question of whether a future Washington R-dkins draftee would ever refuse to join the team based on its mascotting practices.

These decisions by sports journalists and television commentators involve difficult rhetorical choices and require some sacrifices in terms of their overall careers and ethos in the eyes of sports fans, especially those adherents supporting franchises and schools with Native American mascots. In an early study of mascotting culture, media scholar Robert Jensen contended that such a decision requires the contemplation of a two-part test. "For journalists, there are two questions to consider, one general and one specific to their trade," he argued. "First, is it ethically and politically responsible for sports teams that have no connection to Native Americans to use Native American names and images for nicknames and logos? Second, if teams retain those names and logos, should news media outlets independently choose to stop using them in news accounts? The answers offered here are no and yes, respectively."[47] Seemingly, some journalists have agreed with such a two-part test, particularly since the 2005 and 2007 NCAA ban lists and sanctions against universities with Native American mascots, the 2013–2017 R-dskins debacle, and the 2016 ALCS and World Series involving the Cleveland Indians.

When it comes down to the mechanics of changing Native American mascots, anti-mascotters require the ethos of legitimizers. "Insiders," such as members of the sports media, wield influence; they are the mouthpieces through which the public receives, internalizes, and interrogates sport culture, and therefore think, feel, and act on their own sports identities and team fandom. Journalist-citizens who are committed to changing the mascot represent a rare case when members of an institution, of the establishment, can actually work to dismantle colonial practices from the inside. Though we are doubtful they recognize it as such, Costas, Horwath, Dungy, and crew help decolonize the oppressive power dynamics at work in Native American names, logos, and performances.

AVENUE #5: LEGAL CHALLENGES

Finally, as one might imagine, legal challenges will continue to enter into the controversy and will concomitantly catalyze anti-mascotting efforts to retire Native American mascots. In terms of the R-dskins legal case itself, a potential veil might be pierced with Justice Alito's reminder of Lanham's two-part test in the Slants case. In his majority opinion, Alito explained:

> When deciding whether a trademark is disparaging, an examiner at the [US] PTO generally applies a "two-part test." The examiner first considers "the likely meaning of the matter in question, taking into account not only dictionary definitions, but also the relationship of the matter to the other elements in the mark, the nature of the goods or services, and the manner in which the mark is used in the marketplace in connection with the goods or services." "If that meaning is found to refer to identifiable persons, institutions, beliefs or national symbols," the examiner moves to the second step, asking "whether that meaning may be disparaging to a substantial composite of the referenced group."[48]

Certainly, the dictionary definition of "slants" indicates a connotative meaning associated with Asian Americans. However, if context matters—if connotation has any power and commands even a scintilla of importance within a Native-U.S. socialscape—then it is possible the word "r-dskins" satisfies the Lanham Act's test more so than "slants." This is so because the difference between Asian American and Native American milieus is that the latter is ensconced in colonialism and, now, neocolonial logics.

Denotation matters, of course, but so does contextual connotation. As King writes, "['R-dskins'] is best regarded as a racial slur. . . . This should unsettle us. The word has deep connections to the history of anti-Indian violence, marked by ethnic cleansing, dispossession, and displacement. It is a term of contempt and derision that targets indigenous people. As much a weapon as a word, then, it injures and excludes, denying history and humanity."[49] The long-standing history of European-Native contact in North America, and the use of "r-dskin" as an emblem to commit physical violence and social death against Native Americans, deepens the harm associated with the word as a mascot name.

If the fallout from the 2017 *Matal v. Tam* case does *not* positively impact Snyder and the Washington franchise, we may well witness the next domino falling, and a sizable one at that. If the reality of the R-dskins mascot—combined with educational efforts, economic pressure, journalistic protest, and other legal challenges—is its ultimate retirement, the line of declivity will be ripe for, as Roberto Rodriguez has called it, "plotting the assassination of little Red Sambo."[50]

Coda: Mascotted America

Jensen makes perhaps the most cogent point regarding changes to the mascot controversy. He argues, "Clearly, whether a few teams use derogatory names and symbols is not the only, or most important, item on the agenda of Native Americans. But when the costs of change [on the part of pro-mascotters] are so small, there is no credible reason not to change, even if that change is not the single most important issue concerning Native Americans."[51] Indeed, as our quantitative analysis and critical, postcolonial explorations into Native American mascot names, logos, and performances indicate, this is unquestionably the case. Survey respondents find these three realms of the mascot anywhere from modestly to considerably offensive and unacceptable (in different layers depending on the mascot in question); Native American leaders, specifically the nation's largest organization (NCAI), believe the same to be true. Postcolonial analysis reveals how Native American mascots replicate—in neocolonial ways—the logics of settler-colonialism. And, most vitally, those anti-mascotters who have toiled for decades on the ground and in the trenches of the courtroom, stadium, classroom, and conference space disclose how very poisonous the "mascotting of Native America" can be for indigenous peoples and for the nation as a whole.

We hope that sometime in the very near future decolonial activists such as Amanda Blackhorse will never have to utter deflated words in the wake of legal defeat like "This is just another day for Native Americans. This is nothing new for us. There is rarely any justice for Native Americans."[52] Rather, if respect and honor, responsibility and civic engagement, community and cultural sanctity, sensibility and sensitivity, genuinely mean anything in the American *civis*, we will take heart in the words of the National Coalition on Racism in Sports and Media and lifelong mascot activist Charlene Teeters: "For Native leadership and allies working on the mascot issue, the call nationwide is to work towards the elimination of the misrepresentation and abuses of Indian images, names and spiritual way of life. . . . And the rallying call is, American Indians are a People, Not Mascots. . . . We are human beings."[53]

Notes

Introduction

1. John Woodrow Cox, Scott Clement, and Theresa Vargas, "New Poll Finds 9 in 10 Native Americans Aren't Offended by Redskins Name," *Washington Post*, May 19, 2016, https://www.washingtonpost.com/local/new-poll-finds-9-in-10-native-americans-arent-offended-by-redskins-name/2016/05/18/3ea11cfa-161a-11e6-924d-838753295f9a_story.html?utm_term=.7e6a9076b26d.

2. Jacqueline Keeler, "On the Shameful and Skewed 'Redskins' Poll," *The Nation*, May 25, 2016, https://www.thenation.com/article/on-the-shameful-and-skewed-redskins-poll.

3. Cindy Boren and Scott Allen, "Daniel Snyder, Former Coach Pleased with Redskins Name Poll, Ex-Player Upset," *Washington Post*, May 19, 2016, https://www.washingtonpost.com/news/dc-sports-bog/wp/2016/05/19/reaction-to-latest-redskins-name-poll-despite-results-strong-emotions-remain/?utm_term=.dc524a3549d2.

4. Keeler, "On the Shameful and Skewed 'Redskins' Poll."

5. Jay Rosenstein, "How Do Native Americans Really Feel about the Washington Redskins Nickname? Don't Use the Phone," *Huffington Post*, May 31, 2016, http://www.huffingtonpost.com/jay-rosenstein/how-do-native-americans-really-feel-about-redskins-nickname_b_10199688.html.

6. Samuel Alito, "Majority Opinion," *Matal v. Tam*, 582 U.S. __ (2017).

7. Matt Reevy, "The Seven Most Popular Names in Team Sports," *Sports Cheat Sheet*, September 16, 2014, http://www.cheatsheet.com/sports/the-7-most-popular-team-names-in-american-sports.html/?a=viewall.

8. Moni Basu, "Native American Mascots: Pride or Prejudice?" *CNN.com*, April 4, 2013, http://inamerica.blogs.cnn.com/2013/04/04/native-american-mascots-pride-or-prejudice/comment-page-7.

9. Miguel Bustillo, "Bill to Ban Indian Mascots Is Blocked," *Los Angeles Times*, May 29, 2002, http://articles.latimes.com/2002/may/29/local/me-mascot29.

10. Brendan O'Neill, "Is 'Redskins' Really an Offensive Name for a Football Team?," *Reason*, October 20, 2013, http://reason.com/archives/2013/10/20/is-redskins-really -an-offensive-name-for.

11. Theresa Vargas and Annys Shin, "President Obama Says 'I'd Think about Chang-ing' Name of Washington Redskins," *Washington Post*, October 5, 2013, https://www .washingtonpost.com/local/president-obama-says-id-think-about-changing-name -of-washington-redskins/2013/10/05/e170b914-2b70-11e3-8ade-a1f23cda135e_story .html?utm_term=.187e5d8c5e74.

12. Lynn Bartels, "Lamar, Home of the Savages, Defends Mascot as Culture Wars Rage," *Denver Post*, April 2, 2015, http://www.denverpost.com/2015/04/02/lamar -home-of-the-savages-defends-mascot-as-culture-wars-rage.

13. John Oliver, "How Is There a Team Still Called the Redskins?," *Last Week To-night with John Oliver*, June 14, 2014.

14. Laurel R. Davis, "Protest against the Use of Native American Names/Logos: A Challenge to Traditional American Identity," *Journal of Sport & Social Issues* 17 (1993): 9–22.

15. Quoted in Travis Waldron, "MLB Commissioner to Discuss Chief Wahoo Logo with Cleveland Owner after World Series," *Huffington Post*, October 27, 2016, http://www.huffingtonpost.com/entry/rob-manfred-cleveland-indians-logo_us _58123623e4b0990edc2fa7b2.

16. Sudie Hofmann, "The Elimination of Indigenous Mascots, Logos, and Nick-names: Organizing on College Campuses," *American Indian Quarterly* 29 (2005): 156–77.

17. Jennifer Guiliano, *Indian Spectacle: College Mascots and the Anxiety of Modern America* (New Brunswick, NJ: Rutgers University Press, 2015), 117.

18. Jason Edward Black, *American Indians and the Rhetoric of Removal and Allot-ment* (Jackson: University Press of Mississippi, 2015); James V. Fenelon and Clifford E. Trafzer, "From Colonialism to Denial of California Genocide to Mis-Representation: Indigenous Struggles in the Americas," *American Behavioral Scientist* 58 (2014): 3–29; Raka Shome, "Postcolonial Interventions in the Rhetorical Canon: An 'Other' View," *Communication Theory* 6 (1996): 40–59.

19. Ives Goddard, "'I am a Red-Skin': The Adoption of a Native American Expres-sion (1769–1826)," *European Review of Native American Studies* 19 (2005): 1–20.

20. Guiliano, *Indian Spectacle*, 110.

21. Ellen J. Staurowsky, "An Act of Honor or Exploitation? The Cleveland Indians' Use of the Louis Francis Sockalexis Story," *Sociology of Sport Journal* 17 (1998): 299–316; Michelle Renee Jacobs, *Framing Pseudo-Indian Mascots: The Case of Cleveland* (Kent, OH: Kent State University Press, 2007).

22. Steve Wulf, "Why Use of Native American Nicknames Is an Obvious Affront," *ESPN.com*, September 3, 2014, http://www.espn.com/espn/otl/story/_/id/11426021/ why-native-american-nicknames-stir-controversy-sports.

23. Dwanna Robertson, "Invisibility in the Color-Blind Era: Examining Legitimized Racism against Indigenous Peoples," *American Indian Quarterly* 39 (2005): 113–54.

24. R. W. Connell, *Gender and Power: Society, the Person, and Sexual Politics* (Palo Alto, CA: Stanford University Press, 1987); George Gerbner and Lawrence Gross, "Living with Television: The Violence Profile," *Journal of Communication* 26 (1976): 172–99.

25. Erik Brady, "The Real History of Native American Team Names," *USA Today*, August 24, 2016, http://www.usatoday.com/story/sports/2016/08/24/real-history -native-american-team-names/89259596.

26. James V. Fenelon, *Redskins? Sport Mascots, Indian Nations, and White Racism* (New York: Routledge, 2017), 121.

27. Steven Pinker, *The Blank Slate: The Modern Denial of Human Nature* (New York: Penguin Books, 2003).

28. James McWhorter, "Why 'Redskins' Is a Bad Word," *Time*, October 12, 2015, http://time.com/4070537/redskins-linguistics.

29. Chris Rock, "Redskins? That's Not Nice. That's a Racial Slur," Indian Country Media Network, July 30, 2014, https://indiancountrymedianetwork.com/culture/ sports/chris-rock-redskins-thats-not-nice-thats-a-racial-slur.

30. Russell G. Thornton, ed., *Studying Native Americans: Problems and Prospects* (Madison: University of Wisconsin Press, 1998).

31. Elizabeth Cook-Lynn, "Who Stole Native American Studies?," *Wicazo Sa Review* 12 (1997): 9–28; Raymond William Stedman, *Shadows of the Indian: Stereotypes in American Culture* (Norman: University of Oklahoma Press, 1982).

32. S. S. Slowikowski, "Cultural Performance and Sport Mascots," *Journal of Sport & Social Issues* 17 (1993): 23–33.

33. Amy Bass, ed., *In the Game: Race, Identity, and Sports in the Twentieth Century* (New York: Palgrave, 2005), 7.

34. D. Banks, Laurel R. Davis, S. S. Slowikowski, and Lawrence A. Wenner, "Tribal Names and Mascots in Sports," *Journal of Sport & Social Issues* 17 (1993): 5–8.

35. David Anthony Clark, "Wa a o, Wa ba Ski na Me Ska Ta!: 'Indian' Mascots and the Pathology of Anti-Indigenous Racism," in Bass, *In the Game*, 154.

36. Sterling HolyWhiteMountain, "The Great Failure of the Indians Mascot Debate? Thinking of It Only as Racism," *ESPN.com*, October 26, 2016, http://www .espn.com/mlb/story/_/id/17891581/great-failure-indians-mascot-debate-thinking -only-racism.

37. Clark, "Wa a o, W aba Ski na Me Ska Ta!," 140.

38. Guiliano, *Indian Spectacle*, 108.

39. Gavin Clarkson, "Racial Imagery and Native Americans: A First Look at the Empirical Evidence behind the Indian Mascot Controversy," *Cardozo Journal of International and Comparative Law* 11 (2003): 393–407.

40. Fenelon, *Redskins?*, 16.

41. Stuart Hall, *Representation: Cultural Representations and Signifying Practices* (Thousand Oaks, CA, Sage, 1997).

42. Mike McPhate, "California Today: The Debate over Indian Mascots and Imagery," *New York Times*, September 22, 2016, https://www.nytimes.com/2016/09/22/us/california-today-indian-school-mascots.html?_r=0.

43. Quoted in ibid.

44. C. Richard King, *Redskins: Insult and Brand* (Lincoln: University of Nebraska Press, 2016), 14; C. Richard King, "Defensive Dialogues: Native American Mascots, Anti-Indianism, and Educational Institutions," *Studies in Media and Information Literacy Education* 2 (2002): 1–12.

45. C. Richard King and Charles F. Springwood, *Team Spirits: The Native American Mascots Controversy* (Lincoln: University of Nebraska Press, 2001).

46. Scott Freng and Cynthia Willis-Esqueda, "A Question of Honor: Chief Wahoo and American Indian Stereotype Activation among a University-Based Sample," *Journal of Social Psychology* 151 (2011): 577–91.

47. John C. Turner, Michael A. Hogg, Penelope J. Oakes, Stephen D. Reicher, and Margaret S. Wetherell, *Rediscovering the Social Group: A Self-Categorization Theory* (Oxford, UK: Blackwell, 1987).

Chapter 1. Framing the Mascot through Self-Categorization

1. Lawrence R. Baca, "Native Images in Schools and the Racially Hostile Environment," *Journal of Sport & Social Issues* 28 (2004): 71–78.

2. Todd M. Callais, "Controversial Mascots: Authority and Racial Hegemony in the Maintenance of Deviant Symbols," *Sociological Focus* 43 (2010): 61–81; R. W. Connell and James W. Messerschmidt, "Hegemonic Masculinity: Rethinking the Concept," *Gender and Society* 19 (2005): 829–59; Laurel R. Davis, "Protest against the Use of Native American Mascots: A Challenge to Traditional American Identity," *Journal of Sport & Social Issues* 17 (1993): 9–22; Ellen J. Staurowsky, "An Act of Honor or Exploitation? The Cleveland Indians' Use of the Louis Francis Sockalexis Story," *Sociology of Sport Journal* 15 (1998): 299–316; Ellen J. Staurowsky, "Privilege at Play: On the Legal and Social Fictions That Sustain American Indian Sport Imagery," *Journal of Sport & Social Issues* 28 (2004): 11–29.

3. Jackson B. Miller, 'Indians,' 'Braves,' and 'Redskins': A Performative Struggle for Control of an Image," *Quarterly Journal of Speech* 85 (1999): 188.

4. C. Richard King, "Defensive Dialogues: Native American Mascots, Anti-Indianism, and Educational Institutions," *Studies in Media and Information Literacy Education* 2 (2002): 1–12; C. Richard King, "This Is Not an Indian: Situating Claims about Indianness in Sporting Worlds," *Journal of Sport & Social Issues* 28 (2004): 3–10; C. Richard King, "Teaching Intolerance: Anti-Indian Imagery, Racial Politics, and (Anti)racist Pedagogy," *Review of Education, Pedagogy and Cultural Studies* 30 (2008): 420–36; Carol Spindel, *Dancing at Halftime: Sports and the Controversy over American Indian Mascots* (New York: New York University Press, 2000).

5. Stephanie A. Fryberg, Hazel Rose Markus, Daphna Oyserman, and Joseph M. Stone, "Of Warrior Chiefs and Indian Princesses: The Psychological Consequences

of American Indian Mascots," *Basic and Applied Social Psychology* 30 (2008): 208–218.

6. Scott Freng and Cynthia Willis-Esqueda, "A Question of Honor: Chief Wahoo and American Indian Stereotype Activation among a University-Based Sample," *Journal of Social Psychology* 15, no. 5 (2011): 582.

7. Carl Iver Hovland and Muzafer Sherif, *Social Judgment: Assimilation and Contrast Effects in Communication and Attitude Change* (Westport, CT: Greenwood, 1980).

8. Leon Festinger, "A Theory of Social Comparison Processes," *Human Relations* 7 (1954): 117–40.

9. George R. Goethals and John M. Darley, "Social Comparison Theory: An Attributional Approach," in *Social Comparison Processes: Theoretical and Empirical Perspectives*, ed. Jerry M. Suls and Richard L. Miller (Hoboken, NJ: Wiley and Sons, 1977), 86–109; Jerry M. Suls, R. Martin, and Ladd Wheeler, "Social Comparison: Why, with Whom, and with What Effects?," *Current Directions in Psychological Science* 11 (2002): 159–63.

10. Shelli E. Taylor and Marci Lobel, "Social Comparison Activity Under Threat: Downward Evaluation and Upward Contacts," *Psychological Review* 96 (1989): 569–75.

11. Henri Tajfel and John C. Turner, "The Social Identity Theory of Inter-Group Behavior," in *Psychology of Intergroup Relations*, ed. Stephen Worchel and William G. Austin (Chicago: Nelson-Hall, 1986), 7–24.

12. S. Alexander Haslam, Nancy Ellemers, Steven David Reicher, Katherine J. Reynolds, and Michael T. Schmitt, "The Social Identity Perspective Today: An Overview of Its Defining Ideas," in *Rediscovering Social Identity*, ed. Tom Postmes and Nyla R. Branscombe (Sussex, UK: Psychology Press, 2010), 341–56; John C. Turner and Katherine J. Reynolds, "The Story of Social Identity," in Postmes and Branscombe, *Rediscovering Social Identity*, 341–56.

13. John C. Turner, Michael A. Hogg, Penelope J. Oakes, Stephen D. Reicher, and Margaret S. Wetherell, *Rediscovering the Social Group: A Self-Categorization Theory* (Oxford, UK: Blackwell, 1987).

14. John C. Turner, "Towards a Cognitive Redefinition of the Social Group," in *Social Identity and Intergroup Relations*, ed. Henri Tajfel (Cambridge, UK: Cambridge University Press, 1982), 15–40; John C. Turner, *Social Influence* (Buckingham, UK: Open University Press, 1991); John C. Turner, "Explaining the Nature of Power: A Three-Process Theory," *European Journal of Social Psychology* 35 (2005): 1–22; John C. Turner, Penelope J. Oakes, S. Alexander Haslam, and Craig McGarty, "Self and Collective: Cognition and Social Context," *Personality and Social Psychology Bulletin* 20 (1994): 454–63.

15. Rachel A. Smith and Norbert Schwartz, "Language, Social Comparison, and College Football: Is Your School Less Similar to the Rival School Than the Rival School Is to Your School?," *Communication Monographs* 70 (2003): 351–60.

16. Robert B. Cialdini, Richard J. Borden, Avril Thorne, Marcus Randall Walker, Stephen Freeman, and Lloyd Reynolds Sloan, "Basking in Reflected Glory: Three

(Football) Field Studies," *Journal of Personality and Social Psychology* 34 (1976): 366–75.

17. Ingar Mehus and Arnulf Kolstad, "Football Team Identification in Norway: Spectators of Local and National Football Matches," *Social Identities* 17 (2011): 833–45.

18. Alberto Voci, "Relevance of Social Categories, Depersonalization, and Group Processes: Two Field Tests of Self-Categorization Theory," *European Journal of Social Psychology* 36 (2006): 73–90.

19. Ibid., 86.

20. Shaughan Keaton and Christopher Gearhart, "Identity Formation, Identity Strength, and Self-Categorization as Predictors of Affective and Psychological Outcomes: A Model Reflecting Sport Team Fans' Responses to Highlights and Lowlights of a College Football Season," *Communication & Sport* 2 (2014): 363–85.

21. James A. Dimmock and J. Robert Grove, "Relationship of Fan Identification to Determinants of Aggression," *Journal of Applied Sport Psychology* 17 (2005): 37–47.

22. Mark W. Bruner, W. L. Dunlop, and Mark R. Beauchamp, "A Social Identity Perspective on Group Processes in Sport and Exercise," in *Group Dynamics in Exercise and Sport Psychology*, ed. Mark R. Beauchamp and Mark A. Eys (New York: Routledge, 2014), 51.

23. Michael A. Hogg and Barbara A. Mullin, "Joining Groups to Reduce Uncertainty: Subjective Uncertainty Reduction and Group Identification," in *Social Identity and Social Cognition*, ed. Dominic Abrams and Michael A. Hogg (Oxford, UK: Blackwell, 1999), 249–79.

24. Margaret Morse, "An Ontology of Everyday Distraction: The Freeway, the Mall, and Television," in *The Logics of Television*, ed. Patricia Mellencamp (Bloomington: Indiana University Press, 1990), 193–221.

25. Clifford Stott, Paul Hutchison, and John Drury, "Hooligans Abroad? Inter-Group Dynamics, Social Identity, and Participation in Collective 'Disorder' at the 1998 World Cup Finals," *British Journal of Social Psychology* 40 (2001): 359–84.

26. Ibid., 375–76.

27. Elizabeth B. Delia, "The Exclusiveness of Group Identity in Celebrations of Team Success," *Sport Management Review* 18 (2015): 396–406.

28. James A. Dimmock, J. Robert Grove, and Robert C. Eklund, "Reconceptualizing Team Identification: New Dimensions and Their Relationship to Intergroup Bias," *Group Dynamics: Theory, Research, and Practice* 9 (2005): 75–86.

29. Delia, "Exclusiveness of Group Identity," 402.

30. Dimmock, Grove, and Eklund, "Reconceptualizing Team Identification."

31. John C. Turner, "Social Comparison and Social Identity: Some Prospects for Intergroup Behaviour," *European Journal of Social Psychology* 5 (1975): 1–34.

32. Arthur A. Raney and William Kinnally, "Examining Perceived Violence in and Enjoyment of Televised Rivalry Sports Contests," *Mass Communication and Society* 10 (2009): 25–41.

33. Turner, "Social Comparison and Social Identity," 26.

34. Bob Heere, Matthew Walker, Masayuki Yoshida, Yong Jae Ko, Jeremy Jordan, and Jeffrey D. James, "Brand Community Development through Associated Communities: Grounding Community Measurement within Social Identity Theory," *Journal of Marketing Theory and Practice* 19 (2011): 407–422; Daniel L. Wann and Frederick G. Grieve, "Biased Evaluations of In-Group and Out-Group Spectator Behavior at Sporting Events: The Importance of Team Identification and Threats to Social Identity," *Journal of Social Psychology* 145 (2005): 531–45.

35. J. Robert Grove, Maree Fish, and Robert C. Eklund, "Changes in Athletic Identity Following Team Selection: Self-Protection versus Self-Enhancement," *Journal of Applied Sport Psychology* 16 (2004): 75.

36. Michael A. Hogg and Elizabeth A. Hardie, "Social Attraction, Personal Attraction, and Self-Categorization: A Field Study," *Personality and Social Psychology Bulletin* 17, no. 2 (1991): 175–80.

37. E. Nicole Melton and George B. Cunningham, "Examining the Workplace Experiences of Sport Employees Who Are LGBT: A Social Categorization Theory Perspective," *Journal of Sport Management* 28, no. 1 (2014): 21–33.

38. John S. W. Spinda, "Perceptual Biases and Behavioral Effects among NFL Fans: An Investigation of First-Person, Second-Person, and Third-Person Effects," *International Journal of Sport Communication* 5 (2012): 327–47.

39. Synthia S. Slowikowski, "Cultural Performance and Sport Mascots," *Journal of Sport & Social Issues* 17 (1993): 23–33.

40. Susan S. Harjo, "Fighting Name-Calling: Challenging 'Redskins' in Court," in *Team Spirits: The Native American Mascots Controversy*, ed. C. Richard King and Charles F. Springwood (Lincoln: University of Nebraska Press, 2001), 189–207.

41. Mary Jiang Bresnahan and Kelly Flowers, "The Effects of Involvement in Sports on Attitudes toward Native American Sport Mascots," *Howard Journal of Communications* 19 (2008): 165–81; Laurel R. Davis-Delano, "Eliminating Native American Mascots: Ingredients for Success," *Journal of Sport & Social Issues* 31 (2007): 340–73; James V. Fenelon, "Indian Icons in the World Series of Racism: Institutionalization of the Racial Symbols of Wahoos and Indians," *Research in Politics and Society* 6 (1999): 25–46; Jay Rosenstein, "In Whose Honor? Mascots and the Media," in King and Springwood, *Team Spirits*, 241–56; Ellen J. Staurowsky, "The Cleveland 'Indians': A Case Study in American Indian Cultural Dispossession," *Sociology of Sport Journal* 17 (2000): 307–330; Pauline Turner Strong, "The Mascot Slot: Cultural Citizenship, Political Correctness, and Pseudo-Indian Sports Symbols," *Journal of Sport & Social Issues* 28 (2004): 79–87.

42. Dana M. Williams, "Patriarchy and the 'Fighting Sioux': A Gendered Look at Racial College Sports Nicknames," *Race, Ethnicity, and Education* 9 (2006): 325–40; Dana M. Williams, "Where's the Honor? Attitudes toward the 'Fighting Sioux' Nickname and Logo," *Sociology of Sport Journal* 24 (2007): 437–56.

43. Joe Barrett, "Sioux Nickname Yields," *Wall Street Journal*, November 10, 2011, http://www.wsj.com/articles/SB10001424052970204224604577028320279217872.

44. Robert Jensen, "What the 'Fighting Sioux' Tells Us about White People," in *The Native American Mascot Controversy: A Handbook*, ed. C. Richard King (Lanham, MD: Rowman and Littlefield, 2010), 33–40; Charles Fruehling Springwood, "'I'm Indian Too!': Claiming Native American Identity, Crafting Authority in Mascot Debates," *Journal of Sport & Social Issues* 28 (2004): 56–70.

45. David Wahlberg, "Ending the Debate: Crisis Communication Analysis of One University's American Indian Athletic Identity," *Public Relations Review* 30 (2004): 197–203.

46. Steven Fink, *Crisis Management: Planning for the Inevitable* (Lincoln, NE: iUniverse Inc., 2002).

47. Daniel Grow, "Money Apparently Matters in Indian Nickname Dispute," *Minneapolis Star-Tribune*, January 17, 2001.

48. Jared Clinton, "Public Backlash Leads University of North Dakota President to Reconsider Nickname: Committee's Five Name List," *Hockey News,* July 24, 2015, http://www.thehockeynews.com/blog/public-backlash-leads-university-of-north -dakota-president-to-reconsider-nickname-committees-five-name-list.

49. Dave Kolpack, "Fighting Hawks: New Mascot for UND," *U.S. News and World Report*, November 18, 2015, http://www.usnews.com/news/articles/2015/11/18/ fighting-hawks-to-replace-fighting-sioux-at-university-of-north-dakota.

50. Raul Tovares, "Mascot Matters: Race, History, and the University of North Dakota's 'Fighting Sioux' Logo," *Journal of Communication Inquiry* 26 (2002): 76–94.

51. Kristina Rolin, "Standpoint Theory as a Methodology for the Study of Power Relationships," *Hypatia* 24 (2009): 218–26.

52. Tovares, "Mascot Matters," 77–78.

53. James Loewen, *Sundown Towns: A Hidden Dimension of American Racism* (New York: Touchstone, 2006), 178.

54. Richard B. Stolley, "Pekin Choose: The Author's High School Made the Tough Decision the Redskins Haven't," *Sports Illustrated*, November 23, 2015, https://www .si.com/vault/2016/02/11/pekin-choose.

55. Loewen, *Sundown Towns*.

56. David Plotz, "The Washington _____: Why *Slate* Will No Longer Refer to Washington's NFL Team as the Redskins," *Slate*, August 8, 2013, http://www.slate.com/ articles/sports/sports_nut/2013/08/washington_redskins_nickname_why_slate_will _stop_referring_to_the_nfl_team.html.

57. Stolley, "Pekin Choose," 14.

58. Roger Simon, "The Chinks' Nickname: It's Not PC, It's Decency," *Baltimore Sun*, December 5, 1994, http://articles.baltimoresun.com/1994-12-05/news/1994339058_1 _chinks-pekin-high-tribune.

59. Jonathan Zimmerman, "The Ugly Truth about Our Love of Redskins," *Washington Post*, August 30, 2013, https://www.washingtonpost.com/opinions/the-washington -redskins-and-the-ugly-truth-about-our-love-for-the-team/2013/08/30/efce94e6-fed8 -11e2-9711-3708310f6f4d_story.html?utm_term=.e9db9588c1d5.

60. Michelle R. Jacobs, "Race, Place, and Biography at Play: Contextualizing American Indian Viewpoints on Indian Mascots," *Journal of Sport & Social Issues* 38 (2014): 322–45.

61. David Zirin, "The Florida State Seminoles: The Champions of Racist Mascots," *The Nation*, January 7, 2014, http://www.thenation.com/article/florida-state-seminoles-champions-racist-mascots.

62. Steve Wieberg, "NCAA Allowing Florida State to Use Its Seminole Mascot," *USA Today*, August 23, 2005, http://usatoday30.usatoday.com/sports/college/2005-08-23-fsu-mascot-approved_x.htm.

63. George Will, "The Government Decided That 'Redskins' Bothers You," *Washington Post*, June 27, 2014, https://www.washingtonpost.com/opinions/george-f-will-the-government-decided-that-redskins-bothers-you/2014/06/27/669558a6-fd54-11e3-932c-0a55b81f48ce_story.html?utm_term=.4579cd9e016f; Chuck Culpepper, "Florida State's Unusual Bond with Seminole Tribe Puts Mascot Debate in Different Light," *Washington Post*, December 29, 2014, https://www.washingtonpost.com/sports/colleges/florida-states-unusual-bond-with-seminole-tribe-puts-mascot-debate-in-a-different-light/2014/12/29/5386841a-8eea-11e4-ba53-a477d66580ed_story.html.

64. Chris Tomasson, "Redskins' Name Change 'Festered by Liberals,' Former QB Billy Kilmer Says," *St. Paul Pioneer Press*, October 31, 2014, http://www.twincities.com/2014/10/31/redskins-name-change-festered-by-liberals-former-qb-billy-kilmer-says.

65. Zirin, "Florida State Seminoles."

66. Jessica M. Toglia and Othello Harris, "Alumni Perceptions of a University's Decision to Remove Native American Imagery from Its Athletic Program," *Journal of Sport & Social Issues* 28 (2014): 291–321.

67. Ibid., 313.

68. Laurel R. Davis, "Protest against the Use of Native American Names/Logos: A Challenge to Traditional American Identity," *Journal of Sport & Social Issues* 17 (1993): 9–22.

69. James McWhorter, "Why Redskins Is a Bad Word," *Time*, October 12, 2015, http://time.com/4070537/redskins-linguistics.

Chapter 2. The Native American Mascot in the Western Gaze: Reading the Mascot through a Postcolonial Lens

1. Edward W. Said, *Orientalism* (New York: Vintage, 1978); Gayatri Spivak, "Can the Subaltern Speak?" in *Marxism and the Interpretation of Culture*, ed. Cary Nelson and Larry Grossberg (Chicago: University of Illinois Press, 1988), 271–313.

2. Derek Buescher and Kent A. Ono, "Civilized Colonialism: Pocahontas as Neocolonial Rhetoric," *Women's Studies in Communication* 19 (1996): 131.

3. Jason Edward Black, *American Indians and the Rhetoric of Removal and Allotment* (Jackson: University Press of Mississippi, 2015), 11.

4. Jason Edward Black, "A Clash of Native Space and Institutional Place in a Local Choctaw-Upper Creek Memory Site: Decolonizing Critiques and Scholar-Activist Interventions," *American Indian Culture and Research Journal* 36, no. 3 (2012): 23.

5. Susan Silbey, "Let Them Eat Cake: Globalization, Postmodern Capitalism, and the Possibilities of Justice," *Law and Society Review* 31 (1997): 210.

6. Black, "Clash of Native Space," 23.

7. Glen Sean Couthard, *Red Skin, White Masks: Rejecting the Colonial Politics of Recognition* (Minneapolis: University of Manitoba Press, 2014): 6–7; Emma LaRocque, *When the Other Is Me: Native Resistance Discourse, 1850–1990* (Winnipeg: University of Manitoba Press, 2010); Duane Champagne, "In Search of Theory and Method in American Indian Studies," *American Indian Quarterly* 31, no. 2 (2007): 353–72; and Linda Tuhiwai Smith, *Decolonizing Methodologies: Research and Indigenous Peoples* (London: Zed Books, 2007).

8. Couthard, *Red Skin, White Masks*, 6–7.

9. Mary E. Stuckey and John M. Murphy, "By Any Other Name: Rhetorical Colonialism in North America," *American Indian Culture and Research Journal* 25, no. 4 (2001): 75.

10. Jason Edward Black, "Remembrances of Removal: Native Resistance to Allotment and the Unmasking of Paternal Benevolence," *Southern Communication Journal* 72 (2007): 67.

11. Anders Stephanson, *Manifest Destiny: American Expansionism and the Empire of Right* (New York: Hill and Wang, 1995).

12. David G. Gutierrez, "Significant to Whom? Mexican Americans and the History of the American West," in *A New Significance: Re-Envisioning the History of the American West*, ed. Clyde A. Milner III (New York: Oxford University Press 1996), 68.

13. David Rich Lewis, "Still Native: The Significance of Native Americans in the History of the Twentieth-Century American West," in Milner, *New Significance*, 213.

14. According to Robert E. Shalhope, "by 'property' [the U.S. government] almost always meant land" or real property. Robert E. Shalhope, *The Roots of Democracy: American Thought and Culture, 1760–1800* (Boston: Twayne, 1990), 162.

15. Rogers M. Smith, *Civic Ideals: Conflicting Views of Citizenship in U.S. History* (New Haven, CT: Yale University Press, 1997), 183; and Rogan Kersh, *Dreams of a More Perfect Union* (Ithaca, NY: Cornell University Press, 2005), 116.

16. Andrew Jackson, "Draft of First Annual Message, December 8, 1829," in *The Correspondence of Andrew Jackson*, vol. 4, ed. John Spencer Bassett (Washington, DC: Carnegie, 1928), 103. Even anti-Jacksonian Daniel Webster summarily dismissed American Indian territoriality. Writing to a friend in 1826, Webster noted, "There is little [about American Indians as citizens] worth studying or worth knowing." Kersh, *Dreams of a More Perfect Union*, 117.

17. Francis Paul Prucha, *The Indians in American Society: From the Revolutionary War to the Present* (Berkeley: University of California Press, 1985), 11.

18. John Kleinig, *Paternalism* (New York: Rowan and Allenheld, 1983), 171.

19. Mary Jackman, *The Velvet Glove: Paternalism and Conflict in Gender, Class, and Race Relations* (Berkeley: University of California Press, 1994), 14–15.

20. See Michael Paul Rogin, *Fathers and Children: Andrew Jackson and the Subjugation of the American Indian* (New York: Knopf, 1975).

21. Jackman, *Velvet Glove*, 14–15.

22. Prucha, *Indians in American Society*, 11.

23. Thomas Skinner, "Debate on Bill to Provide Lands in Severalty, December 15–16 and January 18, 25, 1887," in *The American Indian and the United States: A Documentary History*, vol. 4, ed. Wilcomb Washburn (New York: Random House, 1973), 1849.

24. Joseph Dolph, "Debate on Bill to Provide Lands in Severalty, December 15–16 and January 18, 25, 1887," in Washburn, *American Indian and the United States*, 4:1878.

25. Laura Anne Whitt, "Cultural Imperialism and the Marketing of Native America," *American Indian Culture and Research Journal* 19 (1995): 8.

26. Brenda Farnell, "The Fancy Dance of Racializing Discourse," *Journal of Sport & Social Issues* 28, no. 1 (2004): 31.

27. Forsyth's Remarks, April 15, 1830, *Gales & Seaton's Register of Debates in Congress*, Senate (April 14, 15, 1830), 333.

28. Jason Edward Black, "Authoritarian Fatherhood: Andrew Jackson's Early Familial Lectures to America's 'Red Children,'" *Journal of Family History* 30, no. 3 (2005): 251.

29. For a detailed discussion of the marketing of Native culture, see S. Elizabeth Bird, "'Indians Are Like That': Negotiating Identity in a Media World," in *Black Marks: Minority Ethnic Audiences and Media*, ed. Karen Ross and Peter Playdon (Burlington, VT: Ashgate, 2001), 105–122; Ward Churchill, *Indians Are Us? Culture and Genocide in Native North America* (Monroe, ME: Common Courage Press, 1994), 65–72; C. Richard King and Charles Fruehling Springwood, "Fighting Spirits: The Racial Politics of Sports Mascots," *Journal of Sport & Social Issues* 24, no. 3 (2000): 282–305; C. Richard King and Charles Fruehling Springwood, *Beyond the Cheers: Race as Spectacle in College Sports* (Albany: State University of New York Press, 2001); Richard Morris and Phillip Wander, "American Indian Rhetoric: Dancing in the Shadows of the Ghost Dance," *Quarterly Journal of Speech* 76 (1990): 164–91; Kent A. Ono and Derek Buescher, "Deciphering Pocahontas: Unpackaging the Commodification of an American Indian Woman," *Critical Studies in Media Communication* 18 (2001): 23–43; Carol Spindel, *Dancing at Halftime: Sports and the Controversy over American Indian Mascots* (New York: New York University Press, 2000); and Hillary N. Weaver, "Indigenous Identity: What Is It, and Who Really Owns It?" *American Indian Quarterly* 25, no. 2 (2001): 240–55.

30. Ono and Buescher, "Deciphering Pocahontas," 35–36.

31. Charles Barnes, "Animals Are Mascots—Seminole Indians Are Symbols," *Florida State Times* (September 2001): 10.

32. Jason Edward Black, "The Mascotting of Native America: Construction, Commodity, and Assimilation," *American Indian Quarterly* 26, no. 4 (2002): 606.

33. Laurel R. Davis, "Problems with Native American Mascots," *Multicultural Education* 9, no. 4 (2002): 11–14.

34. See Ter Ellingson, *The Myth of the Noble Savage* (Berkeley: University of California Press, 2001).

35. Hinton, "Chief Opinion: For," *Inside Higher Ed*, March 1, 2007, http://www.insidehighereducation.com/news/2007/03/07/qt.

36. Brinkmann, "Chief Opinion: Very For," *Inside Higher Ed*, March 7, 2007. Copy in author's possession.

37. Florida State University, "Florida State Seminoles: A Tradition of Tribute," FSU website (n.d.), https://unicomm.fsu.edu/messages/relationship-seminole-tribe-florida/tribute.

38. Ellen J. Staurowksy, "'You Know, We Are All Indian': Exploring White Power and Privilege in Reactions to the NCAA Native American Mascot Policy," *Journal of Sport & Social Issues* 31, no. 1 (2007): 62.

39. See the classic studies on the "savage" myth, Brian Dippie, *The Vanishing American: White Attitudes and U.S. Indian Policy* (Lawrence: University Press of Kansas, 1982); and Roy Harvey Pearce, *Savagism and Civilization: A Study of the Indian and the American Mind* (Baltimore: Johns Hopkins University Press, 1969).

40. Farnell, "Fancy Dance," 34.

41. Barnes, "Animals Are Mascots."

42. Chief Osceola Facebook page, introduction to group (n.d.), http://ua.facebook.com/group.php. (As of August 3, 2007, this Facebook page was removed.)

43. Greenstreet, response to "Illinois Trustees Vote to Retire Chief Illiniwek," ESPN.com, March 13, 2007, http://sports.espn.go.com/ncaa/news/story?id=2796923.

44. See Greg Dickinson, Brian L. Ott, and Eric Aoki, "Memory and Myth at the Buffalo Bill Museum," *Western Journal of Communication* 69, no. 2 (2005): 85–108; and Greg Dickinson, Brian L. Ott, and Eric Aoki, "Spaces of Remembering and Forgetting: The Reverent Eye/I at the Plains Indian Museum," *Communication and Critical/Cultural Studies* 3, no. 1 (2006): 27–47.

45. Staurowksy, "'You Know, We Are All Indian,'" 62.

46. Black, "Mascotting," 614.

47. Save the Chief Facebook page, introduction to group. Version cited is from March 2007. Textual excerpts are in author's possession.

48. Raymond Magyar, "'Seminole' Is Fine," *Florida State Times*, November 2001, 3.

49. Charles Barnes, "'Noles Never Give Up," *Florida State Times*, May 2001, 3.

50. Black, "Mascotting," 613–14.

51. Honor the Chief, "Frequently Asked Questions about the Chief Illiniwek Tradition," *Honor the Chief Society*, (n.d.), http://www.waunakee.k12.wi.us/hs/departments/lmtc/Assignments/McConnellScenarios/mascots3illini_supporters.pdf.

52. Black, "Mascotting," 613–14.

53. Randall Lake, "Between Myth and History: Enacting Time in American Indian Protest Rhetoric," *Quarterly Journal of Speech* 77 (1991): 129.

54. Mark R. Connolly, "What's in a Name? A Historical Look at Native American Related Nicknames and Symbols at Three Universities," *Journal of Higher Education* 71, no. 5 (2000): 530.

55. Whitt, "Cultural Imperialism," 18–21.

56. Richard Morris, "Educating Savages," *Quarterly Journal of Speech* 83 (1997): 161.

57. Charles Fruehling Springwood, "Playing Indian and Fighting (for) Mascots: Reading the Complications of Native American and Euro-American Alliances," in *Team Spirits: The Native American Mascot Controversy*, ed. C. Richard King and Charles Fruehling Springwood (Lincoln: University of Nebraska Press, 2001), 304–327.

58. Board of Indian Commissioners, "Twelfth Annual Report," November 1, 1880, in Carl Schurz, "Annual Report of the Secretary of the Interior," November 1, 1880, *House Executive Document* no. 1, 46th Congress, 3d session, serial 1959, pp. 7–9.

59. Ibid.

60. Farnell, "Fancy Dance," 46.

61. Howard Zinn, Introduction to *The Forging of the American Empire: From the Revolution to Vietnam: A History of U.S. Imperialism*, ed. Sidney Lens (Chicago: Haymarket Books, 2003), xi–xii. See also Max Boot, *The Savage Wars of Peace: Small Wars and the Rise of American Power* (New York: Basic Books, 2002); and Arthur M. Schlesinger Jr., *War and the American Presidency* (New York: Norton, 2004).

62. Lumpkin's Remarks, May 17, 1830, *Gales & Seaton's Register of Debates in Congress*, House (May 17, 1830), 1016.

63. Susan M. Ryan, *The Grammar of Good Intentions: Race and the Antebellum Culture of Benevolence* (Ithaca, NY: Cornell University Press, 2003), 45.

64. Lanier125, "Response to Mascot Decision," National Coalition on Racism in Sports and the Media, AIM Blogspot (n.d.), http://aimggc.blogspot.com.

65. GDang, "Chief Opinion: Very For," *Inside Higher Ed*, March 3, 2007, http://www.insidehighered.com/news/2007/03/07/qt.

66. The Tanker, "Chief Opinion: Very For," *Inside Higher Ed*, February 24, 2007, http://www.insidehighered.com/news/2007/03/07/qt.

67. Chris Smith, "Response to Mascot Decision," National Coalition on Racism in Sports and the Media, AIM Blogspot (n.d.), http://aimggc.blogspot.com.

68. Ibid.

69. Gann, "Response to Mascot Decision," National Coalition on Racism in Sports and the Media, AIM Blogspot (n.d.), http://aimggc.blogspot.com.

70. Brinkmann, "Chief Opinion."

71. Sandy D'Alemberte, "We Honor the Seminole Legend," *Florida State Times*, February/March 1996.

72. Sarah Robinson, "Real Seminoles Say Symbol's OK, Stereotypes Aren't," *Florida State Times* (n.d.). Copy in author's possession.

73. RW, "Front Page Comments," Save the Chief Facebook page (n.d.). Version cited is from March 2007. Textual excerpts are in author's possession.

74. Farnell, "Fancy Dance," 43.

75. An analogy is defined as "reasoning or arguing from parallel cases." See Richard A. Lanham, *A Handlist of Rhetorical Terms*, 2nd ed. (Berkeley: University of California Press, 1991), 188.

76. Andrew Jackson, "Second Annual Message," December 6, 1830, in *U.S. House Journal* (Dec. 6, 1830), 25.

77. Tronson, "Response to Mascot Decision," National Coalition on Racism in Sports and the Media, AIM Blogspot (n.d.), http://aimggc.blogspot.com.

78. rcw3006, "Response to Mascot Decision," National Coalition on Racism in Sports and the Media, AIM Blogspot (n.d.), http://aimggc.blogspot.com.

79. 12 Angry Men Blog, "Morons on Ice," https://12angrymen.wordpress.com/2007/02.

80. Save the Chief Facebook page, introduction to group.

81. See Wake Forest University, *The History of Wake Forest College*, vol. 4, *1943–1967* (Winston-Salem, NC: Wake Forest University, 1988).

82. See David G. Sansing, *The University of Mississippi: A Sesquicentennial History* (Oxford: University Press of Mississippi, 1999).

83. Ono and Buescher, "Deciphering Pocahontas," 35–36.

84. Whitt, "Cultural Imperialism."

85. C. Richard King, Ellen J. Staurowsky, Lawrence Baca, Laurel R. Davis, and Cornel Pewewardy, "Of Polls and Prejudice: *Sports Illustrated*'s Errant 'Indian Wars,'" *Journal of Sport & Social Issues* 26 (2002): 395.

Chapter 3. Online Debate on the Acceptability of the Washington NFL Mascot

1. Melanie Mason, "California Schools Barred from Using 'Redskins' as Team Name or Mascot," *Los Angeles Times*, October 11, 2015, http://www.latimes.com/politics/la-me-pc-redskins-mascot-banned-20151011-story.html.

2. Samantha Cowan, "High Schools Drop 'Redskins' Team Name, but NFL Refuses," Take Part, July 29, 2015, http://www.takepart.com/article/2015/07/29/redskins.

3. Jason Edward Black, "The 'Mascotting' of Native America: Construction, Commodification, and Assimilation," *American Indian Quarterly* 26, no. 4 (2002): 605–622.

4. Ellen J. Staurowksy, "'You Know, We Are All Indian': Exploring White Power and Privilege in Reactions to the NCAA Native American Mascot Policy," *Journal of Sport & Social Issues* 31, no. 1 (2007): 61–76.

5. Laura Stampler, "This Powerful Anti-Redskins Ad Will Play during the NBA Finals," *Time*, June 10, 2014, http://time.com/2852670/washingtonredskins-nba-commercial.

6. National Congress of American Indians, "Proud to Be," YouTube.com, https://www.youtube.com/watch?v=mR-tbOxlhvE, accessed January 23, 2018.

7. Laura Stampler, "Washington Redskins Defend Name with Help from Native Americans," *Time*, August 12, 2014, http://time.com/3104775/redskinsvideo-native-americans.

8. Washington Redskins, "Redskins Is a Powerful Name," YouTube.com, https://www.youtube.com/watch?v=4oSFqadRTQo, accessed January 23, 2018.

9. Jason Edward Black, "Native American Mascotting Reveals Neocolonial Logics," *Spectra* 50, no. 3 (2014): 14.

10. Raka Shome, "Postcolonial Interventions in the Rhetorical Canon: An 'Other' View," *Communication Theory* 6, no. 1 (1996): 41.

11. Black, "Native American Mascotting," 17.

12. Ibid., 16.

13. Kathryn M. Olson, "Detecting a Common Interpretive Framework for Impersonal Violence: The Homology in Participants' Rhetoric on Sport Hunting, Hate Crimes, and Stranger Rape," *Southern Communication Journal* 67 (2002): 215–44.

14. Jason Edward Black, "Extending the Rights of Personhood, Voice, and Life to Sensate Others: A Homology of Right to Life and Animal Rights Rhetoric," *Communication Quarterly* 51 (2003): 312–31.

15. Jason Edward Black and Adam Sharples, "Republican Motherhood, Black Militancy, and Scorching Irony in Sara Stanley's 'What, to the Toiling Millions There, Is This Boasted Liberty?'" *Carolinas Communication Annual* 30 (2014): 1–16.

16. Black, "'Mascotting of Native America'"; Black, "Native American Mascotting"; and Staurowsky, "You Know, We Are All Indian."

17. "NFL Player Poll: Redskin Name OK," September 2, 2014, ESPN.com, http://espn.go.com/nfl/story/_/id/11452022/nfl-nation-confidential-majority-players-support-washington-redskins-nickname; and Scott Clement, "New Poll Says Large Majority of Americans Believe Redskins Should Not Change Name," *Washington Post*, September 2, 2014, http://www.washingtonpost.com/sports/redskins/new-poll-says-large-majority-of-americans-believe-redskins-should-not-change-name/2014/09/02/496e3dd0-32e0-11e4-9e92-0899b306bbea_story.html.

18. Jessica M. Toglia and Othello Harris, "Alumni Perceptions of a University's Decision to Remove Native American Imagery from Its Athletic Program," *Journal of Sport & Social Issues* 28 (2014): 291–321.

19. Michael A. Robidoux, "The Nonsense of Native American Sports Imagery: Reclaiming a Past That Never Was," *International Review for the Sociology of Sport* 41(2006): 201.

Chapter 4. Deconstructing the Mascot, Part 1: Names and Textual Fields

1. Heather Vanderford, "What's in a Name? Heritage or Hatred: The School Mascot Controversy," *Journal of Law and Education* 25 (1996): 381–88.

2. Laurel R. Davis-Delano, "Eliminating Native American Mascots: Ingredients for Success," *Journal of Sport & Social Issues* 31 (2007): 340–73; and Robert Jensen, "Banning 'Redskins' from the Sports Page: The Ethics and Politics of Native American Nicknames," *Journal of Mass Media Ethics* 9 (1994): 16–25.

3. Debra Merskin, "Sending Up Signals: A Survey of Native American Media Use and Representation in the Mass Media," *Howard Journal of Communications* 9 (1998): 333–45.

4. Eric Prisbell, "NCAA Takes Hard Line on Mascots," *Washington Post*, August 5, 2005, http://www.washingtonpost.com/wpdyn/content/article/2005/08/05/AR2005080500648.html.

5. John Woodrow Cox, Scott Clement, and Theresa Vargas, "New Poll Finds 9 in 10 Native Americans Aren't Offended by Redskins Name," *Washington Post*, May 19, 2016, https://www.washingtonpost.com/local/new-poll-finds-9-in-10-native-americans-arent-offended-by-redskins-name/2016/05/18/3ea11cfa-161a-11e6-924d-838753295f9a_story.html?utm_term=.7e6a9076b26d.

6. Dan Steinberg, "The Great Redskins Name Debate of . . . 1972?" *Washington Post*, June 3, 2014, https://www.washingtonpost.com/news/dc-sports-bog/wp/2014/06/03/the-great-redskins-name-debate-of-1972.

7. John S. W. Spinda, "Perceptual Biases and Behavioral Effects among NFL Fans: An Investigation of First-Person, Second-Person, and Third-Person Effects," *International Journal of Sport Communication* 5, no. 3 (2012): 327–47.

8. Cox, Clement, and Vargas, "New Poll."

9. Danielle Endres, "American Indian Permission for Mascots: Resistance or Complicity within Rhetorical Colonialism," *Rhetoric and Public Affairs* 18, no. 4 (2015): 655.

10. Glen Sean Couthard, *Red Skin, White Masks: Rejecting the Colonial Politics of Recognition* (Minneapolis: University of Minnesota Press, 2014), 6–7.

11. Amy Lonetree, *Decolonizing Museums: Representing Native America in National and Tribal Museums* (Chapel Hill: University of North Carolina Press, 2012), 8–9.

12. Brief of *Amici Curiae*, Native American Organizations in Support of Appellees, *Pro-Football, Inc. (plaintiff and appellant) v. Amanda Blackhorse, Marcus Briggs-Cloud, Phillip Glover, Jillian Pappan, Courtney Tsotigh (defendants and appellees)*; United States of America (intervenor-appellee), In the United States Court of Appeals for the Fourth Circuit, no. 15-1874.

13. C. Richard King, *Redskins: Insult and Brand* (Lincoln: University of Nebraska Press, 2016), 1.

14. Timothy Burke, "Redskins Mentions Down 27% on NFL Game Broadcasts in 2014," *Deadspin*, December 30, 2014, http://deadspin.com/redskins-mentions-down-27-on-nfl-game-broadcasts-in-1676147358.

15. Quoted in King, *Redskins*, 2.

16. See John W. Bower, Donovan J. Ochs, Richard J. Jensen, and David P. Schulz, *The Rhetoric of Agitation and Control*, 3rd ed. (Long Grove, IL: Waveland Press, 2010); Jason Del Gandio, *Rhetoric for Radicals: A Handbook for 21st-Century Activists* (Gabriola Island, BC, Canada: New Society Publishers, 2008); John P. McHale, *Communicating for Change: Strategies of Social and Political Advocates* (Lanham, MD: Rowman and Littlefield, 2004); and Charles J. Stewart, Craig Allen Smith, and Robert E. Denton Jr., *Persuasion and Social Movements*, 6th ed. (Long Grove, IL: Waveland Press, 2012).

17. "Letter from Washington Redskins Owner Dan Snyder to Fans," *Washington Post*, October 9, 2013, https://www.washingtonpost.com/local/letter-from-washington -redskins-owner-dan-snyder-to-fans/2013/10/09.

18. Carl Hulse and Elena Schneider, "Citing N.B.A. Example, Senators Urge N.F.L. to Act on Redskins' Name," *New York Times*, May 22, 2014, https://www.nytimes.com/ 2014/05/22/sports/football/citing-nba-example-senators-urge-nfl-to-act-on-redskins -name.html.

19. Dan Steinberg, "Maria Cantrell Explains the Senate's Letter to the NFL about the Redskins," *Washington Post*, May 22, 2014, https://www.washingtonpost.com/ news/dc-sports-bog/wp/2014/05/22/maria-cantwell-explains-the-senates-letter-to -the-nfl-about-the-redskins/?utm_term=.f826a709bf13.

20. Erik Brady, "Redskins Trademarks Cancelled by U.S. Patent Office," *USA Today*, June 18, 2014, https://www.usatoday.com/story/sports/nfl/redskins/2014/06/18/ redskins-trademark-revoked-us-patent-office/10735053.

21. Eugene Volokh, "ACLU Argues That Cancellation of Redskins Trademark Violates First Amendment," *Washington Post*, March 6, 2015, https://www.washington post.com/news/volokh-conspiracy/wp/2015/03/06/aclu-argues-that-cancellation-of -redskins-trademark-violates-the-first-amendment/?utm_term=.01c78fcf3e8c.

22. These groups were the American Indian Council; American Indian Science and Engineering Society at the University of Minnesota; American Indian Student Alliance at California State University San Marcos; American Indian Student Cultural Center at the University of Minnesota; American Indian Studies Association; American Indians in Film and Television; Americans for Indian Opportunity; Association of Native Americans at Yale University; Association of Tribal Archives, Libraries, and Museums; Association on American Indian Affairs; Blue Feather Drum Group; California Indian Culture and Sovereignty Center at California State University San Marcos; California Indian Museum and Cultural Center; Capitol Area Indian Resources Inc.; Center for Indigenous Peoples Studies, College of Social and Behavioral Sciences, California State University, San Bernardino; Change the Mascot Campaign; Council of Fire Native American Leadership and Debate Society; First Nations at the University of Washington; Gamma Delta Pi; "Indian" Mascot and Logo Taskforce; Indigenize OU; Indigenous and American Indian Studies Club at Haskell Indian Nations University; Indigenous Law and Policy Center at the Michigan State University College of Law; International Indian Treaty Council; Midwest Alliance of Sovereign Tribes; National Indian Education Association; National Indian Youth Council; National Congress of American Indians; National Native American Law Students Association; Native American Contractors Association; Native American Journalists Association; Native American Law Students Association at the University of Washington School of Law; Scholars of Stereotypes of Native Americans in Sport; Society of American Indian Government Employees; Society of Indian Psychologists; Southern California Tribal Chairmen's Association; Morning Star Institute; United

South and Eastern Tribes; UNLV Native American Community; and Wisconsin Network for Peace and Justice.

23. "What Is a Racial Slur? Fight over Washington Redskins Name Raises Questions about Race and Language," *National Post*, June 21, 2014, http://nationalpost.com/sports/football/nfl/what-is-a-slur-fight-over-washington-redskins-name-raises-many-questions-about-race-and-language/wcm/105cdbd0-28bb-41a0-a7f9-ccdb 6f148b19.

24. Volokh, "ACLU Argues."

25. King, *Redskins*, 17.

26. Jerry M. Suls, R. Martin, and Ladd Wheeler, "Social Comparison: Why, With Whom, and With What Effects?" *Current Directions in Psychological Science* 11 (2002): 159–63.

27. George D. Smithers, "Why Do So Many Americans Think They Have Cherokee Blood? The History of the Myth," *Slate*, October 1, 2015, http://www.slate.com/articles/news_and_politics/history/2015/10/cherokee_blood_why_do_so_many _americans_believe_they_have_cherokee_ancestry.html.

28. Endres, "American Indian Permission," 656.

29. Bryan McKinley Jones Brayboy, "Toward a Tribal Critical Race Theory in Education," *Urban Review* 32, no. 5 (2006): 425–46.

30. Kent Ono and Derek T. Buescher, "Deciphering Pocahontas: Unpackaging the Commodification of a Native American Woman," *Critical Studies in Media Communication* 18, no. 1 (2001): 26–27.

31. Brenda Farnell, "The Fancy Dance of Racializing Discourse," *Journal of Sport & Social Issues* 28, no. 1 (2004): 43.

32. See King, *Redskins*, 91–107.

33. Quoted in ibid., 13.

34. See ibid., 31–32.

35. Jason Edward Black, "The 'Mascotting' of Native America: Construction, Commodification, and Assimilation," *American Indian Quarterly* 26, no. 4 (2002): 605–622.

36. Casey Kelly, "Detournement, Decolonization, and the American Indian Occupation of Alcatraz (1969–1971)," *Rhetoric Society Quarterly* 44, no. 2 (2014): 173.

37. See Jason Edward Black, "Extending the Rights of Personhood, Voice, and Life to Sensate Others: A Homology of Right to Life and Animal Rights Rhetoric," *Communication Quarterly* 51, no. 3 (2003): 312–31; Kathryn Olsen, "Detecting a Common Interpretive Framework for Impersonal Violence: The Homology in Participants' Rhetoric on Sport Hunting, Hate Crimes, and Stranger Rape," *Southern Communication Journal* 67 (2002): 215–44; and Stephen M. Underhill, "Urban Jungle, Ferguson: Rhetorical Homology and Institutional Critique," *Quarterly Journal of Speech* 102, no. 4 (2016): 396–417.

38. Waziyatawin Angela Wilson and Michael Yellow Bird, *For Indigenous Eyes Only: A Decolonization Handbook* (Santa Fe, NM: School of American Research, 2005), 5.

39. For more, see Jason Edward Black, *American Indians and the Rhetoric of Removal and Allotment* (Jackson: University Press of Mississippi, 2015).

40. Kelly, "Detournement," 174.

41. Randall Lake, "Between Myth and History: Enacting Time in American Indian Protest Rhetoric," *Quarterly Journal of Speech* 77 (1991): 129.

42. Jason Edward Black, "Native American Mascotting Reveals Neocolonial Logic," *Spectra* 50, no. 3 (2014): 14–17.

43. "What Is a Racial Slur?" *National Post*.

44. Ibid.

45. Eva Marie Garroutte, *Real Indians: Identity and Survival of Native America* (Berkeley: University of California Press, 2003).

46. Stuart Hall, *Representation: Cultural Representations and Signifying Practices* (Thousand Oaks, CA: Sage, 1997).

Chapter 5. Deconstructing the Mascot, Part 2: Visual Symbols

1. Cornel Pewewardy, "Playing Indian at Halftime: The Controversy over American Indian Mascots, Logos, and Nicknames in School-Related Events," *Clearing House* 77 (2004): 180–85.

2. Sudie Hofmann, "The Elimination of Indigenous Mascots, Logos, and Nicknames: Organizing on College Campuses," *American Indian Quarterly* 29 (2005): 156–77; Dana Williams, "Where's the Honor? Attitudes toward the Fighting Sioux Nickname and Logo," *Sociology of Sport Journal* 24 (2007): 437–56.

3. Geoffrey Nunberg, "When Slang Becomes Slur," *The Atlantic*, June 23, 2014, http://www.theatlantic.com/entertainment/archive/2014/06/a-linguist-on-why-redskin-is-racist-patent-overturned/373198; John McWhorter, "Why Redskins Is a Bad Word," *Time*, October 12, 2015, http://time.com/4070537/redskins-linguistics.

4. Terry Pluto, "Cleveland Indians Owner Paul Dolan Says Team Is Keeping Chief Wahoo, but Not as Main Logo," *Cleveland Plain-Dealer*, April 1, 2016, http://www.cleveland.com/pluto/index.ssf/2016/04/cleveland_indians_owner_paul_d_7.html.

5. Ibid.

6. Lya Wasraska, "Is It Time for Utah's Drum and Feather to Go?" *Salt Lake City Tribune*, February 19, 2013, http://archive.sltrib.com/story.php?ref=/sltrib/sports/55810828-77/utes-feather-tribe-drum.html.csp.

7. Annalisa Purser, "U Mascot Swoop Turns 20," August 29, 2016, http://unews.utah.edu/u-mascot-swoop-turns-20.

8. Gene Sapakoff, "Catawba Chief: Redskins Is 'Derogatory,'" *Charleston (SC) Post and Courier*, July 11, 2014, http://www.postandcourier.com/sports/catawba-chief-redskins-is-derogatory/article_58710479-b850-53c6-b090-140ab848c8f5.html.

9. Donnie Webb, "Goodbye, Orangemen: Syracuse Cleans Up Nickname as Part of Identity Remake," Syracuse.com, March 23, 2015, http://www.syracuse.com/orangesports/index.ssf/2004/05/goodbye_orangemen_orangewomen_syracuse_cleans_up_nickname_as_part_of_identity_re.html.

10. Mark Keeley, "No, the Syracuse Orange Should Never Go Back to Being Orangemen," *SB Nation*, March 25, 2015, http://www.nunesmagician.com/2015/3/25/8286985/no-the-syracuse-orange-should-never-go-back-to-being-orangemen.

11. Max Brantley, "Meet the New ASU Mascot," *Arkansas Times*, March 13, 2008, http:// www.arktimes.com/ArkansasBlog/archives/2008/03/13/meet-the-new-asu-logo.

12. Allan Brettman, "Florida State to Adopt New Nike-Designed Logo, Controversy Ensues," *Oregon Live*, April 4, 2014, http://www.oregonlive.com/playbooks-profits/ index.ssf/2014/04/florida_state_to_adopt_new_nik.html.

13. Amy Wimmer Schwarb, "Where Pride Meets Prejudice," *NCAA Champion Magazine*, Winter 2016, http://www.ncaa.org/static/champion/where-pride-meets -prejudice/index.php.

14. "Bolt, the Savage Storm Mascot," Southeastern Oklahoma State University, (n.d.), www.se.edu/bolt.

15. Josh Cooper, "First Nations Chief Supports Blackhawks Logo Redesign with Blackhawk," *Yahoo! Sports*, November 5, 2013, http://sports.yahoo.com/blogs/nhl -puck-daddy/first-nations-chief-supports-blackhawks-logo-redesign-of-black -hawk-210325573.html.

16. Rory Boylen, "NHL Logo Rankings, No. 1: Chicago Blackhawks," *Hockey News*, August 22, 2014, http://www.thehockeynews.com/news/article/nhl-logo-rankings -no-1-chicago-blackhawks.

17. James V. Fenelon, "Symbolic Racism: Chief Wahoo and the Cleveland Indi- ans," paper presented to the American Sociological Association annual convention, Toronto, Canada, August 1997; C. Richard King and Charles F. Springwood, eds., *Team Spirits: The Native American Mascot Controversy* (Lincoln: University of Ne- braska Press, 2001); Cornel Pewewardy, "Playing Indian at Halftime: The Controversy over American Indian Mascots, Logos, and Nicknames in School-Related Events," *Clearing House* 77, no. 5 (2004): 180–85; and Ellen Staurowsky, "'You Know, We Are All Indian': Exploring White Power and Privilege in Reactions to the NCAA Native American Mascot Policy," *Journal of Sport & Social Issues* 31, no. 1 (2007): 61–76.

18. Ellen Staurowsky, "The Cleveland 'Indians': A Case Study in American Indian Cultural Dispossession," *Sociology of Sport Journal* 117 (2000): 307–330.

19. Michael Dorris, quoted in Laurel Davis, "The Problems with Native American Mascots," *Multicultural Education* 9 (2002): 13.

20. Scott Freng and Cynthia Willis-Esqueda, "A Question of Honor: Chief Wahoo and American Indian Stereotype Activation among a University-Based Sample," *Journal of Social Psychology* 15, no. 5 (2011): 586.

21. National Congress of American Indians, "Ending the Legacy of Racism in Sports and the Era of Harmful 'Indian' Sports Mascots," NCAI website, October 2013, http:// www.ncai.org/resources/ncai-publications/Ending_the_Legacy_of_Racism.pdf, 6.

22. Bobby Mueller, "Cleveland Indians: Is It Time to Retire the Chief Wahoo Logo?" *Call to the Pen*, January 28, 2017, http://calltothepen.com/2017/01/28/cleveland-indians -time-retire-chief-wahoo-logo.

23. Staurowsky, "Cleveland 'Indians,'" 311.

24. Jackson B. Miller, "'Indians,' 'Braves,' and 'Redskins': A Performative Struggle for Control of an Image," *Quarterly Journal of Speech* 85 (1999): 180.

25. Mueller, "Cleveland Indians."

26. Ellen J. Staurowsky, "An Act of Honor or Exploitation? The Cleveland Indians' Use of the Louis Francis Sockalexis Story," *Sociology of Sport Journal* 15 (1998): 305.

27. Ibid., 306–307.

28. Pluto, "Cleveland Indians Owner Paul Dolan"; Sam Allard, "Why Chief Wahoo Is Still Grinning," *Slate*, October 26, 2016, http://www.slate.com/articles/sports/sports_nut/2016/10/why_the_protests_against_chief_wahoo_never_work.html.

29. Mueller, "Cleveland Indians."

30. Staurowsky, "Act of Honor or Exploitation," 300–301.

31. Miller, "'Indians,' 'Braves,' and 'Redskins,'" 188.

32. "Appeals Court Orders Reconsideration in Chief Wahoo Protest Case," *Mercury News*, September 1, 2004, https://web.archive.org/web/20040917193012/http://www.mercurynews.com/mld/mercurynews/sports/9557017.htm.

33. Charlene Teters, "American Indians Are People, Not Mascots," American Indian Movement, (n.d.), http://www.aimovement.org/ncrsm.

34. John Holyoke, "Penobscots Seeking Ban of Cleveland's Mascot: Chief Wahoo Found as Offensive," *Bangor Daily News*, December 8, 2000, https://news.google.com/newspapers?id=KqVJAAAAIBAJ&sjid=mgoNAAAAIBAJ&pg=6178%2C2496892.

35. Native American Journalist Association, "Reading Red Report: A Call for the News Media to Recognize Racism in Sports Team Nicknames and Mascots," 2003, http://www.ais.illinois.edu/documents/2003_reading-red.pdf.

36. Peter Edwards, "Jerry Horwath Refuses to Say Cleveland Team Name," *Toronto Star*, October 11, 2016, https://www.thestar.com/sports/bluejays/2016/10/11/jerry-howarth-refuses-to-say-cleveland-team-name.html.

37. Allard, "Why Chief Wahoo Is Still Grinning."

38. Mueller, "Cleveland Indians."

39. Paul Lukas, "Hail to De-Chiefing," ESPN.com, April 2, 2014, http://www.espn.com/mlb/story/_/id/10715887/uni-watch-some-fans-removing-chief-wahoo-logos-protest.

40. Fenelon, "Symbolic Racism," 4.

41. Susan Silbey, "'Let Them Eat Cake': Globalization, Postmodern Colonialism, and the Possibilities of Justice," *Law and Society Review* 31 (1997): 207–235.

42. Jason Edward Black, "A Clash of Native Space and Institutional Place in a Local Choctaw–Upper Creek Memory Site: Decolonizing Critiques and Scholar-Activist Interventions," *American Indian Culture and Research Journal* 36, no. 3 (2012): 23.

43. Freng and Willis-Esqueda, "Question of Honor," 580.

44. Fenelon, "Symbolic Racism", 3.

45. Ibid., 4.

46. Staurowsky, "'You Know, We Are All Indian,'" 66.

47. "Redskins, Sambos, and Whities—Racism in Sports Mascots," untitled photo, Change from Within website, December 10, 2010, https://changefromwithin.org/2010/12/10/redskins-sambos-and-whities-racism-in-sports-mascots.

48. David Leonhardt, "Cleveland's Unthinking Racism," *New York Times*, October 29, 2016, https://www.nytimes.com/2016/10/28/opinion/clevelands-unthinking-racism.html.

49. Jason Miller, photo captioned "Cleveland Indians Fans express their hops [*sic*] for the post season during the game between the Cleveland Indians and the Chicago White Sox at Progressive Field on September 24, 2013 in Cleveland, Ohio," *CBS DC*, April 30, 2014, http://washington.cbslocal.com/2014/04/30/not-just-redskins-native-americans-call-for-ban-of-indians-chief-wahoo.

50. Philip J. Deloria, *Playing Indian* (New Haven, CT: Yale University Press, 1998).

51. Ibid., 7.

52. Jamie Squire and Jason Miller, untitled photos in Sam Allard, "Why Chief Wahoo Is Still Grinning," *Slate*, October 26, 2016, http://www.slate.com/articles/sports/sports_nut/2016/10/why_the_protests_against_chief_wahoo_never_work.html.

53. Staurowsky, "Cleveland 'Indians,'" 311.

54. Jason Miller, untitled photo in Cork Gaines, "MLB Commissioner Rob Manfred to Meet with Cleveland Indians Owner over Use of Controversial 'Chief Wahoo' Logo," *Business Insider*, October 25, 2016, http://www.businessinsider.com/rob-manfred-cleveland-indians-future-of-chief-wahoo-logo-2016-10.

55. Leonhardt, "Cleveland's Unthinking Racism."

56. Linda Tuhiwai Smith, *Decolonizing Methodologies: Research and Indigenous Peoples* (London: Zed Books, 2007), 33.

57. "Not Just Redskins: Native Americans Call for Ban of Indians' 'Chief Wahoo,'" *CBS DC*, April 30, 2014, http://washington.cbslocal.com/2014/04/30/not-just-redskins-native-americans-call-for-ban-of-indians-chief-wahoo.

58. Untitled images, National Coalition on Racism in Sports and Media website, (n.d.), http://www.aimovement.org/ncrsm.

59. Quoted in Katie Bieri, "Mascot Protests at D-Backs Game Draw Mixed Reactions," *Arizona Republic*, June 24, 2014, http://www.azcentral.com/story/news/local/phoenix/2014/06/25/cleveland-indian-protests-abrk/11341355.

60. Duane Champagne, "In Search of Theory and Method in American Indian Studies," *American Indian Quarterly* 31, no. 2 (2007): 362.

61. Associated Press, image captioned "A protester stands outside Progressive Field before a postponed baseball game between the Boston Red Sox and the Cleveland Indians in Cleveland," *Daily Herald*, April 4, 2016, http://www.dailyherald.com/article/20160404/sports/304049843.

62. Miller, "'Indians,' 'Braves,' and 'Redskins,'" 189.

63. Jason Edward Black, *American Indians and the Rhetoric of Removal and Allotment* (Jackson: University Press of Mississippi, 2015), 12.

64. See Newberry Library, "Can You Imagine?" *Indians of the Midwest*, ©1997 *Philadelphia Enquirer*, http://publications.newberry.org/indiansofthemidwest/indian-imagery/challenging-stereotypes/sports-imagery.

65. Leonhardt, "Cleveland's Unthinking Racism."

66. Quoted in Lukas, "Hail to De-Chiefing."

67. Ebenezer Samuel, "Indians' Chief Wahoo Logo Is Racist Caricature, Something LeBron James, Outspoken on Racial Injustice, and Many Others Fail to See," *New York Daily News*, October 25, 2016, http://www.nydailynews.com/sports/baseball/indians-chief-wahoo-logo-derogatory-racist-article-1.2844958.

68. Lukas, "Hail to De-Chiefing."

69. Quoted in ibid.

70. National Congress of American Indians, "Ending the Legacy of Racism in Sports," 6.

71. Craig Calceterra, "Topps Has Eliminated Chief Wahoo from Both New and Throwback Card Designs," NBC Sports, July 21, 2017, https://sports.yahoo.com/topps-eliminated-chief-wahoo-both-174455807.html.

72. Staurowsky, "Act of Honor or Exploitation?" 299–300.

73. Freng and Willis-Esqueda, "Question of Honor," 587.

Chapter 6. Deconstructing the Mascot, Part 3: Rituals and Performances

1. Michael Taylor, *Contesting Constructed Indian-ness: The Intersection of the Frontier, Masculinity, and Whiteness in Native American Mascot Representations* (Lanham, MD: Rowman and Littlefield, 2014); Daniel L. Wann and Nyla R. Branscombe, "Die-Hard and Fair-Weather Fans: Effects of Identification on BIRGing and CORFing Tendencies," *Journal of Sport and Social Issues* 14 (1990): 103–117; and Arthur A. Raney, "Why We Watch and Enjoy Mediated Sports," in *Handbook of Sport and Media*, ed. Arthur Raney and Jennings Bryant (Mahwah, NJ: Erlbaum): 313–29.

2. C. Richard King, "On Being a Warrior: Race, Gender, and American Indian Imagery in Sport," *International Journal of the History of Sport* 23 (2006): 313–29.

3. L. V. Anderson, "When Did People Start Doing the Tomahawk Chop?—and It Is Racist, Right?" *Slate*, September 26, 2012, http://www.slate.com/articles/news_and_politics/explainer/2012/09/origins_of_the_tomahawk_chop_scott_brown_s_staffers_mocking_elizabeth_warren_are_continuing_a_long_tradition_.html.

4. Debbie Kelley, "Cheyenne Mountain Working with Students, Supporters to End Indian Stereotypes," *Colorado Springs Gazette*, November 3, 2016, http://gazette.com/cheyenne-mountain-working-with-students-supporters-to-end-indian-stereotypes/article/1589351.

5. Maria Mooshil, "Ten More Things to Know about the Bears' Fight Song," *Chicago Tribune*, December 1, 2006, http://articles.chicagotribune.com/2006-12-01/features/0611300370_1_fight-song-chicago-bears-philadelphia-eagles.

6. Robert Andrew Powell, "Florida State Can Keep Its Seminoles," *New York Times*, August 24, 2005, http://www.nytimes.com/2005/08/24/sports/florida-state-can-keep-its-seminoles.html; "Traditions," Tallahassee Seminole Club website, 2016, http://www.tallahasseeseminoleclub.com/fsu-traditions.

7. One might think about NASCAR fans raising three fingers to the sky on the third lap of every race to celebrate the sport's stock car messiah, Dale Earnhardt, who drove the number 3 car and lost his life on the track at the most holy of NASCAR meccas, Daytona International Speedway. His martyred death was a sacrifice to the betterment of safety in NASCAR, which has not lost a driver since Earnhardt's death in 2001.

8. Daniel A. Grano, *The Eternal Present of Sport: Rethinking Sport and Religion* (Philadelphia: Temple University Press, 2017), 16.

9. Roberto Rodriguez, "Plotting the Assassination of Little Red Sambo: Psychologists Join War against Racist Campus Mascots," *Black Issues in Higher Education* 15, no. 8 (1998): 20.

10. Ellen J. Staurowsky, "An Act of Honor or Exploitation? The Cleveland Indians' Use of the Louis Francis Sockalexis Story," *Sociology of Sport Journal* 15 (1998): 304.

11. Jason Edward Black, "The Mascotting of Native America: Construction, Commodity, and Assimilation," *American Indian Quarterly* 26, no. 4 (2002): 607–608.

12. Jim Joanos, "Seminole Traditions at FSU," *Seminole Spotlight*, August 2011, http://www.nolefan.org/garnet/seminole62.html.

13. Florida State University, "Relationship with the Seminole Tribe of Florida: A Tradition of Tribute," University Communications, (n.d.), https://unicomm.fsu.edu/messages/relationship-seminole-tribe-florida/tribute.

14. Staurowsky, "Act of Honor or Exploitation?" 63.

15. Florida State University, "Relationship with the Seminole Tribe: Tradition of Tribute."

16. Diane Morris Bernstein, *We Dance Because We Can: People of the Powwow* (Atlanta: Longstreet Press, 1996).

17. Florida State University, "Relationship with the Seminole Tribe: Tradition of Tribute."

18. Florida State University, "Relationship with the Seminole Tribe of Florida: Frequently Asked Questions," University Communications, (n.d.), https://unicomm.fsu.edu/messages/relationship-seminole-tribe-florida/faqs.

19. James E. Billie, "Like the Old Florida Flag: 'Let Us Alone!'" *Seminole Tribune*, October 24, 2013.

20. Jackson B. Miller, "'Indians,' 'Braves,' and 'Redskins': A Performative Struggle for Control of an Image," *Quarterly Journal of Speech* 85 (1999): 190.

21. Billie, "Like the Old Florida Flag."

22. Carol Spindel, *Dancing at Halftime: Sports and the Controversy over American Indian Mascots* (New York: New York University Press, 2000), 265–66.

23. Palm Beach County Seminole Club, "FSU Songs and Chants," (n.d.), http://www.pbnoles.com/FSUSongsandChants.

24. "FSU Traditions," Tallahassee Seminole Club, (n.d.), http://www.tallahasseeseminoleclub.com/fsu-traditions.

25. NCAA, "NCAA Executive Committee Issues Guidelines for Use of Native American Mascots at Championship Events," NCAA Press Release Archive, August 5, 2005, http://fs.ncaa.org/Docs/PressArchive/2005/Announcements.

26. Ellen Staurowsky, "'You Know, We Are All Indian': Exploring White Power and Privilege in Reactions to the NCAA Native American Mascot Policy," *Journal of Sport & Social Issues* 31, no. 1 (2007): 61–76.

27. Florida State University, "Relationship with the Seminole Tribe of Florida: A Seminole Timeline at Florida State University," University Communications, (n.d.), https://unicomm.fsu.edu/messages/relationship-seminole-tribe-florida/timeline.

28. Florida State University, "Relationship with the Seminole Tribe of Florida."

29. "War Chant and Tomahawk Chop: From Seminoles to Republicans," *Indian Country Today*, September 29, 2012, https://indiancountrymedianetwork.com/news/war-chant-and-tomahawk-chop-from-seminoles-to-republicans-via-braves-diddy-and-a-40-foot-cow.

30. Billie, "Like the Old Florida Flag."

31. Florida State University, "Relationship with the Seminole Tribe of Florida, FAQs."

32. Billie, "Like the Old Florida Flag."

33. Native Appropriations, "Interest Convergence, FSU, and the Seminole Tribe of Florida," January 22, 2013, http://nativeappropriations.com/2013/01/interest-convergence-fsu-and-the-seminole-tribe-of-florida.html.

34. Danielle Endres, "American Indian Permission for Mascots: Resistance or Complicity within Rhetorical Colonialism," *Rhetoric and Public Affairs* 18, no. 4 (2015): 655.

35. Raymie McKerrow, "Critical Rhetoric: Theory and Praxis," *Communication Monographs* 56, no. 2 (1989): 91–111.

36. Miller, "'Indians,' 'Braves,' and 'Redskins,'" 191.

37. Ibid., 189.

38. Charles Fruehling Springwood and C. Richard King, "'Playing Indian': Why Native American Mascots Must End," *Chronicle of Higher Education* 48, no. 11 (2001): 1–4. See also Philip J. Deloria, *Playing Indian* (New Haven, CT: Yale University Press, 1998).

39. Miller, "'Indians,' 'Braves,' and 'Redskins,'" 195.

40. Palm Beach County Seminole Club, "FSU Songs and Chants," http://www.pbnoles.com/FSU%20Songs%20and%20Chants.

41. Joanos, "Seminole Traditions at FSU."

42. "War Chant and Tomahawk Chop," *Indian Country Today*.

43. Brenda Farnell, "The Fancy Dance of Racializing Discourse," *Journal of Sport & Social Issues* 28, no. 1 (2004): 34.

44. Spindel, *Dancing at Halftime*, 16–17.

45. These comments were gathered as a part of the methodology described in the analytical portion of chapter 4.

46. Farnell, "Fancy Dance," 35.

47. Staurowsky, "Act of Honor or Exploitation?" 304.

48. Staurowsky, "'You Know, We Are All Indian,'" 65.

49. "FSU Seminoles Fans Are Told to Stop Wearing Native American Headdresses to Athletic Games Because They Are Representative of Other Tribes," *Daily Mail*, May 3, 2016, http://www.dailymail.co.uk/news/article-3572152/FSU-student-reps -No-headdresses-Seminoles-games.html.

50. Staurowsky, "Act of Honor or Exploitation?" 64.

51. Black, "'Mascotting' of Native America," 614–15.

52. Jason Edward Black, *American Indians and the Rhetoric of Removal and Allotment* (Jackson: University Press of Mississippi, 2015).

Chapter 7. What Is Lost? The Perceived Stakes of Recent and Potential Mascot Removals

1. Graham Noble, "Why the Fuss over Washington Redskins Is Demeaning to Native Americans," *Guardian Liberty Voice*, October 12, 2014, http://guardianlv.com/ 2014/10/why-the-fuss-over-washington-redskins-is-demeaning-to-american-indians; Genevieve Wood, "If You Are Offended, Get Over It: Redskins Should Get to Decide Their Own Name," *Daily Signal*, August 26, 2014, http://dailysignal.com/2014/08/26/ youre-offended-get-redskins-get-decide-name; Charlotte I. Harris, "Whiteness as Property," *Harvard Law Review* 106 (1993): 1710–91; and C. Richard King, *Redskins: Insult and Brand* (Lincoln: University of Nebraska Press, 2016).

2. Carol Spindel, *Dancing at Halftime: Sports and the Controversy over Native American Mascots* (New York: New York University Press, 2002).

3. James Klatell, "Fighting Illini Say Goodbye to the Chief," *CBS News*, February 16, 2007, http://www.cbsnews.com/news/fighting-illini-say-goodbye-to-the-chief; and Walbert Castillo, "University of Illinois' Chief Illiniwek Mascot Lives On at School Despite Ban," *USA Today*, February 2, 2016, http://college.usatoday.com/2016/02/18/u-of -illinois-chief-illiniwek-mascot-lives-on-at-school-despite-ban.

4. Shannon Ryan, "Illinois to Select New Mascot; Chief Illiniwek Backers 'Not Going to Stop,'" *Chicago Tribune*, May 13, 2016, http://www.chicagotribune.com/sports/ college/ct-university-of-illinois-mascot-chief-illiniwek-20160502-story.html.

5. George Will, "The Government Decided That 'Redskins' Bothers You," *Washington Post*, June 27, 2014, https://www.washingtonpost.com/opinions/george-f-will -the-government-decided-that-redskins-bothers-you/2014/06/27/669558a6-fd54-11 e3–932c-0a55b81f48ce_story.html?utm_term=.4579cd9e016f; and David Zirin, "The Florida State Seminoles: The Champions of Racist Mascots," *The Nation*, January 7, 2014, http://www.thenation.com/article/florida-state-seminoles-champions-racist -mascots.

6. Rich Lowry, "Liberals Fabricate Outrage over Redskins, *National Review*, October 8, 2013, http://www.nationalreview.com/article/360614/liberals-fabricate-outrage-over -redskins-rich-lowry.

7. Robert Andrew Powell, "Florida State Can Keep Its Seminoles," *New York Times*, August 24, 2005, http://www.nytimes.com/2005/08/24/sports/florida-state-can-keep-its-seminoles.html?_r=0.

8. Chuck Culpepper, "Florida State's Unusual Bond with Seminole Tribe Puts Mascot Debate in a Different Light," *Washington Post*, December 29, 2014, https://www.washingtonpost.com/sports/colleges/florida-states-unusual-bond-with-seminole-tribe-puts-mascot-debate-in-a-different-light/2014/12/29/5386841a-8eea-11e4-ba53-a477d66580ed_story.html.

9. Philip L. Deloria, *Playing Indian* (New Haven, CT: Yale University Press, 1998).

10. John Woodrow Cox, Scott Clement, and Theresa Vargas, "New Poll Finds 9 in 10 Native Americans Aren't Offended by Redskins Name," *Washington Post*, May 19, 2016, https://www.washingtonpost.com/local/new-poll-finds-9-in-10-native-americans-arent-offended-by-redskins-name/2016/05/18/3ea11cfa-161a-11e6-924d-838753295f9a_story.html?utm_term=.7e6a9076b26d.

Chapter 8. W(h)ither the Mascot?
Pathways through the Logics of Native American Mascotting

1. Brief of *Amici Curiae*, Native American Organizations in Support of Appellees, *Pro-Football, Inc. (plaintiff and appellant) v. Amanda Blackhorse, Marcus Briggs-Cloud, Phillip Glover, Jillian Pappan, Courtney Tsotigh (defendants and appellees)*; United States of America (intervenor-appellee), in the United States Court of Appeals for the Fourth Circuit, no. 15-1874.

2. Ibid.

3. "Owner: Redskins Will 'Never' Change Name," *ESPN.com*, May 10, 2013, http://www.espn.com/nfl/story/_/id/9259866/daniel-snyder-says-washington-redskins-never-change-team-name.

4. Quoted in Jason Edward Black, "Native American Mascotting Reveals Neocolonial Logics," *Spectra* 50, no. 3 (2014): 17.

5. National Congress of American Indians, "National Congress of American Indians and Change the Mascot Respond to Disappointing Supreme Court Ruling Upholding Derogatory Trademark," NCAI.org, June 19, 2017, http://www.ncai.org/news/articles/2017/06/19/national-congress-of-american-indians-and-change-the-mascot-respond-to-disappointing-supreme-court-ruling-upholding-derogatory-trademark.

6. Raka Shome and Radha S. Hegde, "Postcolonial Approaches to Communication: Charting the Terrain, Engaging the Intersections," *Communication Theory* 12 (2002): 258. See also Jason Edward Black, "A Clash of Native Space and Institutional Place in a Local Choctaw–Upper Creek Memory Site: Decolonizing Critiques and Scholar-Activist Interventions," *American Indian Research and Culture Journal* 36, no. 3 (2012): 19–44.

7. Quoted in C. Richard King, *Redskins: Insult and Brand* (Lincoln: University of Nebraska Press, 2016), 162.

8. "What Is a Racial Slur? Fight over Washington Redskins Name Raises Questions about Race and Language," *National Post*, June 21, 2014, http://nationalpost.com/ sports/football/nfl/what-is-a-slur-fight-over-washington-redskins-name-raises -many-questions-about-race-and-language/wcm/105cdbd0-28bb-41a0-a7f9-ccdb6 f148b19.

9. Samuel Alito, "Majority Opinion," *Matal v. Tam*, 582 U.S. __ (2017).

10. Ibid.

11. Chuck Schilken, "Redskins Are 'Thrilled' by the Supreme Court Decision Striking Down Law Banning Offensive Trademarks," *Los Angeles Times*, June 19, 2017, http://www.latimes.com/sports/sportsnow/la-sp-redskins-trademark-supreme -court-20170619-story.html.

12. Erik Brady, "Redskins Owner Dan Snyder Thrilled with Supreme Court Decision," *Chicago Sun-Times*, June 19, 2017, http://chicago.suntimes.com/sports/redskins -owner-dan-snyder-thrilled-with-supreme-court-decision.

13. Alito, "Majority Opinion."

14. Ibid.

15. Brady, "Redskins Owner Dan Snyder Thrilled."

16. Schilken, "Redskins are 'Thrilled.'"

17. Darren Heitner, "Supreme Court Ruling Is Great for Washington Redskins in Trademark Battle," *Forbes*, June 19, 2017, https://www.forbes.com/forbes/welcome/ ?toURL=https://www.forbes.com/sites/darrenheitner/2017/06/19/supreme-court -ruling-is-great-for-washington-redskins-in-trademark-battle/&refURL=https:// search.yahoo.com&referrer=https://search.yahoo.com.

18. Brady, "Redskins Owner Dan Snyder Thrilled."

19. Brian McNally, "Dan Snyder 'Thrilled' with Supreme Court Decision That Benefits Redskins," *CBS Washington*, June 19, 2017, http://washington.cbslocal.com/ 2017/06/19/redskins-owner-dan-snyder-thrilled-with-supreme-court-decision.

20. Martin Luther King Jr., "Letter from a Birmingham Jail (April 19, 1963)," African Studies Center, University of Pennsylvania, https://www.africa.upenn.edu/ Articles_Gen/Letter_Birmingham.html.

21. Stephen Whyno, "Redskins Clear Supreme Court Hurdle, but Trademark War Still Rages," *Washington Times*, June 20, 2017, http://www.washingtontimes.com/ news/2017/jun/20/supreme-court-pushes-redskins-name-fight-back-to-s.

22. Brief of *Amici Curiae*.

23. NCAI, "National Congress of American Indians."

24. Quoted in Whyno, "Redskins Clear Supreme Court Hurdle."

25. NCAI, "National Congress of American Indians."

26. Whyno, "Redskins Clear Supreme Court Hurdle."

27. National Congress of American Indians, "Ending the Legacy of Racism in Sports and the Era of Harmful 'Indian' Sports Mascots," *NCAI.org*, October 2013, p. 6, http://www.ncai.org/news/articles/2013/10/10/ncai-releases-report-on-history-and -legacy-of-washington-s-harmful-indian-sports-mascot.

28. Quoted in ibid.

29. Brief of *Amici Curiae*.

30. King, *Redskins*, 1.

31. Quoted in ibid., 2.

32. NCAI, "National Congress of American Indians."

33. Jason Edward Black, "The 'Mascotting' of Native America: Construction, Commodification, and Assimilation," *American Indian Quarterly* 26, no. 4 (2002): 605–622.

34. Brenda Farnell, "The Fancy Dance of Racializing Discourse," *Journal of Sport & Social Issues* 28, no. 1 (2004): 46.

35. Susan M. Ryan, *The Grammar of Good Intentions: Race and the Antebellum Culture of Benevolence* (Ithaca, NY: Cornell University Press, 2003), 45.

36. King, *Redskins*, 169.

37. Quoted in ibid., 162.

38. Whyno, "Redskins Clear Supreme Court Hurdle."

39. Ibid.

40. Jill Lane, "Digital Zapatistas," *Drama Review* 74, no. 2 (2003): 134.

41. Quoted in Whyno, "Redskins Clear Supreme Court Hurdle."

42. Phaedra C. Pezzullo, "Contextualizing Boycotts and Buycotts: The Impure Politics of Consumer-Based Advocacy in an Age of Global Ecological Crisis," *Communication and Critical/Cultural Studies* 8, no. 2 (2011): 124–45.

43. Whyno, "Redskins Clear Supreme Court Hurdle."

44. Charles J. Stewart, Craig Allen Smith, and Robert E. Denton Jr., *Persuasion and Social Movements*, 6th ed. (Long Grove, IL: Waveland Press, 2012), 62–71.

45. Peter Edwards, "Jerry Horwath Refuses to Say Cleveland Team Name," *Toronto Star*, October 11, 2016, https://www.thestar.com/sports/bluejays/2016/10/11/jerry-howarth-refuses-to-say-cleveland-team-name.html.

46. Quoted in National Congress of American Indians, "Ending the Legacy of Racism."

47. Robert Jensen, "Banning 'Redskins' from the Sports Page: The Ethics and Politics of Native American Nicknames," *Journal of Mass Media Studies* 9, no. 1 (1994): 18.

48. Alito, "Majority Opinion."

49. King, *Redskins*, 1.

50. Roberto Rodriguez, "Plotting the Assassination of Little Red Sambo: Psychologists Join War against Racist Campus Mascots," *Black Issues in Higher Education* 15, no. 8 (1998): 20–24.

51. Jensen, "Banning 'Redskins,'" 24.

52. Brady, "Redskins Owner Dan Snyder 'Thrilled.'"

53. Charlene Teters, "American Indians Are People, Not Mascots," National Coalition on Racism in Sports and Media, http://www.aimovement.org/ncrsm.

Index

ANDREW C. BILLINGS is Professor and Ronald Reagan Chair of Broadcasting in the Department of Journalism and Creative Media at the University of Alabama. He is the author of *Olympic Television: Broadcasting the Biggest Show on Earth* and *Media and the Coming Out of Gay Male Athletes in American Team Sports*.

JASON EDWARD BLACK is chair and professor of communication studies at the University of North Carolina at Charlotte. His books include *Decolonizing Native American Rhetoric: Communicating Self-Determination, American Indians and the Rhetoric of Removal and Allotment*, and *An Archive of Hope: Harvey Milk's Speeches and Writings*.

The University of Illinois Press
is a founding member of the
Association of American University Presses.

—————————————————————

Composed in 10.5/13 Minion Pro
with Univers LT Std display
by Lisa Connery
at the University of Illinois Press
Manufactured by Sheridan Books, Inc.

University of Illinois Press
1325 South Oak Street
Champaign, IL 61820-6903
www.press.uillinois.edu